NEGROES

AND

NEGRO "SLAVERY:"

THE FIRST AN INFERIOR RACE:

THE LATTER ITS NORMAL CONDITION.

BY

J. H. VAN EVRIE, M.D.

I0029046

ISBN: 978-1-63923-756-2

Printed: February 2023

Published and Distributed By:
Lushena Books
607 Country Club Drive, Unit E
Bensenville, IL 60106
www.lushenabks.com

ISBN: 978-1-63923-756-2

PREFACE.

Since the first edition of this work was issued, startling and deplorable events have occurred. The great " Anti-Slavery" delusion, that originated with European monarchists more than fifty years ago, has culminated in disunion and civil war, as its authors always predicted it would. A party strongly imbued with the false theories and absurd assumptions of British writers and abolition societies, is in possession of the Federal Government, which it stands pledged to use to reduce its assumptions to practice. It holds that the negro, except in color, is a man like themselves, and naturally entitled to the same liberty—that to deny him this liberty, is to enslave him —that, therefore, Southern society is wrong, and should be revolutionized, and it avows it to be its mission to accomplish this—to institute a policy that shall finally abolish or destroy the supremacy of the white man, and secure " impartial freedom" for negroes! To this the South replies, that this government was created for white men alone, and *their* posterity, as declared in the preamble to the Constitution—that the Supreme Court has recently declared the same great truth—that, seizing the government by a mere sectional vote, and placing it in distinct conflict with the social order of the South, with the avowed purpose of penning up its negro population, in order to bring about some day the extinction or overthrow of the existing condition, is, therefore, an overthrow of the Constitution—that the object avowed necessarily involves their future destruction, and to save themselves from the wild delusion and malignant fanaticism of the North, they are forced, in self-defense, to withdraw from the Union, hitherto, or until this hostile and dangerous party entered the field, so beneficial to all sections of the country.

So stands the case between the sections. If the "anti-slavery" party was based on truth—if the negro, except in color, was a man like ourselves—if social subordination of this negro was wrong, and the four millions of these people at the South entitled to the same liberty as ourselves—and if the men who made this government designed it to include the inferior races of this continent, and it were really beneficial to equalize and fraternize with these negroes, then, though it may be doubted, if using the common government to bring it about were proper, the *end* in view would be so beneficent, and such a transcendent act of justice to these assumed slaves, that all honest, earnest, and patriotic citizens should promptly sustain the party now striving to accomplish it. But, on the contrary, if this party is based on a stupendous falsehood—if the negro is a different and inferior being, and in his normal condition at the South—and if the men who made this government, designed it for white men alone—then the length and breadth and width and depth of the "anti-slavery" delusion, and the crime of the "anti-slavery" party, which has broken up the Union in a blind crusade after negro freedom, will be fully comprehended by the American people. The whole mighty question, therefore, with all its vast and boundless consequences, hinges on the apparently simple question of *fact*—is the negro, except in color, a man like ourselves, and therefore naturally entitled to the same liberty?

It is absolutely certain that neither the liberty, the rights, nor the interests of one single northern citizen is involved; nothing whatever but a blind and foolish theory of "negro slavery" which is attempted to be forced on the South. If the people of the two great sections of the country could change places, the vast "anti-slavery" delusion would be exploded in sixty days. But as this is impossible, the next best thing is to explain the actual condition of things in the South to the northern mind. This great work the author has undertaken, not to defend an imaginary slavery, for it needs no defense, but to explain the social order—to demonstrate to the senses, as well as the reason, that the negro is a different and subordinate being, and in his normal condition at the South; and thus to show the enormous and fathomless folly, crime, and impiety wrapped up in the great "anti-slavery" delusion of the day. The former edition of this work was put to press so hurriedly, that it contained many errors, but the present one has been carefully revised; and, moreover, the introductory chapter has been rewritten, in order to present a more distinct history of the origin and progress of the great British "anti-slavery" imposture which is now working out its legitimate and designed purpose in the destruction of the American Union.

In conclusion, the author begs to say, that mere literary display or fine writing is with him quite a subordinate consideration. He only desires to be understood, and, that the grand and momentous truths described in this book shall be clearly comprehended by the masses, with the confident assurance that when they come to understand that their own liberty, welfare, and prosperity are all hazarded in a blind crusade after that which, could it be accomplished, would be the greatest calamity ever inflicted on a civilized people, the causeless and senseless, but frightful sectional conflict now raging will be speedily terminated by the universal uprising of the northern masses in favor of a government of WHITE MEN, and UNION with the South.

CONTENTS.

CHAPTER IV.

HISTORICAL OUTLINE.

CHAPTER V

COLOR.

CHAPTER VI.

FIGURE.

CHAPTER VII.

THE HAIR.

CHAPTER VIII.

THE FEATURES.

CHAPTER IX.

LANGUAGE.

CHAPTER X.

THE SENSES,

CHAPTER XI.

THE BRAIN.

CHAPTER XII.

GENERAL SUMMARY.

PART II.

CHAPTER XIII.

HYBRIDISM.

CHAPTER XIV.

THE "SLAVE TRADE," OR THE IMPORTATION OF NEGROES.

CHAPTER XV.

NORMAL CONDITION OF THE NEGRO.

CHAPTER XIX.

MARRIAGE.

CHAPTER XX.

CLIMATIC AND INDUSTRIAL ADAPTATION.

CHAPTER XXI.

NORTH AND SOUTH—THE ORIGIN OF THE AMERICAN IDEA OF GOVERNMENT.

CHAPTER XXII.

THE ALLIANCE OF NORTHERN AND SOUTHERN PRODUCERS.

CHAPTER XXIII.

THE FUTURE OF THE NEGRO.

CHAPTER XXIV.

CONCLUSION.

CHAPTER I.

CAUSES OF POPULAR DELUSION.

"AMERICAN SLAVERY," though having no existence in fact, is a phrase which, for the last forty years, has been oftener heard than *American democracy;* yet the latter is one of the great powers of the earth, and destined, in the course of time, to revolutionize the world. But in this prominence of an *abstraction*, and indifference, or apparent indifference, to the grandest *fact* of modern times, is witnessed the wide-spread and almost despotic influence of the European over the American mind. What is here termed "American slavery," is the *status* of the negro in American society—the social relation of the negro to the white man—which, being in accord with the natural relations of the races, springs spontaneously from the necessities of human society. The white citizen is superior, the negro inferior; and, therefore, whenever or wherever they happen to be in juxtaposition, the human law should accord, as it does accord in the South, with these relations thus inherent in their organizations, and thus fixed forever by the hand of God. And were America isolated from Europe—did that sea of fire, which Mr. Jefferson once wished for, really divide the Old World and the New, and thus separate us from the mental obliquities and moral perversities of the former—then any other relation than that now common to the South, would be an impossible conception to the American mind.

The words "slave" and "slavery" were scarcely heard a hundred years ago, as indeed they will be unheard a hundred years hence; and prior to the Revolution of 1776, the people of America were quite unconscious of that mighty "evil," now so oppressive to many otherwise sensible minds, though this imaginary slavery then spread over the whole continent. All new communities are distinguished by a certain advance in civilization over the elder ones, however rude the former may appear in some respects, or whatever may be the over-refinement, or seeming refinement, of the latter. Truth lives forever—"the eternal years of God are hers;" and all real knowledge, all true progress made by the race, is treasured up, and carried with it in all its wanderings, whether from the Nile to the Tiber, or from the Thames to the Hudson; while the errors, the foolish traditions and vicious habits, mental and moral, that gather about it, and weaken, and sometimes so overlie and conceal the truth as to render it useless, are left behind. We see this even in our own energetic and progressive society. The younger States are the most enlightened States; and the West, whatever may be its wants, or supposed wants among a certain class, is really more civilized than the East. That community which is the most prosperous—where there is the greatest amount of happiness—where there is relatively the greatest number of independent citizens—is *per se* and of necessity the most civilized; for the end of existence, the object of the All-wise and beneficent Creator —happiness for His creatures—is here most fully accomplished.

And when we contemplate the history of this continent, and compare the character of the early colonists, their history, and their influence over the present condition of things, it will be found that they remained stationary in exact proportion as they clung to the ideas and habitudes of the Old World; or advanced towards a better and higher condition just as they cast off these influences, and lived in natural accord with the circumstances that surrounded them. The Spanish conquerors were often the pets and favorites of the court, and always the faithful sons of the Church, and brought with them the pomps and vanities of the former, and the rigid ecclesiastical observances of the latter. When Cortez and Pizzaro took possession of a province, they pompously paraded the titles and dignities of the emperor before the wondering savages, and added vast multitudes of "Christian converts" to "Holy Church" with a zeal and fervor that the Beechers and Cheevers of our times might envy, but surely could not equal. The English colonists, on the contrary, were almost all disaffected, or at all events, were charged with disaffection to the mother country. This, it is true, was masked under religious beliefs and scruples of conscience, but was none the less hostile to the political order under which they had been persecuted and suffered so long. As soon, therefore, as they found themselves in a New World, and relieved from the tyranny of the Old, they abandoned, to a great extent, the forms, as they already had abandoned many of the ideas, of the latter. They recognized the nominal sovereignty of the mother country, or rather of the Crown; but from the landing at Jamestown, as well as at Plymouth, all the British colonists really governed themselves, made their own laws, provided for their own safety, and, except the governor, and occasionally some subordinate officials, elected their own rulers. The result was a corresponding prosperity; for not only did the discipline of self-reliance strengthen the character, and call out a higher phase of citizenship among the English colonists, but in casting off the habitudes of the old societies, and adopting those that were suited to the circumstances surrounding them, they soon exhibited a striking contrast to those of Spain and of other European powers, who clung to the ideas and habits of Europe.

But this drawback on American progress—this clinging to the habitudes of the Old World, which kept the Spanish and French colonies in abject submission to the mother country, and which England, at a later period, sought to force on her colonies—was not the sole embarrassment in the progress of the colonists. They were confronted by wild and ferocious savages, who disputed every step of the white European; and though, previous to the independence of the colonies, the mother country united with the latter against the former, from the breaking out of hostilities in 1776 to the close of the War of 1812 the interests of monarchy and savagism may be said to have been inseparable, and to have formed a common barrier against the march of republicanism. Indeed, it is a truth, attested by the whole history of the past, and equally so by the circumstances of the present, that the subordinate races of this continent—the Indian, Negro, Mongrel, etc.— constitute the material, the very stock in trade, of European monarchists, to embarrass the progress of American institutions; and in every instance where we have been engaged in Indian wars, that portion of our people who, in their ignorance and blindness, have condemned the course of their own government, have been the unconscious instruments of the enemies of their country, and in their sickly sentimentality and folly, they have sought to obstruct the progress of American civilization. Monarchy consists in artificial distinctions of kings, nobles, peasants, etc., or it may be defined as the rule of classes of the same race, and, from the inherent necessities of its organization, it is forced to make war on the natural distinction of races. Prior to the breaking out of the American Revolution, there was no necessity for calling in the aid of the Negro or the Indian to crush out the liberty of the white man. The colonists, as has been observed, were practical republicans, and substantially governed themselves; but they had not questioned the European system or theory of monarchism. When they did this, however, in that grand Declaration of Mr. Jefferson, that all men (meaning, of course, his own race) were created free and equal, the British monarchists instinctively and, indeed necessarily, resorted to the means at hand—to the subordinate races of America—to demoralize and break down this immortal truth. An English judge, anticipating the coming rebellion of the Americans, had already ruled that "slavery," or social subordination of the negro to the white man, was a result of municipal law—a creature of the *lex loci;* and though this was in language that led vast numbers of people into error, its technical as well as absolute falsehood is apparent, when we remember that no such "law" has ever existed, either now or at any other time, in American history, from the Canadian Lakes to Cape Horn. But it served as a foundation and stand-point for that wide-spread imposture and world-wide delusion which has since so overshadowed the land, and, with the best intentions on their part, so deluded Americans themselves into a blind warfare against the progress, prosperity, and indeed the civilization, of their country and continent. In the seven years' war waged to crush out the rebellion of the Colonies, England subsidized the savage Indian tribes wherever it was possible to do so; and in the subsequent War of 1812, her agents partially succeeded in combining all the savages on our western border, under Tecumseh, with the design of shutting us out forever from the country west of the Mississippi. The result of this monstrous alliance of European monarchists and American savages to beat back the advancing civilization of the New World, to hold in check, and, if possible, to defeat and overthrow republicanism, has ended in the destruction and almost utter annihilation of the North American Indians. General Jackson's campaigns in Florida, as well as those of Harrison in the West, and, to a certain extent, even the later Seminole War, all had their origin in the same causes, the open or secret intrigues of British agents, stimulating the savages to resist the onward march of American civilization. Nor was it anything like the former contests of the agents of England and France to enlist the aid of the savages against each other; for, repulsive and iniquitous as it may be for men of the same race to employ subordinate races against their own blood, they were struggling for possession of a continent, and all means, doubtless, seemed legitimate that should give them victory. But in this case it was a war against Americanism —against a new order of political society—against a system based on a principle of utter antagonism to monarchism, and which if permitted to develop its legitimate results, to grow into a new and grander order of civilized society than the world had ever yet witnessed, the rotten and worn-out systems of Europe were doomed to certain and perhaps early overthrow. It is true, the agents employed did not know this—indeed, their European masters were ignorant, perhaps, of the principles involved; but the instinct of self-preservation, the instinct inherent in hostile systems impelled them forward, while the ends to be reached, or the consequences of success, were always too apparent to be mistaken. But their savage instruments were destroyed in the conflict, in the uses to which they were applied by their European allies; and what-ever may be the future fate of the Aborigines in Spanish America, the North American Indian is virtually annihilated. A few wild tribes of the West and South-west, whose means for preserving existence are every day growing less, still remain, and some remnants of semi-civilized tribes, which are perishing even more rapidly than the former, are to be found on our Western frontier; but the time is not distant, perhaps, when they will be wholly and absolutely extinct.

What might have been, it is useless to conjecture; but the notion of a certain class of sentimentalists among us, that we have done the Indian great wrong, and that, had we treated him with kindness and justice, he might have become civilized, and a part of our permanent population, of course, is absurd; for it is founded on that foolish dogma of a single race, which Europe has fastened on the American mind, and which supposes the Indian, as the Negro, etc., to have the same nature as themselves. Nor is the notion of others, that the Indian is incapable of civilization, and therefore destined to give way before the advance of the white man, worthy of any consideration; for this involves the paradox of being created without a purpose, a supposition not to be entertained a moment; for the most insignificant beings in the lowest forms of organic life have their uses, and the human creature, surely, was not created in vain. The simple truth is, that we need to know what the Indian is in fact, his true nature and true relations to our own race, and then, as we have done in the case of the Negro, adapt the social and governmental machinery to the wants of both races. But this employment and consequent destruction of the Indians of America by the monarchists of Europe, though often inflicting great temporary evil on our border settlements, did not retard our progress in the least, nor did England, to any appreciable extent, succeed in her objects. The theory or dogma of a single race, which her writers and publicists had set up about the time of the Revolution, produced, however, immense practical results both in Europe and America. The doctrines of the American Revolution, as was foreseen by British statesmen, soon became universally accepted in France, and threatened to overturn monarchy all over the Continent, and indeed in England itself. Dr. Johnson, Wilberforce, Pitt, and all the great writers and leaders of England, naturally enough adopted the notion that

Indians, Negroes, etc., were men like themselves, except in color, cultivation, etc.; but they were impelled, by the necessities of their system and the preservation of monarchical institutions, to practicalize this theory to the utmost extent in their power, and thus divert the attention of their own oppressed white people from *their* wrongs, by holding up before them continually the *imaginary* wrongs of "American slaves." They said, "It is true, you laborers of Yorkshire and operatives of Birmingham have a hard life, a life of constant toil and privation; but you are free-born Englishmen, and your own masters, and in all England there is not a single slave; while in America, in that so-called land of freedom, where there is no king, or noble, or law of primogeniture, and where, in theory, it is declared that all men are created free and equal, one sixth of the population are slaves, so abject and miserable that they are sold in the public markets, like horses and oxen. What, then, are your oppressions or your wrongs in comparison with those of American slaves? or what are the evils or the injustice of monarchy when contrasted with those dark and damning crimes of American democracy, that thus, in these enlightened times, dooms one sixth of the population to open and undisguised slavery?" Such was the argument of the British writers, and it was unanswerable if it had rested on *fact*— if the foundation were true, then the inference, of course, was unavoidable. If the so-called American slave was created free and equal with his master, then all that the British writers charged would have been true enough, and American slavery, in comparison with British liberty—or what passed for such in Yorkshire and Birmingham—would have been a wrong, so deep, damning, and fathomless, that no words in our language would be able to express its enormity. How was the poor, ignorant, and helpless laborer, or even his defenders, Fox, Sheridan, and other liberal leaders of the day, to answer this

argument? They did not attempt it. They admitted that
" American slavery" was all that it was charged to be—that it
was a wrong and evil immeasurably greater and more atrocious than any of those which the people of France had risen
against, or that the masses in England suffered under; but
they hoped that the great principle of the American Revolution
was strong enough to overcome this wrong, and in the process of time, to " abolish slavery," and that liberty would become universal among Americans. Indeed, some of those who
had been the most devoted believers in the great American doctrine, both in England and France, were so painfully impressed
by the seeming wrong done the negro, that they lost their interest, to a great extent, in the real wrongs of the white man,
and devoted all their efforts to the former. Societies were
formed in London and Paris, funds contributed, books published, tracts distributed, and extensive arrangements entered
into, with the sole purpose of relieving the " American slave"
from the fancied wrongs that were heaped on him; and their
societies, these " *Amis des Noirs*," patronized by Robespierre and other leaders of the people, which were formed in
almost every town in France and England, popularized the
movement, and so identified the imaginary cause of the negro
with that of the European masses, that to this day they doubtless seem inseparable. And even in our own times, we have
witnessed the sorry spectacle of English laborers contributing
of their wretched pittance to glorify some abolition hero or
heroine of the " Uncle Tom" pattern, under the deplorable
misconception, of course, that these blind tools of the enemies
of liberty were faithful defenders of a common cause, when, in
truth, they were vastly more dangerous to that cause than
the open and avowed friends of despotism. But this very
natural mistake of the friends of freedom in Europe, this ignorance and misconception of the negro nature and relations

2

to the white man, which led Fox in England, and Robespierre
in France, to confound the cause of the oppressed multitudes
of their own race with the imaginary interests of negrodom,
extended and unfortunate as it was and still is, was surpassed
by a still more insidious and more extended influence. Wilberforce, who, more than any other man, gave form and direction to the great " anti-slavery" delusion of modern times, was
eminently pious—as piety is accepted by a large portion of the
religious world. He was an Episcopalian in form, but pre-
eminently a Puritan in practice ; and, while doubtless sin-
cere in his belief, and perfectly correct in his religious habits,
he was one of the most complete bigots, religious, political,
and social, the world ever saw. Belonging to the ruling class,
and possessed of a considerable fortune, he believed that his
own *status* was the stand-point, and himself the model, for the
government of society, and therefore was as doggedly and
bitterly opposed to any change in England, or to any reform
in English society, as he was earnest in his efforts to relieve
the " sufferings of the slave" in America. In a public career
of some forty years, as a member of Parliament, he never failed
to record his vote against any increase of popular freedom, or
any change that tended to ameliorate the condition of the white
masses, and just as steadily and uniformly labored to " elevate"
the negro to the *status* of the English laborer, or, at all events,
to favor that final " abolition of slavery," which he himself
was not, however, destined to witness in the British American
possessions. But throughout he regarded the question rather
as a religious than a political one, and at an early period, in
this respect, impressed his own character on it. Identified
with the Church, all his notions those of the High Church
party—substantially the notions that Archbishop Laud entertained two centuries before—by birth and association connected with the landed aristocracy, and yet distinguished for

practical piety, for a zeal and devotion to his religious duties
that the most zealous among the Dissenters and Evangelicals
might imitate but could not surpass, this was just the man
to impress a great movement with his own characteristics, and
the " anti-slavery cause" became the cause of religion as well
as of liberty with the religious world.   Nor was it confined to
the " American slave ;" it embraced the whole world of heath-
endom ; and a religious crusade sprang up, that finally became
more extended, and, in some respects, more permanent, than
the great political movement inaugurated by Jefferson a few
years before.   And if the Father of Lies, Lucifer himself, had
plotted a plan or scheme for concealing a great truth, and
embarrassing a great cause, he could have accomplished nothing more effective than the movement that Wilberforce inaugurated for the professed benefit of the negro and other subordinate races of mankind, which, masked under the form of
religious duty, and appealing to the conscience, the love of
proselytism, the enthusiasm, and even the bigotries of the
religious world, has, for more than half a century, held in
thrall the conscience as well as the reason of Christendom.
Robespierre, and other patrons of the *Amis des Noirs*, could
only present a common cause, that " universal liberty" which
they declared to be the birthright of *all* men, and which it
were better that every conceivable calamity should happen
rather than this " great principle" should perish ; but when it
became the duty of every Christian man and woman, every
follower of Christ and professor of religion, to work and
pray for " the deliverance of the slave," then a power was
aroused that nothing could resist, for it became an immediate and sacred duty to labor in this cause.   Missionary societies were organized, money contributed by millions both
in Europe and America, enthusiastic men and women offered
their services, even children were taught to give their pocket-

money for a cause so holy as that of redeeming the " slave,"
while all this time innumerable multitudes of their own race,
their own blood, those whom God had created their equals,
and endowed with like capacities, instincts, and wants, and
therefore designed for the same happiness as themselves, were
left to grovel in midnight darkness and abject misery.

It is not intended to sneer at or to indulge in unkind criti-
cism on missionary efforts. On the contrary, it is frankly admitted that they sprang from the sincerest conviction, and were
generally pursued with an utter disregard of selfish and mercenary considerations; but in not understanding the diversity of
races, these efforts were more likely to do harm than good. A
man's first duties are to his own household ; and no amount or
extent of benefits conferred on strangers, can excuse him for
neglecting the former; and even if the " heathen"—the Negro,
Indian, and Sandwich Islander—had been benefited by the
efforts of Wilberforce and his followers, the neglect of the ignorant, darkened, and miserable millions of their own race,
was a wrong that scarcely has a parallel in history. But they
did not benefit the subordinate races, but, on the contrary,
assuming them *to be beings like themselves*, when they were
widely different beings, they necessarily injured them; and
when it is reflected that they not only neglected the ignorant
and degraded multitudes of their own race, but got up a false
issue, in order to distract the attention and conceal the wrongs
of their own people, then an unequalled crime was committed.

. The government of England, which is simply an embodiment of the class to which Wilberforce belonged, acted in concert with these religious efforts ; and thus we see the leaders
of the popular cause in the Old World, Fox and Robespierre,
the Church and Aristocracy, all acting together in a common
cause, and laboring, in fact, to retard the progress and the
liberation of millions upon millions of their own race, under

the pretence, and doubtless with many, in the belief, that they were laboring for the benefit of the negro and other subordinate races. The government expended about a thousand millions to crush out American liberty in 1776; but it is quite likely that an almost equal sum, expended for the professed benefit of the negro, has accomplished vastly more than all other things together to protract the liberation of her own masses. It has been estimated that six hundred millions have been expended nominally to put down the slave trade, but in reality to pervert the natural relations of races, and force the subordinate negro to the *status* of the British laborer. The interest on this enormous sum is annually drawn from the sweat and toil of the English masses; and every hut and cottage in the British Islands is forced to surrender a portion of its daily food, or of the daily earnings of its owner, to pay the interest on money squandered on the negro in America! The amount thus paid, properly expended, would be amply sufficient to give a good English education to the entire laboring class; but that would be an overwhelming calamity to the governing class, who could not retain their power for a single day after the masses were thus enlightened.

A few years since, famine and pestilence swept over Ireland, carrying off some three millions of the Irish people, all of whom might have been saved if the annual amount wasted on negroes in America had been applied to this beneficent and legitimate purpose. Indeed, it is quite possible that if the money wrung from the sweat and toil of Irishmen alone, for the pretended benefit of the negro, had been appropriated to the relief of the suffering multitudes of that unhappy people, few would really have perished. The mortgage on the bodies and souls of future generations of British laborers, for the avowed purpose of "doing good" to the negro, enormous as the amount may be—and it has been estimated as high as one thousand million dollars—is only a portion of the vast waste and wholesale destruction of property involved in the British Free Negro policy, or so-called schemes of philanthropy. Farms and plantations in Jamaica and other islands, valued at fifty thousand pounds prior to the "emancipation," were afterward sold with difficulty at ten and even five thousand pounds; and indeed extensive districts were abandoned by their unfortunate owners. An infamous system of fraud and inhumanity, practiced of late years on the ignorant and simple Chinese and other Asiatics, has enabled some planters to recover and restore their wasted and plundered estates; and the vile hypocrites who filled the world with their doleful lamentations over the sorrows of Africa, not only wink at this infinitely greater wrong practiced on Asiatics, but resort to the *effects* attending it, as a proof that emancipation has not ruined these beautiful islands! Could audacity and hypocrisy surpass, or did they ever surpass, this shameless fraud? But this new and vastly more atrocious system of "man-stealing," is transitional and temporary. The Mongol or Asiatic is rapidly worked up and destroyed in the West Indies; and, as no females are introduced, they can never become an essential or permanent element of the population.

The negro, forced from his normal condition, and into unnatural relation to the white man, must relapse into his African habits, just as fast as the white element disappears; and as the latter is relatively feeble, the time must soon come, unless we take possession and restore the natural order, when civilization itself will utterly perish, and the great heart of the continent be surrendered to African savagism! The eternal and immovable laws fixed forever in the heart and organism of things, can not be changed or modified by human folly, fraud, or power; and therefore the climate, the soil, the products, and the *means* that the Almighty has ordained shall be used to make them tributary to human welfare, have their fixed and everlasting relations since time began. The brain of the white man and the muscles of the negro, the mind of the superior and the body of the inferior race, in natural relation to each other, are the vital principles of tropical civilization, without which it is as impossible that civilization should exist in the great centre of the continent, as that vegetation should spring from granite, or animals exist without atmospheric air; and, therefore, thrusting the negro from his natural sphere into unnatural relations with the white man, necessarily destroys the latter, and drives the other into his inherent and original Africanism.

The delusion, the folly, or the fraud of Wilberforce and his associates, in presenting a false issue to their own wronged and oppressed millions, and thus diverting their attention from their own oppressions to the imaginary sufferings of negroes and other subordinate races, is so transcendent, its magnitude so enormous, that we have no terms in our language that can express it; but great and indeed awful as may be this wrong on the white man, it is in some respects really surpassed by the evils, if not the wrongs, inflicted on the negro. More than one million of negroes are believed to have perished, through the means resorted to to suppress the slave trade; and now it is admitted that those attempts have not prevented the importation of one single negro! The world needed the products of the tropics; the labor of a certain number of negroes were needed to furnish these products; and therefore, when fifty thousand were required in Cuba, eighty thousand were shipped on the African coast, thus leaving a margin of thirty thousand to be destroyed by interference with the laws of demand and supply. Who can contemplate these frightful results without awe, and sorrow, and pity, not alone for the victims, but for the authors of such wide-spread

and boundless calamity. The crusades of the middle ages are
now recognized as utterly baseless—simple human delusions,
in which millions of lives were sacrificed, not to an idea, but
to a false assumption—an assumption that the Holy Sepulchre
could be recovered at Jerusalem. That crusade of "humanity," in behalf of the subordinate races, set up by Wilberforce
and his associates in modern times, is also a simple delusion,
based on a false assumption, the assumption that negroes are
black-white men, or men like ourselves, and though not so
fatal to human life as the former, its effects or influences on
human welfare are vastly and immeasurably more deplorable.

Such is the great "anti-slavery" delusion of our times. It
is wholly European and monarchical in its origin ; and leaving
out of view all other considerations, its mere existence among
us, or that any considerable number of Americans could be so
deluded and mentally so degraded, as to embrace it, will aston-
ish posterity to the latest generations. We are in contact
with the negro—we see he is a negro—a different being from
ourselves. We will not—even the most deluded Abolitionist
will not, in his own case or family, act on the assumption that
he is a being like himself, indeed, would rather see his child
carried to the grave than intermarried with a negro, however
rich, cultivated, and pious ; and rather than thus live out his
own professed belief, he would prefer the death of his whole
household. The European, on the contrary, naturally enough
supposes the negro to differ only in color ; and the monarchist
—the enemy of Democracy—the man opposed to the great
principle of equality underlying our system—just as naturally
demands that we shall be consistent and apply it to negroes.
But instead of enlightening this European ignorance, and
indignantly rejecting this monarchical impudence, which pro-
poses that we shall degrade our blood and destroy our institutions, by including a subordinate race in our political system,

we have foolishly, wickedly, and .abjectly assented to the European assumption, and millions of Americans have based their
reasonings, and to a certain extent their actions, on this pal-
pahle, fundamental, and monstrous falsehood. Those portions
of the country most directly under the mental dictation of the
Old World, are those, of course, most given up to the delusion, but nearly the whole northern mind has adopted it as a
mental habit. The time, however, has come when it must be
exploded, and the *reason* of the people restored, or it will drag
after it consequences and calamities that one shudders to contemplate. Eighty years ago it was an abstraction, universally
assented to, and just as universally rejected in practice ; for
all the States save one then recognized the legal subordination
of the negro as a social necessity, whatever the speculative
notions were on this subject. They generally believed that,
in some indefinite or mysterious manner, it would—or rather
that the negro would—become extinct ; and as the industrial
powers of this element of the general population was not
specifically adapted to our then territory, all perhaps were
willing to hope that it should some day disappear. But the
vast acquisition of Southern territory, the discovery and opening up of new channels of industry, and the extensive cultivation of those great staples so essential to human welfare, which
are only to be attained on this continent by the labor of the
negro when directed by the white man ; and, moreover, the
rapid increase of this population, and the certainty that it
must remain forever an element of our population, demand
that this mighty delusion shall be exposed, as it is in fact
the vilest and most infamous fraud on the freedom, dignity,
and welfare of the white millions ever witnessed since the
world began.

CHAPTER II.

THE organic world is separated into two great divisions, animal and vegetable, or into animate and inanimate beings. In regard to the vegetable kingdom, as it is termed, it is not necessary to say a word; those desirous of obtaining a thorough knowledge of animal life, however, had better begin their studies with the more elementary and simple forms of vegetable being. Many persons suppose that the whole animate existence is linked together by connecting or continuous gradations. In a certain sense this may be said to be so; nevertheless, absolutely considered, each family or form of being is a complete and independent creation. There are resemblances and approximations as well as gradations, yet each is perfect in itself, and makes up an entire world of its own. The Almighty Creator, in His infinite wisdom, has provided against chance, or accident, or human caprice, and placed each and every one of His works in a position of such absolute independence, that one of them, or more, perhaps, might utterly perish, and yet the beauty and harmony of nature would remain unimpaired. It is certain that some species of animals belonging to the existing order have utterly disappeared, and it is quite probable that some species of men have perished; but the grand economy of nature is unaffected by it. It is thought that the aborigines of this continent will, in time, utterly perish, and yet no one supposes that that event will disturb the operations of nature or deface the fair form of creation. This shows that there is no continuous or connecting link even among species of the same family or form of being. If there were such—if all the forms of life were continuous and connecting gradations —then it is evident that the destruction of one of these connecting links would cast the whole economy of being into utter confusion. In a watch, or any other elaborate machinery of human contrivance, a single wheel, or cog, or link, however minute, torn from its place, involves the disruption, if not absolute destruction, of the whole machine. And so it is in the economy of individual life, for, though one organ may be disabled, another, to a certain extent, and for a given time, supplies its place; yet the vital forces are enfeebled from the instant of such accident, and life, if not interrupted, is always impaired. But a species, a genus, a class, perhaps, a great number of these, might disappear, utterly vanish from existence, and those remaining would preserve the integrity and completeness the Creator had endowed them with at the beginning. While each and every form of life is, therefore, perfect in itself and independent of all others, there are resemblances and approximations that must be regarded as of vital importance.

Naturalists have divided or separated the organic world into classes, orders, genera, species and varieties. Classes are those like the mammalia—that is, all animals where the female nourishes its offspring by mammary glands. Orders are those like the quadrumana—all those having four hands. A genus, or a family proper, is composed of species; and a species includes varieties, or possible varieties, of the same being under different circumstances. But these classifications are, to a considerable extent, arbitrary; and though they serve the purpose of facilitating our studies, they may also lead us astray, if too closely followed. Genera, or families proper, in many cases at least, are, however, susceptible of very exact definitions. So, too, are species. For example:—The simiadæ, or monkey family, are so entirely distinct that they will not be or need not be confounded with anything else. Some ignorant or superficial persons, with the false notion of continuous and connecting gradations, have supposed the negro something midway between men and animals. But there is no such monstrosity in nature, for, as already observed, each form of being is a complete and independent creation in itself. A genus is composed of a given number of species, all diff——ant from each other, and, it need not be repeated, independent of each other. These genera are believed to be incapable of interunion with other genera, though this has been questioned in some cases. Species are capable of a limited interunion, though it may be doubted if such interunion ever occurs in a wild or savage state. And as each species is different in form and character from others, so the limited capacity for interunion varies, or in other words, hybrids—the product of different species—vary in their virility or power of reproduction. The given number of species of which a genus is composed, ascends or descends in the scale of being, that is, there is a head and base to the generic column. The one next above the most inferior has all the qualities of the latter, but these qualities have a fuller development, that is, the organization is more elaborate and the corresponding faculties are of a higher order. And indeed this is not confined to mere species or genera even, but is true of widely separated beings. Thus, the exalted and elegant Caucasian mother—the habitue of the Fifth avenue or St. Germain—nourishes her offspring by the same process common to the meanest of the mammalia. So, too, in the process of gestation, the function of mastication, deglutition, digestion, the sense of taste, of sight, etc.—the function is absolutely the same, but what a world of difference in the mode of its manifestation, that distinguishes the human being from the animal!

Investigations made by some French physiologists would seem to show that the mysterious problem of animal life might be simplified, and clearly grasped by the human intellect, by simply tracing this great fact to its elementary sources. It is said that the embryo (Caucasian) fœtus passes through all the forms of an innumerable number of lower gradations before it reaches its own specific development. And be this as it may, enough is seemingly established to demonstrate its truth in respect to a genus or family, and especially is it demonstrated in the human creation. At a certain stage of fœtal development there is the cranial manifestation of the Negro, then the aboriginal American, the Malay, the Mongolian, and finally the broad expansion and oval perfection of the most perfect of all, the superior Caucasian. Nor can these demonstrations be mistaken, for it is not a mere question of size but of form. The negro brain is small and longitudinal—thus approximating to the si niadæ and other animals. The aboriginal is larger and quadrangular, almost square in its general outline. The Mongolian pyramidal, and still larger than either of the others. Finally, at the period of complete gestation, there is the full and complete oval development, alone peculiar to the Caucasian. The force of these distinctions may be easily grasped by the non-scientific reader by bearing in mind that a female of either of these races or species could no more give birth to a child with the cranial development of a race different from her own, than she could to that of an inferior animal. The distinctions of nature, or the boundaries which separate even species from each other, are absolutely impassable; each has the hand of the Eternal impressed upon it forever, which neither accident nor time can modify in the slightest particular. They have, it is true, a limited capacity for interunion, and we sometimes witness the disgusting spectacle of a white woman with a so-called negro husband. But while the offspring of this unnatural connection is limited in number, they partake of the nature of both the parents, and thus the birth becomes possible, though at the expense of great physical suffering to the mother and perhaps in every case shortening her existence. In another place this subject will be more especially discussed; it is only referred to in this connection to show the perfect order and harmony in the economy of animal life. The primal steps—the process of reproduction—the starting point of creation—being in complete harmony with the laws governing the being, man or animal, after it has reached its mature development.

The same eternal separation of all the forms of being and the same eternal approximations, however varied the manifestations may be at different periods, remain unaltered and unalterable. Linnæus ventured to place "man" in the category or class mammalia, while at the same time he separated the mammalia from birds and other forms of being—thus assuming that the human creation had a closer union with pigs and dogs, than the latter have with birds, etc. At this every Christian and believer in a future state of being must revolt, for though there are certain approximations that cannot be disregarded, nevertheless it is absolutely certain that the human creation is separated by an interval wider than that separating any of the forms of mere animal life, and therefore his classification must be wrong.

It is not intended to make this a scientific work, but on the contrary, to popularize for the general reading of the people, some few elementary truths of zoology and physiology in order that they can better comprehend the subject really to be discussed, viz.:—the specific differences and specific relations of the white and black races. But the author feels himself con-

scientiously impelled to dissent from the classifications of Linnæus, and those modern naturalists who follow him, not only as
being untrue in point of fact, but pregnant with mighty mischief. Linnæus placed "man" in the category mammalia, but
made him an order, a genus and species by himself. This is
false as a matter of fact, for in the entire world of animal
existence there is no such fact as a single species. All the
forms of life are made up of groups or families, properly genera, and each of these is composed of a certain number of
species. These species, as already observed, differ from each
other. They begin with the lowest, or simplest, or grossest
formation, and rise, one above the other, in the scale of being,
until the group is completed; so that they are all, not only
specifically different from each other, but absolutely unlike
each other in every thing, in the minutest particle of elementary matter as well as in those things palpable to the sense.
Generally considered, they resemble each other, but specifically
considered, they are absolutely distinct, and, it need not be
repeated, the distinctions in each case or each individual species are also specific.

That Linnæus and other European naturalists, and especially
the ethnologists, should make such a mistake, and suppose that
the human creation is composed of a single species, is perhaps
natural enough, for they saw but one—the two hundred millions of Europe, except a few thousand Laplanders, being all
Caucasians. But then it is strange how those so ready to
class men with animals should so widely depart from the spirit
and order of their own classification. They must have known
that in the whole world of animate existence there was no such
fact as a single species, and therefore when assuming only a
single human species, that they directly contradicted or ignored the most constant, universal and uniform fact in organic
life, a fact underlying and forming the very basis of all with

which they were dealing. This mistake, or misconception, or ignorance of European ethnologists, however, is of no particular importance. They saw no other and therefore could know of no other species of men except their own, and though its effect on ourselves has been mischievous, the cause of their misconception is so palpable to men's common sense that it only needs to be pointed out to be utterly rejected. It is about as respectable as the assumptions of the northern Abolitionists, who, though not even venturing out of Massachusetts, affect to know, and doubtless really believe that they do know, more about the internal condition of South Carolina or Virginia than the people of those States themselves. But facts are stubborn things, and, as the Spanish proverb says, " seeing is believing." It is impossible that the northern Abolitionist who never ventured out of New England can comprehend a condition of society that he has never seen. So, too, the authority of European writers, necessarily ignorant of the subject, will be rejected by those whose very senses assure them that negroes are specifically different from white men. And that mental dominion which, beginning with the early planting of European colories on this continent, has continued long after political independence has been secured, only needs to be cast off altogether, to convince every one of the utter absurdity of European teachings on the subject.

But there is an objection to the Linnæan classification infinitely more important than this misconception in regard to species. He places his one human species (Caucasian) in the class mammalia, and therefore assumes that the human creation has a closer connection with a class of animals, than these animals themselves have with some other forms of animal life. For example : men (and white men, too) approximate more closely to dogs and cats than the latter do to owls and eagles ! It does not help the matter to say that this is only in their animal structures, for there is an invariable and imperishable unity between the material organization and the external manifestations or faculties, which is fixed forever, and the conclusion or inference from the Linnæan assumption is unavoidable —if men approximate more closely to a class of animals than these animals do to some other class, then it is absurd to suppose the purposes assigned them by the Almighty are so widely different as our reason and instinct alike impel us to believe. To hope for or to believe in immortality, or in a destiny so transcendent, while beings that closely resembled us perished with this life, in common with those still farther separated from themselves, was such a contradiction to reason, that men involuntarily shrunk from it, and the result has been to repel vast numbers of people from the study and investigation of this most essential element of all knowledge. The Materialists promptly accepted it, and wielded it with tremendous effect in advancing their gloomy and forbidding philosophy, while those impelled by that innate and indescribable consciousness of the soul itself, which, in its Godlike knowledge, rises high beyond the realms of reason and mere human will, and assures them of a life immortal and everlasting, shrunk from all study or investigation of the laws of physical life, as if it involved consequences fatal to that higher life of the soul. The former said, and said truly, if men have a closer union with the quadrumana than the latter have with birds, etc., then it is all nonsense to suppose that they have an eternity of life, while those separated by a still wider interval are limited to the present. And the only reply to their reasoning has been the refusal to investigate the subject or to study the laws of God, and to admit, inferentially at least, that there was a contradiction between the word and the works of the Almighty.

Nothing is more common than to find men of great intelligénce on almost every subject except this, the most vital, indeed the foundation and starting point of all real knowledge. Especially are clergymen ignorant, and those who assume to be the interpreters of the laws of God are not unfrequently the most ignorant of the most palpable and fundamental of these laws. This should not be so, and in all reasonable probability would not be so had it not been for the untruthful and unfortunate classification of Linnæus. Instead of meeting the Materialists on their own ground, and showing them that however approximating to certain forms of animal life, the human creation was yet separated by an absolutely boundless as well as impassable interval—for the distinctions between them are utterly unlike those separating mere animal beings— they tacitly admitted the truth of their assumptions, and met it by a blind and foolish refusal to investigate the matter, indeed have generally cast their influence on the side of ignorance, and advised against the study of nature and the noblest works of God.

But there can be no contradiction; God cannot lie; and whatever seeming conflict there may be at times between His word and His works, a further search is alone needed to show their perfect uniformity. It is true that the physical resemblances between men and beings of the class mammalia seem closer than those of the latter and some other forms of life, but while there is also an eternal correspondence between structure and functions, it is rational and philosophical to suppose that the difference in the qualities or external manifestations is the safest standard of comparison. Or in other words, whatever may be the seeming physical resemblances, the differences in the faculties show that the former are not reliable. For example: in contemplating the intelligence of certain quadrupeds and birds, can any one suppose or believe for a moment that the difference between them in this respect equals

or even approaches to that separating both from human beings? And in the present state of our knowledge, our ignorance of the elementary arrangement of organic life, it is surely
safer and more philosophical to be governed by our reason
rather than our senses—to accept the differences which separate human intelligence from the animal world as boundless
and immeasurable when compared with the apparent physical
approximations which seem to unite us with a class of the
latter.

In conclusion, it is scarcely necessary to repeat that there is
a fixed, uniform, and universal correspondence between structure and function, or between organism and the purpose it is
designed to fulfil. We do not know nor need to know the
cause of this or the nature of this unity. We only know, and
are only permitted to know, that it exists, and are not bound
to accept the dogma of the Materialists, that function is the
result of organism; nor that of their opponents, who still more
falsely imagine results without causes, or that there can be
functions without organism. Truth, in this instance, lies between extremes:—functions or faculties cannot exist without a
given structure or organism, but they are not a result of that
organism. They exist together inseparably, universally, eternally dependent on each other, but not a result of either. To
see there must be eyes; to hear, ears; to walk, the organism
of locomotion; to manifest a certain extent of intelligence
there must be a corresponding mental organism, but there is
no such thing proper as cause and effect, nothing but fact—
the fact of mutual existence.

CHAPTER III.

THE human creation, like all other families or forms of being, is composed of a genus, which includes some half dozen or more species. It has been the fashion to call these permanent varieties, and almost every writer on ethnology has made his own classification, or rather has created what number he pleased of these "imaginary varieties." Agassiz, unquestionably the greatest of American naturalists, but unfortunately not much of a physiologist, and therefore unprepared to deal with the higher truths of ethnology, supposes several species of white men, and, in regard to the subordinate races, would doubtless multiply them *ad infinitum*. But at this time, or in the existing state of our knowledge, the number actually known to exist cannot be assumed beyond that already named. They are thus:—1st. The Caucasian. 2d. The Mongolian. 3d. The Malay or Oceanic. 4th. The Aboriginal American. 5th. The Esquimaux; and 6th. The Negro or typical African.

The Caucasian can be confounded with no other, for though in some localities, climate and perhaps other causes darken the skin, sometimes with a deep olive tint, and extending, as with the Bedouins and the Jews of the Malabar coast, to almost black, the flowing beard (more constant than color), projecting forehead, oval features, erect posture and lordly presence, stamp him the master man wherever found.

The Mongolian, though less distinctive, is, however, sufficiently so, for his yellow skin, squat figure, beardless face,

pyramidal head, and almond eyes, can scarcely be confounded
with any other form of man. The Malay is less known, and
therefore more difficult to describe. They are darker than the
Mongol, though in some islands of a bright copper color, and
indeed, vary from light olive to dark brown, and as in the case
of the Australians, to deep black, but with no other approximation to the Negro.

The vast populations known under the term Papuan, and
mainly Malay, are doubtless extensively mixed with the Negro, for however remote the time, or whatever the form or
mode, real negro populations have resided in tropical Asia,
and left behind them these remains of their former existence.
In some islands, like New Zealand, etc., the ruling dynasties or principal families have a considerable infusion of Caucasian blood, which is shown in their tall, erect form, more
or less beard, fair complexion, and manly presence, and intellectually in their prompt and often intelligent acceptance of
Christianity.

The Indian, American, or Aboriginal, needs no description;
suffice it to say that, from the mouth of the Columbia River to
Cape Horn, they are the same species. It is quite possible,
indeed probable, that some species, fomerly existing on this
continent, have disappeared—utterly perished. The investigations of Dr. Tschudi warrant this belief, though his nice dis-
criminations in regard to some of the bones of the head are of
little or no importance, as all this might be, and doubtless was,
the result of artificial causes. But crania discovered in Southern Mexico and Yucatan, as well as in Peru and Brazil, are
sufficient evidence to warrant the belief that a still inferior race
did once really inhabit this continent, but whether aboriginal
or brought here by some superior race, may never be known.
The remains of ancient structures in Yucatan, in Peru, in Mexico, in Brazil, all over the southern portion of the continent,

show simply the traces of Caucasian intrusion. It has been generally supposed that Columbus and his companions were the first white men that ever visited this continent, but it may have been discovered, and to a certain extent, occupied, at least certain localities occupied, before even Europe itself, or before the period of authentic history. Any one visiting Mexico, Puebla, or other cities of Spanish America, is amazed and bewildered with the contrast between the vast and magnificent structures that meet his eye, and the existing population. He involuntarily asks himself, "Can these people be the authors of all this art, this beauty, strength and magnificence? Can these miserable, barefooted, blanketed, idle and stolid-looking creatures have built these palaces, these churches, these bridges, these mighty structures, which seem to have been built for eternity itself, so strong and secure are their foundations?" Some years hence this contrast would be still more palpable, and, left to themselves, a time would come when it would be obvious that the existing population had nothing to do with these structures, for the mixed blood would have disappeared, and there would be only the simple, unadulterated "native American," as discovered by the Spaniards three centuries ago. And we have only to apply this to the antiquities of America to understand its history, at all events, to understand the meaning of those half-buried monuments so frequently found on its surface. Adventurers, often, doubtless, shipwrecked mariners, were cast upon the coasts of America. Possibly in some cases before Rome was founded, or Babylon itself was the mighty capital of a still more mighty empire, these enterprising or unfortunate men found themselves undisputed sovereigns of the New World. We know that Northmen found their way here in the eighth century, and doubtless they were preceded at intervals by numerous other Caucasians. Settling in some localities they reigned undisputed masters, built cities, organized governments, framed laws, and laid the foundations of a civilized society. But intermarrying with the natives, they were swallowed up by mongrelism, and, in obedience to an immutable law of physical life, doomed to perish, and at a given period, the white blood extinct, there remained nothing to denote its former existence, except the half-buried palaces' and ruined monuments yet to be traced over large portions of the continent. The Toltecs, Aztecs, etc., are simply the remnants of these extinct Caucasians, just as the present population, if left alone in Mexico, the latest portion of it, with Caucasian blood, would be the ruling force, and perhaps retain somewhat or some portion of the Spanish habitudes.

The pure native mind is capable of a certain development, but that is fixed and determinate, and beyond which it can no more progress than it can alter the color of its skin or the form of its brain. Powhatan's empire in Virginia was undoubtedly aboriginal and probably called out the utmost resources and reached the utmost limit of the Indian mind. The Indian has, and does manifest to a certain extent, a capacity of mental action, but this is too feeble and limited to make a permanent impression on the physical agents that surround him, and therefore he can have no history, for there are no materials—nothing to record. The term, therefore, "Indian antiquities," is a misnomer and the great congressional enterprise under the editorship of Mr. Schoolcraft an obvious absurdity.

The Polar or Esquimaux race has been least known of all, and prior to the explorations of that true hero and true son of science, the late Dr. Kane, was scarcely known except in name. It is both Asiatic and American, but which continent is its birth-place is matter of doubt. The facilities for passing from one continent to the other were doubtless much greater at some former period than at present, and not only men but ani-

mals may have done so with ease. Except a few well-known
species of animals and vegetables, which are essential to the
well-being of the Caucasian, and which have accompanied
him in all his migrations, each species has its own centre of
existence, beyond or outside of which it is limited to a determinate existence. The Arctic animals are quite numerous, and
differ widely from all others, but they are absolutely the same
in Asia as in America, and therefore must have passed from
one to the other, and man, however subordinate or inferior
to other races endowed by nature with ample powers of locomotion and migration, could meet with only trifling obstacles
in passing from one continent to the other. This race, though
thus far of little or no importance, is doubtless superior to the
Negro, for the necessities of its existence, the terrible struggle for very life in those bleak and desolate regions, infer the
possession of powers superior to those of a race whose centre
of life is in the fertile and luxuriant tropics, where nature produces spontaneously, and where the idle and sensual Negro
only needs to gather these products to exist and multiply his
kind.

Finally, we have the Negro—last and least, the lowest in
the scale but possibly the first in the order of Creation, for
there are many reasons in the nature and structure of things
that indicate, if they do not altogether warrant, the inference
that the Negro was first and the Caucasian latest in the programme or order of Creation. The typical, woolly-haired Negro may have been created in tropical Asia, and carried thence
to Africa, as in modern times he has been carried to tropical
America. Like other subordinate races, it never migrates, but
the extensive traces of its former existence in Asia show beyond doubt that that was either its primal home, or that it
had been carried there by the Caucasian long anterior to the
historic era. But it is now found in its pure state or specific

form in Africa alone, and even here large portions of it have undergone extensive adulteration. Our knowledge of Africa is very limited and consequently very imperfect. African travelers, explorers, missionaries, etc., ignorant of the ethnology, of the physiology, of the true nature of the Negro, and moreover, bitten by modern philanthropy, a disease more loathsome and fatal to the moral than small-pox or plague to the physical nature, have been bewildered, and perverted, and rendered unfit for truthful observation or useful discovery before they set foot on its soil or felt a single flush of its burning sun. With the monstrous conception that the Negro was a being like themselves, with the same instincts, wants, etc., and the same (latent) mental capacities, all they saw, felt, or reasoned upon in Africa was seen through this false medium, and therefore of little or no value. Thus Barth and Livingston encountering a mongrel tribe or community, with, of course, a certain degree or extent of civilization—the result of Caucasian inervation, or perhaps the remains of a former pure white population, note it down and spread it before the world as evidence of Negro capacity, and an indication of the future progress of the race! Myriads and countless myriads of white men have lived and died on the soil of Africa; vast populations and entire nations have emigrated to that continent. At one time there were half a million of Christians (white) and forty thousand inmates of religious houses in the valley of the Nile alone, while three hundred Christian Bishops assembled at Carthage, and it will be a reasonable assumption to say that since the Christian era, there have been five hundred millions of whites in Africa. What has become of them? They have not emigrated—have not been slaughtered in battle, nor destroyed by pestilence, nor devoured by famine, and yet these countless hosts, these innumerable millions, these Christian devotees and holy bishops have all disappeared, as utterly

3

perished as if the earth had opened and swallowed them up.
With the downfall of the Roman empire, civilization receded
from Africa, and the white population were gradually swallowed up by mongrelism. The Negro, being the predominant
element, absorbed, or rather annihilated, the lesser one, and the
result is now seen in numerous, almost countless, mixed hybrid
or mongrel tribes and populations spread all over that continent. It is certainly possible, indeed probable, that there are two
or three, or more species of men, closely approximating, it is
true, nevertheless specifically different from the woolly-haired
or typical Negro. One of these (the Hottentots or Bushmen)
with the true negro features but of dirty yellow color, it would
seem almost certain must be a separate species; but until some
one better qualified to judge, than those hitherto relied on,
has investigated this subject, it is only safe to assume but a
single species, and that the other and numerous populations
of Africa, however resembling or approximating to the typical
Negro, are hybrids and mongrels, the effete and expiring remains of the mighty populations and imposing civilizations
that once flourished upon its soil. There may be also other
species besides the Mongol in Asia, and beside the Malay in
Oceanica, and it is quite probable that some species have
totally perished. But it is certain that those thus briefly discussed now exist; that their location, their history, as far as
they can be said to have a history, their physical qualities and
mental condition, in short, their specific characters, are plainly
marked and well understood. Nevertheless, and though all
this belongs to the domain of fact, and it is as absurd to question it as it would be to question the existence of diverse species in any of the genera or families of the animal creation, the
" world" generally holds to the notion of a single human race.
It is not designed to expressly argue this point, for, to the
American mind, it is so obvious, if not self-evident, that the

Human Creation is composed of diverse species, that argument is misplaced if not absolutely absurd. The European people rarely see the Negro or other species of men, and therefore the notion of a single human race or species (with them) is natural enough, indeed a mental necessity. Ethnologists—men of vast erudition, of noble intellect and honest and conscientious intentions—have devoted their powers to this subject, and volume upon volume has been published to demonstrate the assumption of a single race. Buffon, Blumenbach, Tiedemann, Prichard, even Cuvier himself, have given in their adherence to this dogma, or rather it should be said have set out with the assumption of a single race and collected a vast amount of material—of fact or presumed fact—to demonstrate its supposed truth. Nor is it an easy matter to explode their sophistries or to disprove their assumptions. With great and admitted claims to scientific acquirement and powers of reasoning, they combine undoubted honesty of intention and seemingly careful and patient investigation, and the amount or extent of evidence adduced, the elaborate and mighty array of fact, of learned and imposing authority appealed to, and the fatiguing if not unwarrantable argument put forward, made it, and still make it difficult to reply to them or to disprove their assumptions. Any question, no matter what its nature, or however deficient in the elements of truth, still admits of argument, and falsehood may often lead astray the reason even when the judgment itself is convinced to the contrary. And these European advocates of the dogma of a single race have such a boundless field for discussion, can so bewilder and fatigue the reason as well as pervert the imagination by their plausible arguments, drawn from the analysis of animal life, that it is not wonderful they should lead astray the popular mind; nor is it surprising that those among us claiming to be men of science should bow to their authority, for though common sense

rejects their arguments, there are few of sufficient mental independence to withstand that authority, when backed up by
such an imposing array of distinguished names. But the
strong common sense that distinguishes our people will not
be, indeed, cannot be, deceived on this subject. The American
or the Southern knows that the Negro is a Negro, and is not
a Caucasian, just as clearly, absolutely and unmistakably as he
knows that black is black and is not white, that a man is a
man and is not a woman—that a pigeon is a pigeon and is not
a robin—or a shad a shad and not a salmon. He sees negro
parents have negro offspring; that Indians have Indian offspring; and that whites have white offspring, " each after its
kind," with the same regularity, uniformity and perfect certainty that is witnessed in all other forms of existence. There
is not a white man or woman in the Union who, if told of
such a thing as white parents with negro offspring, or negroes
with white offspring, would believe it, even if sworn to by a
million of witnesses. Such a belief or such a conception would
be as monstrous, and indeed impossible, as to suppose that
robins had begotten pigeons or horses asses. And the constant witnessing of this—this undeviating and perpetual order
in the economy of animal life, demonstrates the specific character of the Negro beyond doubt or possible mistake. Irishmen, Germans, Frenchmen, etc., come here, settle down, become citizens, and their offspring born and raised on American
soil differ in no appreciable or perceptible manner from other
Americans. But Negroes may have been brought here three
centuries ago, and their offspring of to-day is exactly as it was
then, as absolutely and specifically unlike the American as
when the race first touched the soil and first breathed the air
of the New World. It is not intended, as already observed,
to argue this matter, for it is a palpable and unavoidable fact
that Negroes are a separate species; and though in succeeding

chapters of this work the specific qualities are examined in detail, these detailed demonstrations are merely designed to present the physical differences in order to determine the moral relations, and not by any means to demonstrate a fact always palpable to the senses. Even those foolish people, disposed to pervert terms or play upon words—to admit the fact, thus palpable, but ready to confound and distort the reason by the application or use of false terms, cannot avoid the inevitable conclusion of distinct species. To conceal or keep out of sight this truth, some have thus admitted these every day seen and unmistakable specific differences in dividing races, but a silly as strange perversity has prompted them to use the term "permanent varieties" instead of "species," as if white and black were variations and not specialties. It is a fact, an existing, unalterable, demonstrable, and unmistakable fact, that the Negro is specifically different from ourselves—a fact uniform and invariable, which has accompanied each generation, and under every condition of circumstances, of climate, social condition, education, time and accident, from the landing at Jamestown to the present day. The Naturalist, reasoning alone on this basis of fact, says, that which has been uniform and undiviating for three hundred years, in all kinds of climate and under all kinds of circumstances, in a state of "freedom" or condition of "slavery," under the burning Equator and amid the snows of Canada, without change or symptom of change, must have been thus three thousand years ago. And he reasons truly, for the excavations of Champolion and others demonstrate the specific character of this race four thousand years ago, with as absolute and unmistakable certainty as it is now actually demonstrated to the external sense of the present generation. And the Naturalist, reasoning still further on this basis of fact, says, "that which has existed four thousand years, without the slightest change or modification, which in

all kinds of climate and under every condition of circumstances
preserves its integrity and transmits, in the regular and normal order, to each succeeding generation the exact and complete type of itself, must have been thus at the beginning, and
when the existing order was first called into being by the
Almighty Creator." And contemplating the subject from this
stand-point, and reasoning from analogy, or exactly as we do
in respect to other and all other forms of existence, the conclusion is irresistible and unavoidable that the several human
races or species originally came into being exactly as they now
exist, as we know they have existed through all human experience, and without a re-creation, must continue to exist so long
as the world itself lasts, or the existing order remains. But a
large portion of the "world" believe that the Bible teaches
the descent of all mankind from a single pair, and consequently
that there must have been a supernatural interposition at some
subsequent period, which changed the human creation into its
actual and existing form of being. And if there has been, at
any time a special revelation made to man, and supernatural
interposition in regard to other things, then this alteration or
re-creation of separate species is no more irrational or improbable than other things pertaining to that revelation, and which
are universally assented to by the religious world. A revelation is necessarily supernatural—that is, in direct contradiction
to the normal order; but it may be said that the Creator is
not the slave of His own laws, and in His immaculate wisdom
and boundless power might see fit to change the order of the
human creation; and certainly the same Almighty power which
took the Hebrews over the Red Sea on dry land, that saved a
pair of all living things in the ark of Noah, or dispersed the
builders of Babel, could, with equal ease, reform, or re-create
human life, and in future ordain that instead of one there
should be several species of men. This is a matter, however,

in regard to which the author does not assume to decide, to
question, to venture an opinion, or even to hazard a conjecture.
It is clearly and absolutely beyond the reach of human intelligence, and therefore not within the province of legitimate
enquiry. The Almighty has, in His infinite wisdom and boundless beneficence, hidden from us many things, a knowledge of
which would doubtless injure us, and the origin of the human
races belongs to this catalogue. Men may labor to investigate
it, to tear aside the veil the Creator has drawn about it, to
unlock the mystery in which He has shrouded it, and after millions of years thus appropriated, come back to the starting-
point, the simple, palpable, unavoidable truth. They exist,
but why or wherefore, whither they came or whence they go,
is beyond the range of human intelligence. We only know,
and are only permitted to know, that the several species now
known to exist have been exactly as at present in their physical natures and intellectual capacities, through all human experience and without a supernatural interposition or re-creation,
must continue thus through countless ages, and as long as the
existing order of creation itself continues. This we *know*
beyond doubt or possible mistake, while, whether it was thus
at the beginning, or changed by a supernatural interposition
at some subsequent period, is now, and always must be, left to
conjecture. Those who interpret the Book of Genesis, or who
believe that the Book of Genesis teaches the origin of the human family from a single pair, will, of course believe that the
Creator subsequently changed them into their present form,
while those who do not thus interpret the Bible will believe,
with equal confidence perhaps, that they were created thus at
the beginning. It is not, nor could it be of the slightest benefit to us to really and truly know the truth of this matter.
All that is essential to our welfare we already know, or may
know, if we properly apply the faculties with which the Cre-

ator has so beneficently endowed us. We only need to apply these faculties—to investigate the question—to study the differences existing among the general species of men, and compare their natures and capabilities with our own, to understand our true relations with them, and thus to secure our own happiness as well as their well-being, when placed in juxtaposition with them. All this is so obvious, and the remote and abstract question of origin so hypothetical and entirely non-essential, that it seems impossible that intelligent and conscientious men would ever seek to raise an issue on it, or that they would overlook the great practical duties involved in the question and engage in a visionary and unprofitable discussion about that of which they neither do nor can know anything whatever. Nevertheless, some few persons seem to be especially desirous to provoke an issue on this matter, not only with science but with common sense, and a certain reverend and rather distinguished gentleman has publicly and repeatedly declared "that the doctrine of a single human race underlies the whole fabric of religious belief, and if it is rejected, Christianity will be lost to mankind!" What miserable folly, if nothing worse, is this! It is a virtual declaration that we must believe or pretend to believe, what we *know* to be a *lie*, in order to preserve what we *believe* to be a truth. The existence of different species of men belongs to the category of physical fact—a thing subject to the decision of the senses, and belief neither has nor can have anything to do with the matter. It is true, the reverend gentleman in question may shut *his* eyes and remain in utter ignorance of the fact, or rather of the laws governing the fact, and while thus ignorant, may believe, or pretend to believe, that widely different things constitute the same thing—that white and black are identical—that white parents had at some remote time and in some strange and unaccountable manner given birth to Negro offspring; but

what right has he to say, to those who are conscious of the
fact of different species, and who *know*, moreover, that negroes
could no more originate from white parentage than they could
from dogs or cats, that they shall stultify themselves and
dishonestly pretend to believe otherwise, on pain of eternal
reprobation, or what he doubtless considers such, the loss of
Christianity to the world? It is not the desire of the writer to
either reconcile the merits of science with those peculiar interpretations of the Bible, or to exhibit any contradictions with
those interpretations. An undoubting believer himself in the
great doctrines of Christianity, he finds no difficulty whatever
in this respect, and would desire to simply state the *facts* or
what he knows to be truth, and leave the reader to form his
own conclusions. But the seemingly predetermined design of
some to make an issue on this matter, to appeal to a supposed
popular bigotry and fanaticism in order to conceal the most
vital and most stupendous truth of modern times—a truth underlying all our sectional difficulties, and which, truly apprehended by the mind of the masses, will instantly explode those
difficulties—renders it an imperative duty to expose the folly
and sophistry of those who strive to keep it out of sight.
They assume that the Bible teaches the origin of all mankind
from a single pair—that the Mongol, Indian, Negro, etc., with
the same origin, have the same nature as the white man, and
consequently have the same natural rights, and that we owe
to them the same duties that we owe to ourselves or to our own
race. And, moreover, they proclaim a belief in this assumption as essential to salvation, or, in other words, that if it be
rejected Christianity will disappear from the world. It need
not be repeated that the writer will not condescend to argue a
self-evident, actually existing, every-day palpable and unavoidable physical fact, or insult the reader's understanding by presenting proofs to show that the Negro is specifically different

3*

from himself—that is a matter beyond the province of rational discussion, and entirely within the domain of the senses;
yet, as already observed, in the subsequent chapters of this
work the *extent* of these differences separating whites and
blacks will be demonstrated, their physical differences and
approximations shown, in order to determine their moral
relations and social adaptations.   But the assumption that
belief in the dogma of a single human race or species is vital
to the preservation of Christianity needs to be exposed, as
it is in reality as monstrous in morals as stupid and absurd in
fact.   We cannot *believe* that which we *know* to be untrue,
and to affect such belief, however good the motive may seem,
must necessarily debauch and demoralize the whole moral
structure.   There are many things—such as the belief in the
doctrine of election, original sin, of justification by faith,
that admit of belief—honest, earnest, undoubting belief—for
they are abstractions and purely matters of faith that can never
be brought to the test of physical demonstration, or to the
standard of material fact, but the question of race—the fact of
distinct races or rather the existence of species of Caucasian, Mongols, Negroes, etc., are physical facts, subject to the
senses, and it is beyond the control of the will to refuse assent
to their actual presence.   Can a man, by taking thought, add
a cubit to his stature ?   Can he believe himself something else
—a woman, a dog, or that he does not exist—that black is
white, or that red is yellow, or that the Negro is a white man?
It is possible to deceive and delude ourselves, and believe or
think that we believe many things which our interest, our
prejudices, and our caprices prompt us to believe, but they
must be things of an abstract nature, where there are no physical tests to embarrass us or to compel the will to bow to that
fixed and immutable standard of truth which the Eternal has
planted in the very heart of things, and which otherwise the

laws of the mental organism absolutely force us to recognize. But the existence of distinct species of men does not belong to this category. It is fact, a palpable, immediate, demonstrable and unescapable fact. We know, and we cannot avoid knowing, that the negro is a negro and is not a white man, and therefore we cannot believe, however much we may strive to do so, that he is the same being that we are, or in other words, that all mankind constitute a single race or species. All that is possible or permissible is to make liars and hypocrites of ourselves—to pretend to believe in a thing that we do not and cannot believe in—to force this hypocrisy and pretended belief on others who may happen to have confidence in our honesty and respect for our ability; and finally, as a salve for our outraged conscience, to deceive ourselves with the notion that our motives are good, and the end justifies the means.

But the advocates of the European theory of a single race are faced by other difficulties, which are quite as unavoidable as those thus briefly glanced at. They demand that the world shall believe in the dogma of a single race, but not one among them will act upon it in practice, or convince others of their sincerity by living up to their avowed belief. If the Negro had descended from the same parentage, or, except in color merely, was the same being as ourselves, then there could be no reason for refusing to amalgamate with him as with the several branches of our race. But on the contrary, the reverend and distinguished gentleman who has ventured to declare that the belief that the Negro is a being like ourselves, is essential to Christianity, would infinitely prefer the death of his daughter to that of marriage with the most accomplished and most pious Negro in existence! If he believed in his own assertions in regard to this matter, then it would be his first and most imperative duty, as a Christian minister, to set an example to others, to labor night and day to elevate this (in that case) wronged and outraged race—indeed, to suffer every personal inconvenience, even martyrdom itself, in the performance of a duty so obvious and necessary. And when this theory was at last reduced to practice, and all the existing distinctions and "prejudices" against the Negro were obliterated, and the four millions of Negroes amalgamated with the whites, society would be rewarded by the increased morality and purity that would follow an act of such transcendent justice. But will any one believe in such a result—that, reducing to practice the belief, or pretended belief of a single race, will or would benefit American society? No, indeed; on the contrary, every one *knows*—even the wildest and most perverted abolitionist *knows*—that to reduce this dogma to practice, to honestly live out this pretended belief, to affiliate with these negroes, would result in the absolute destruction of American society. Nothing, therefore, can be more certain than the hypocrisy of those who pretend to believe in this single-race doctrine, for it need not be repeated, that they do not and cannot believe in it in reality. But why should they deem this absurd doctrine essential to *their* interpretation of the Bible? That the Almighty Creator subsequently changed the order of the human creation is in entire harmony with the universally received history of the Christian Revelation. All the Christian sects of the day admit the doctrine of miracles, or supernatural interposition, down to the time of the Apostles, and the largest of all (the Roman Catholics) credit this interposition at the present day, and therefore those ready to recognize it in such numerous instances, many, too, of relatively trifling importance, but, determined to reject it in this matter of races, are only imitating their brethren of old, and straining at gnats while swallowing camels with the greatest ease. To many persons the great doctrines of the Christian faith carry with them innate and irresistible proof of their divine origin, but the professional teachers of theology depend mainly upon supernatural interposition to convince the world of its truth, and yet by a strange and unaccountable perversity, some of them would reject it in the most important, or, at all events one of the most important instances in which it ever did or ever could occur. But will the sensible and really conscientious Christian priest or layman venture to persist in forcing this assumption, this palpable, demonstrable, unmistakable falsehood, that the single race-dogma is essential to the preservation of Christianity, upon the public? If he does, and if it is accepted by those who look upon him as a teacher, then it is certain that he will inflict infinite mischief on the cause of Christianity. To assume that all mankind have white skins, or straight hair, or any other specific feature of our own race, involves no greater absurdity, indeed, involves the exact absurdity, that the assumption of a single human species does. If it were assumed that we must stultify ourselves, and believe, or pretend to believe, that all mankind have white skins, or Christianity would be lost to the world, there is not a single man in this Republic that would not reject such an assumption with scorn and contempt. White and black are, of course, specialties, but no more so than (as will hereafter be shown) all the other things that constitute the negro being, and therefore the assumption put forward substantially and indeed exactly, is thus : We must believe that whites, Indians, Negroes, etc., have the same color, or the whole fabric of Christianity will be overthrown and lost to mankind!

But enough—all Americans know—for they cannot avoid knowing—that negroes are negroes and specifically different from themselves; they know, moreover, that they differed just as widely when first brought to this continent, and all who understand the simplest laws of organization know that they must always remain thus different from ourselves, and therefore

they know that they were made so by the act and will of the
Almighty Creator, while when, or how, or why they are thus,
is beyond the province of human enquiry, and of no manner
of importance whatever.

CHAPTER IV.

THE white or Caucasian is the only historic race—the race which is alone capable of those mental manifestations which, written or unwritten, leave a permanent impression behind. What was its first or earliest condition upon the earth? This, except the meagre account given by Moses, is unknown, nor is it of much importance that it should be known, for though it never was nor could be savage or barbarous, as these terms are understood in modern times, still its intellectual acquisitions were doubtless so limited that if really known to us, they would be of little or no service. Moses scarcely attempts any description of social life before the time of Abraham, and that then presented does not differ very materially from what exists in the same locality at the present day. The pastoral habitudes of Abraham, Isaac and Jacob, the sale of Joseph to the Ishmaelites by his brethren, his purchase in Egypt, and sudden exaltation at the court of the Egyptian Monarch, is an almost exact counterpart of scenes witnessed now, and with little varieties in the same lands, for the last four thousand years. The starting-point—the locality where the race first came into being, is equally hidden as the time or period of its creation. Biblical writers have usually supposed somewhere in Asia Minor, on the banks of the Euphrates, while ethnologists are inclined to believe that the high table lands of Thibet and Hindoo Koosh may have been the cradle of the race. Nor is a knowledge of this material, or indeed of the slightest consequence, except as an aid in determining its true centre of existence—that is, its physical adaptation or specific affinities for a certain locality. But this is determined by experience; and it is demonstrated beyond doubt that while the elaborate and relatively perfect structure of the Caucasian Man enables him to resist all external agencies, and to exist in all climates capable of supporting animal life, he can only till the soil or perform manual labor in the temperate zones. It is, therefore, immaterial when or where he first came into being, or what was the starting point of the race—its centre of existence is alike in all the great temperate latitudes of Asia, Africa, Europe, and America. The history of the race may be said to be divided into three great cycles or distinct periods; all, however, connecting with each other, and doubtless mainly resembling each other in their essential nature, however widely different in their external manifestation. The first period, beginning with its actual existence on the earth, may be said to terminate in the era of authentic history. The second, or historic era, may be assumed as extending to the overthrow of the Roman Empire by the so-called northern barbarians, or, perhaps, to what is usually termed the dark ages. And finally, there is another grand cycle in human destiny, which, beginning with the restoration of learning, comes down to and includes our own times. In regard to the first, we actually know little of it, for, leaving out of view the Sacred Scriptures, we have only a few imperfect glimpses of the actual life of the countless millions that preceded the historic period. What little knowledge we have depends on tradition and mythology, sometimes, perhaps, true enough, but the greater portion thus transmitted to our times we know is false, because conditions are assumed that are in contradiction with the laws that govern our animal being. If the race, however, was created in Asia, we know that portions of it migrated to Africa, at a very remote period; indeed, leaving the Bible out of view, the first knowledge we have of its existence, or the earliest traces of its existence, is in Africa. Caucasian tribes or communities entered the valley of the Nile possibly before the delta of the lower country was sufficiently hardened to admit of cultivation, as they evidently occupied localities considerably removed from the outlet of that great river. These early adventurers conquered the aboriginal population, subjected them to their control, compelled them to labor for them, built magnificent cities, temples, palaces, founded a mighty Empire and advanced, to a certain extent, in civilization. But wealth and luxury, with their effeminate consequences, probably, too, injustice and crime in the rulers, and certainly, and worst of all, interunion and affiliation with the conquered races, tempted purer and hardier branches of the race to invade them, and indeed the delicious climate and fertile soil must have always tempted Caucasian tribes into the Valley of the Nile, from the earliest periods, and whenever they felt themselves strong enough to attack the existing community. Of course we can only deal in conjecture in regard to this matter, but it is probable that numerous invasions took place, each passing through much the same course as its predecessors. First came conquest, then the erection of a mighty Empire, followed by a grand civilization; then came effeminacy, affiliation with the subject races, debauchment and debility inviting a new conquest by pure Caucasians, and they, in their turn, going through the same round of glory and decay, of conquest and degradation. Such seems to have been the condition of Egypt when the Romans invaded it, and made it a province of that great Empire. The effete remains of these Egyptian populations afterward, became known to the Roman writers, and, to a certain extent, may be said still to exist. The great

Asiatic empires were doubtless similar to the Egyptian, except
in respect to the debauchment of blood. The Assyrians, Persians, Chaldeans, Babylonians, Hebrews, etc., each in their
turn, were conquerors and conquered, masters and slaves, but
their downfall, in one essential respect, differed widely from
those of Africa. They were pure, unmixed Caucasians, for at
that time the Mongol element was unknown in that portion of
Asia, and the Negro, except a few household servants, never
existed on that continent. The Mongolian race was first
known about five hundred years anterior to the Christian
Era, and whether originally it existed in a more northern
region, or had not reached a full development as regards numbers, can not be known, on account of our limited knowledge
of the earth at that time. The old Caucasian populations of
Asia knew nothing of it, and had no admixture of Mongolic
blood. But all is conjecture, mystery, doubt and uncertainty, in
regard to these ancient and extinct Empires. We know that
they existed—that they were white men—beings like ourselves .
—our own ancestors, with the same wants, the same instincts,
in short, the same nature that we have, and therefore, in the
main, acted, as we do now. Of course we call them heathens,
pagans, savages, barbarians, etc., but were they thus?

In the modern times there are no white barbarians or heathens. In all modern history, wherever found, white men are
much the same ; why, then, should it not have been so always?
The fanatic Jew called all others gentiles, savages; the super-
cilious Greek called even their Roman conquerors barbarians;
even the manly and liberal Roman did not rise above this foolish bigotry, and not only called the Gauls, Britons, Germans,
etc., barbarians, but reduced them to slavery, as if they were
inferior beings. We witness the same ignorance and folly in
our own enlightened times. The Englishman believes that the
English are alone truly Christian and civilized ; the French-

man honestly believes that *La Belle* France is at the head of
modern civilization; even the advanced and liberal American
Democrat thinks, and perhaps correctly, that the Americans
alone are truly civilized; while some among us would exclude
all from the privilege of citizenship who happen to be born
elsewhere, as rigidly as the Jew did the uncircumcised Gentile
or the Moslem the dog of a Christian. Is not this notion of
" outside barbarians," therefore, the result of ignorance, or
foolish egotism, without sense or reason? Some nations or
communities were doubtless advanced more than others in
ancient times, as at present, but in the main the race must
have approximated to the same common standard we witness now. If it is said that in early times the obstacles in the
way of frequent intercourse prevented this general approximation to a common standard of enlightenment, it may be re-
plied that the same obstacles would also prevent a wide departure, and when we know that they had the same wants, the
same instincts, the same tendencies, etc., the conclusion seems
unavoidable that no nation or community could at any time in
history assume, with any justice, that others were barbarians,
or that they alone were civilized. The traditions and imperfect knowledge which we have hitherto possessed in respect
to these long-buried populations, may, perhaps, be replaced by
that which is almost or quite as reliable as written history itself.
Within a few years past a class of men have sprung up who,
excavating the dead remains of long forgotten empires, promise
revelations that will bring us face to face with the buried generations that we now only know through the dim perspec-
tive of uncertain tradition. Champolion, Belzoni, Rawlinson,
Layard and their companions have already made discoveries
in Egypt and Nineveh that open to our minds much of the
social condition and daily life of those remote times, and future
explorations, it is probable, will give us nearly as accurate a

knowledge as we have of those embraced within the cycle of
authentic history.

The next great period in the history of the race—the historic era—is supposed to be entirely within the province of real
knowledge. It begins with the history of the Greeks—not
the symbolic but the real—that grand and glowing intellectualism which, in many respects, may be said to equal the intellectual development of our own times. The history of
Greece and Rome is in truth the history of the race, of the
world, of mankind. There were cotemporary nations of great
power, extent and cultivation, but the Greeks and Romans, •
and the subject or servile populations that acknowledged their
supremacy, made up the larger portion of the race. It is true
the Persians were then pure Caucasians, and, in respect to
numbers, largely surpassed the Greeks, but while they did not
differ much in their general character, they were on the decline before the Greeks had reached their full national development. The latter always referred to Egypt as the source
of their civilization, but it is more probable that they borrowed
from Asia most of those things supposed to be of foreign
origin. It is, however, quite possible that the earliest civilization was developed in Africa, that it receded from thence to
Asia, as we know it afterwards did from the latter to Europe,
and as we now witness it, passing to America. But what is
civilization? It is, or it may be defined as, the result of intellectual manifestation. A nation or people who have most
deeply studied and understood the laws of nature or the nature
of things, and applied their knowledge to their own welfare,
are the most civilized or we might say, in a word, that the
nation that has the most knowledge is the most civilized. The
Greeks, certainly, surpassed all cotemporary nations in the
most essential of all knowledge, yet even this seems to have
been rather a thing of chance than otherwise. Political intel-

ligence, or a knowledge of men's social relations to each
other, is the most vital they can possess. The Greeks may
be said both to have possessed this knowledge and to have
been entirely deficient in it. Athens, with thirty thousand
citizens all recognized as political equals, was a Democracy,
but this so-called Democracy, with, perhaps, a hundred thousand slaves, was a burlesque on a democratic government.
The Helots of Greece, the servile and subject population of
which history gives no account, except to refer to them, were
white men—men with all the natural capacities of Socrates,
Demosthenes, or Alcibiades, but the Greek orators and writers
of the day never even seemed to imagine that they had
any rights whatever. They had much the same relation to
the Greeks that the Saxons had to the Normans, that the
Irish have to the English, and yet with all their political
enlightenment and high intellectual development, the Greeks
gave them no rights, and treated them as different and subordinate beings. The notion, therefore, taught in our schools,
that the Greeks were the authors of political liberty, is unsound
—they neither practised nor understood liberty, and the external forms mistaken for democracy had no necessary connection
with it. Aristotle could not form even a conception of a political system that did not rest upon slavery, and this was doubtless the general condition of the Greek mind. It was merely
accidental that the Greek States assumed a democratic form,
or rather approximated to a democratic form; but while they
were utterly ignorant of individual relations they certainly had
clear views of the relations of states and the duties that independent communities owe to each other. The Asiatic nations
seem to have had no conception wha ever of these duties—
conquest or slavery were the only alternatives. A nation
must conquer or be conquered—a dynasty must destroy all
others, or expect to fall itself—and the Asiatic character still

partakes largely of these habitudes. Except, therefore, in the mere externals or outward arrangements of political society, the Greeks can hardly be said to have done anything for political liberty or to advance political science. The Romans did more—vastly more—but they had little or no conception of democracy or of individual liberty. The proud boast, "I am a Roman citizen," unlike the idea of the American democrat, partook of the spirit of a British aristocrat of our own days, claiming the privileges of his order. The men who founded the city of Rome, though doubtless fillibusters and adventurers, perhaps even outcasts of the neighboring populations, were assumed to be superior to the later emigrants, and their descendants especially claimed exclusive privileges. And when Rome expanded into a mighty empire and ruled the world, the senatorial order ruled the empire—at all events, until Cæsar crossed the Rubicon and seized the supreme power. The change from a republic to an empire had little or no bearing upon the question of liberty, for the condition of the great body of the people remained the same. Rome conquered all, or nearly all, the then known world, for, except the Persians, and perhaps some few populations in the far North, the whole Caucasian race recognized the Romans as their rulers. The Parthians, so often waging desperate war with the Romans, were doubtless a mixed people, something like the modern Turks, and very possibly their ancestors. Following the rude code of early times, the Romans enslaved the conquered populations. All the prisoners of war were deemed to have forfeited their lives, and were parceled out among the Roman conquerors, while the rural populations were compelled to pay tribute to the Roman civil officers. It is quite probable that the Romans conquered some of the inferior races, but except the Numidians, Lybians, Ethiopians, etc., of Africa, Roman writers are silent on the subject. It has been said that the history of the Romans was the history of the Caucasian race, and that was the history of the world. This is literally true, for though we cannot suppose that the conquered populations were the miserable barbarians that the Roman writers represent them to have been, Rome was the most advanced portion of the race, and therefore the embodiment of its civilization and intellectual life. At this moment Paris represents all France; and the city of Rome bore a somewhat similar relation to the populations that composed the empire, however distant they may have been from the capital. It was not an unusual thing for the same general that commanded in Britain or that had conquered in Gaul, to administer the government of the African provinces or to conduct a campaign against the Persians on the bank of the Euphrates. And however much the vanity of Roman authors may have been gratified by assuming that they alone were civilized, it is altogether irrational to suppose that the conquered populations, with the same nature and same capacities as themselves, and moreover, in frequent and often intimate intercourse with themselves, could have differed widely or remained barbarians, even if such when conquered. The Romans advanced far beyond the Greeks in political knowledge, but with them also the state was every thing and the individual nothing. As with the Greeks, the great majority were slaves; and Roman citizenship, or the rights claimed by a Roman citizen, was at best a special privilege; and prior to the advent of Christianity, the idea of individual rights, of equality, of democracy, seems never to have dawned upon the intellectual horizon of the race. Nor did the primitive Christians (even) accept it in theory, though they lived it out in practice. Their mental habits were formed under the old social order, and though the spirit of the new doctrine impelled them to live it out in practice, few, if any, ever adopted it in theory. Christ had said, "love each other," and "do unto

others as you would have them do unto you," that is, "grant
to others the rights claimed for yourselves," but while they
often lived together, owning things in common like the modern communists and socialists, perhaps not one in a million
ever thought of applying their doctrines to the state, or even
supposing for a moment that the artificial distinctions which
separated classes could ever be altered or modified. Even the
forced and unnatural relation of master and slave, which necessarily violated the fundamental doctrine of their religion, was
clung to and respected in theory, and it needed several centuries of practice and faithful obedience to the spirit of the new
faith before this ancient barbarism was finally obliterated from
the Roman world. The conquest of Rome, by the so-called
northern barbarians, was followed by an eclipse of learning—by
a mental darkness in Western Europe at least, that is fitly enough
denominated the dark ages. Was this irruption of the northern
nations into Italy the true cause of this darkness? For several centuries previous there had been an immense and almost
continuous emigration from Asia, not of individuals, as we
witness in the present day, to America, but of tribes, communities, whole nations. History is indeed imperfect, if not
altogether silent, in respect to the cause of these mighty migrations which so long pressed upon Europe. But there can be
little doubt that the Mongolian race about this time changed,
to a considerable extent, its location, and pressing down on the
old Caucasian populations of Asia, impelled those vast masses
to seek shelter and safety, if not homes and happiness, in Europe. In the mighty invasions of Italy in the fifth century
by Attila, the truth of this is certainly demonstrated. He
himself was doubtless a white man, and so were his chiefs; but
the mighty populations he ruled over, and which extended
from the Danube to the frontiers of China, were mainly Mongolian. But no Mongolians settled permanently in Europe—

none but Caucasians, and except the modern Turks, none but
pure Caucasians—and, being the same men as the Romans
themselves, why should they be barbarians? They were conquerors; a pretty good proof that, though not so refined perhaps, certainly not so effeminate as the Romans had become,
they could not have been barbarians. Other things being
equal, the nation that has made the greatest advance in
knowledge will be able to conquer, because it has only to
apply its knowledge to this object to succeed. There can be
no doubt that we ourselves surpass all the nations of our times
in knowledge, or in our capacity to apply our knowledge to
the purposes of material existence. Our railroads, canals,
public works, our ship-building, commerce, etc., prove this,
and we have only to apply this knowledge to purposes of
offence or defence, to invade others or to defend ourselves,
to demonstrate our immense superiority. Nevertheless, if we
should conquer Spain, or any other ancient and effete empire,
doubtless their writers would take their revenge in calling us
barbarians, as indeed the poor, feeble, and adulterated hybrids
of Mexico actually did thus represent us when in possession
of their capital. Nothing, therefore, can be more improbable
than the theory of Gibbon and others, that the nations that
conquered Rome were barbarians, and that the dark ages were
the result of that conquest. But there was a cause for the
subsequent darkness which so long spread over the European
world much more palpable. Christianity had become generally accepted, and bad and ambitious men, in the then general ignorance of the masses of the populations, might wield
it with stupendous effect in advancing their ambition and
securing their own personal objects. The assumption that
Christ had delegated a power on earth to interpret the will
of Heaven, both as to temporal as well as religious interests,

4

was enough; of course all human investigation and mental activity terminated, and was denounced as impiety.

The subordinate clergy were often, perhaps generally, faithful to the great truths transmitted by the primitive Christians, but, dependent on tradition, and subject to the rule of their sacerdotal superiors, they in vain resisted these influences, and these truths became in time so corrupted as scarcely to retain any resemblance to the original faith. It is believed that, except in these "dark ages," the Caucasian mind has never retrograded or indeed remained stationary. Progress is the law, the instinct, the necessity of the Caucasian mind, and however much some branches or some nations may decline, there is always some portion, nationality, or community, that embodies the wants of the race, and that moves forward in pursuit of that indefinite perfectability which is its specific and distinguishing characteristic. But it is easily understood how this might have suffered an eclipse under the circumstances then existing. A great proportion of the so-called barbarian conquerors of Rome were ignorant of Christianity, and when they became the converts of the conquered Romans, they naturally exalted their teachers as beings almost superhuman in their superior knowledge; and the general ignorance of the times favored any pretension of the priests, however absurd it might be. In fact a body of men claiming to be, and universally believed to be, the interpreters of the will of the Almighty, necessarily interrupted all inquiry into the laws of nature (the real laws of God), and though some monks themselves, immured in their cells, continued to think, to experiment, to acquire knowledge, as well as in many instances to preserve that already acquired by others, the great mass of the people as well as the great body of the clergy looked upon everything of the kind as wicked, impious, and heretical. And we have only to suppose an intellectual activity and freedom corresponding with our own times throughout these dark centuries, to realize the stupendous evil inflicted on the world by this priestly arrogance and ambition.

The races, so-called, that figured most prominently during the period beginning with authentic history and terminating in the dark ages, are first, the Semitic, which included the Egyptians, Carthaginians, Persians, Syrians, Hebrews or Jews, Saracens, Arabians, etc., indeed under the term Semitic may be included all the Orientals, except the Parthians, who were doubtless a mixed people, and those northern tribes, historically known as Scythians, afterwards the conquerors of Egypt and the progenitors of that extraordinary military autocracy known in modern times by the name of Mamelukes. The second great branch was the Pelasgian, which included the Macedonians, the Romans, the Hellenic tribes, Dorians, Thracians, etc., and of which the Romans were for nearly two thousand years the main representatives. Between these great branches of the Caucasian—for they were both doubtless, typical Caucasians, though Agassiz thinks that the Semitic constituted a separate species—there was almost constant war, from the very beginning of history to the capture of Constantinople. The Greek and Trojan war was doubtless a collision of this kind—and so were the wars of the Greeks and Persians—the conquests of Alexander, which, for a time, almost annihilated the Persian empire—the terrible life-and-death struggle of the Romans and Carthaginians, and finally the invasion and conquest of Spain by the Arabians, with their ultimate defeat by the Franks under Charles Martel. Indeed, coming down to more modern times, we find the Crusades, when nearly all Europe, in a fit of uncontrollable phrensy, precipitated itself on Asia; and in the collapse which followed, Asiatic hordes, though not exactly Semitic, again seeking to penetrate into Europe, and actually conquering the remains of the old Roman empire, in the eastern capital of

which they are now firmly established. Historians are wont to
magnify the results of these contests, especially the defeat of Hannibal and the overthrow of the Carthaginians by the Romans,
and the defeat of the Arabians by the Franks, as of vital importance to the world and the best interests of mankind; but it is
quite possible that they over-estimate these things, especially
the victory of the Romans over the Carthaginians. They were
both of the same species of men, both branches of the Caucasian, with the same nature, the same tendencies, and, under
the same circumstances, the same beings. The Carthaginians
were, for the time, highly civilized. They were the heirs of
the Egyptian and Asiatic civilizations, as Rome was of that of
the Greeks. They were a great commercial people, with
boundless wealth, science, arts, manufactures, everything but
a warlike spirit; while Rome, at the time without commerce,
poor and torn by factions, was a mere military aristocracy, and
the capital itself little more than a military encampment.
Why, then, should the defeat of the former have been beneficial to the progress of the race, or to the general interests of
mankind?

In regard to the defeat of the Arabians by the Franks, the
case is altogether different. They were the same species, and
doubtless, at that time, more advanced than the Europeans,
but they were Mohammedans, and in the full flush of enthusiasm for their faith, which they invariably propagated by the
sword. And if they had overrun Europe as they did Asia,
somewhat similar results would doubtless have followed, for
though it is altogether improbable, indeed, in view of its
Divine origin, impossible, that they could have exterminated
the Christian religion, they would have done it and the general cause of civilization incalculable injury. But both of
these great branches of the race have long since disappeared
from history. The Semitic element can scarcely be said to exist

at all. In Africa it is adulterated by the blood of the Negro, and perhaps the blood of some race or races not so low in the scale as the Negro. In Asia it is mixed with the Mongolian blood, and though the Arab and Persian populations of our day are mainly white, there is more or less taint pervading all the Asiatic communities. The great Pelasgian branch has long since disappeared and been swallowed up in the more modern branches of the race, and though the modern Italian claims to be, and doubtless is, the lineal descendant of the ancient Roman, no portions of the race are wider apart than the ancient Roman and his modern descendant, a striking proof that accidental consanguinity does not affect the universality of the race.

The last great cycle of history, commencing with the Reformation, comes down to and includes our own times. It is quite unnecessary to dwell upon it, as all intelligent persons have much the same view of it. With the downfall of the Roman empire, however, new varieties of the Caucasian, or, as historians have termed them, new races, have emerged into view, and in their turn struggled for the empire of the world. The hordes that, under Alaric and other leaders, overran Italy, were generally known as Goths, a generic term that is applied to great numbers of very different people, though, of course, all were white men, and therefore of the same race or species. But after varying fortunes, and passing through numerous mutations, all these races have subsided into several well-marked and well-known divisions or families now existing. There are—*First*. The Celts—including a large portion of the French, Italians, Spanish, Portuguese, and the remains of the primitive people of the British Islands. *Second*. The Teutonic or German, including the Germans of all kinds, the Swiss, the mythical Anglo-Saxon and perhaps the Danes, the Scandinavians, etc. *Third*. The Sclavonians, embracing the Russians,

Poles, Serbs, Croats, Montenegrins, etc. There are some few
populations that, either in language or historical facts, have
little or no connection with those enumerated. These are the
modern Hungarians, the European Turks, the Circassians, etc,
They are, however, Caucasians: even the Turks and Circassians are, in our times, pure or mainly pure Caucasians.
Finally there remain our own people, the offspring of every
country and of every variety of the race, and as the more the
blood is crossed the more energetic and healthy the product
or progeny, the American people should become, as it doubtless will become, the most powerful and the most civilized
people in existence.

Such, briefly considered, is an imperfect summary or outline
of the history of our race, the only race that has a history or
that is capable of those mental manifestations whose record
constitutes history. It is a favorite theory of most historians
to represent the mental development of the race as divided
into distinct categories, not as the author has ventured, into
historic periods, but into different phases of intellectual manifestation. They have supposed that men (white men) were
first hunters and lived wholly by the chase—that after a while
they became shepherds, and lived on their herds or flocks—
that then they made another advance and became cultivators,
and finally artisans, merchants, etc. Each of these conditions,
it has been supposed, were dependent on, or were associated
with, a corresponding mental development. The hunter had
intellect enough to run down the stag or wit sufficient to entrap
the game necessary for his support, but had not sufficient
capacity to take care of his flocks or sense sufficient to till the
earth! This notion has doubtless arisen from observing the
habits of the subordinate races of men, though it is quite
possible that our own race has passed through some such
stages as those suggested. But there has never been any vari-

ations in its actual intellectual powers. The mental capacities given it in the morning of creation were just what they are now, and what they will be millions of years hence. Thus is explained the (to many persons) seeming anomaly that in the very dawn of history there were men like Homer, Plato, Socrates, Pythagoras, and others, with a breadth and depth of intellect corresponding to the most intellectual men of our own times. Mental power, like physical strength, remains always the same through all ages and mutations of human society, while knowledge, or the uses made of the intellectual forces, is constantly varying from age to age, and changing from one country to another. The miserable Italian organ-grinder under our window, it is somewhat difficult to suppose, embodies the high intellect and powerful will, which two thousand years ago, made his ancestors masters of the world, but such is the fact, however latent, unknown or unfelt by himself may be these powers. The amount or extent or degrees of knowledge, the perceptions of external things, their relations, the laws that govern them, their uses, their influences on our well-being or the contrary, in short, our capacities for acquiring knowledge, for comprehending ourselves and the things about us, are limitless, and therefore progress and indefinite perfectibility are the specific attributes of the Caucasian. Each generation applies its capabilities and acquires a certain amount of knowledge which the succeeding one is heir to, and which, in turn, transmits its acquisition to those following; thus its march is ever onward, and except during the " dark ages" it is believed that the great law of progress which God has imposed on the race as a duty as well as given it as a blessing, has never been interrupted.

But the inferior races of mankind present a very different aspect in this respect. The Negro, isolated by himself, seems utterly incapable of transmitting anything whatever to the

succeeding generation, and the Aboriginal American, Malay,
etc., doubtless approximate to him in these respects. The
Aztecs and Peruvians, at the time of the Spanish conquest,
however, had advanced to the grade of cultivators, and were
therefore, doubtless, capable of a limited or imperfect trans-
mission of their knowledge. The Malay is probably capable
of still greater development in these respects; but its limitations are too decided to be mistaken., The Mongolian, on the
contrary, approximates much closer to ourselves, and while it
cannot be said to have a history in any proper sense, it is
doubtless capable of transmitting its knowledge to future generations to a much greater extent than others, but it, too, is at
an immeasurable distance from the Caucasian in this respect.
The Chinese, it is true, pretend to trace back their history to
a period long anterior to our own, but this claim is itself sufficient proof of its own worthlessness. No one will suppose
that the individual Chinaman has a larger brain or greater
breadth of intellect than the individual Caucasian, and if not,
what folly to suppose that the aggregate Chinese mind was
capable of doing that which is impossible to the aggregate
Caucasian intellect! The truth is, what is supposed to be
Chinese history is a mere collection of fables and nonsensical
impossibilities, and it may be doubted if they can trace back
their annals even five hundred years with any certainty or
with sufficient accuracy to merit a claim to historic dignity.
There can be no doubt, however, that at some remote period,
a considerable portion of the Chinese population was Cauca-
casian, as indeed a portion is still Caucasian, and it is perhaps
certain that Confucius and other renowned names known to
the modern Chinese, were white men, and what shadowy and
uncertain historical data they now possess are therefore likely
to have originated from these sources. The Mongolian race
was in fact unknown to ancient writers, though there has

doubtless been contact with these races from a very early period.

It is supposed by Hamilton Smith and others, that the Mongolian formally existed much further North than at present, and that its immense development in regard to numbers finally pressed so heavily on the Caucasian populations of Central Asia, that it displaced them, and hence that those mighty migrations into Europe, a short time after the beginning of the Christian era, were the results of this pressure in their rear. Be this as it may, it is certain that those vast inundations which at times swept over the Asiatic world, and also threatened Europe with their terrible results, were mainly composed of Mongolic elements. Attila was of pure Caucasian blood, and his chiefs were doubtless also white men or of a predominating Caucasian innervation; but it is equally certain that the larger portion of his terrible hordes were Mongolians. His seat of empire was on the Danube and somewhere near the modern Buda, from which he threatened France as well as Rome and the Italian Peninsula, while his dominion extended to the frontiers of China, and embraced the vast regions and almost countless populations intervening between these widely separated points. His invasion of France, and his repulse if not defeat at Chalons, is one of those transcendent events that, for good or evil, change the order of history, and for centuries affect the fortunes of mankind. Had this not happened—had his march been uninterrupted—had his terrible legions swept over Western as they already had over Eastern Europe, and a vast Mongolian population become permanently settled there, the destinies of mankind would have been widely different. But his repulse—his desperate retreat and his subsequent death, which occurred soon after—changed the current of events, and his desolating hordes instead of effecting a permanent lodgement in the heart of Europe, vanished so utterly that, except

4*

a few thousand Laplanders, they have left no trace or e·idence ··
of their terrible invasion of the European world.

Genghis Khan, in the twelfth century, was the next great
conqueror and mighty leader of those vast Mongolic hordes
which, at various times, have inundated the ancient world,
and in their desolating march swept away numerous empires
and extinguished whole populations. Genghis Khan, though
of predominating Caucasian blood, was mixed with Mongolian, but his successors for several centuries after were mainly
Caucasians or the children of Caucasian mothers. Finally, the
the last and the greatest of these terrible conquerors, Tamerlane,
in the sixteenth century, made a conquest of nearly the whole
of Asia, penetrating even into Africa and conquering Egypt,
while his defeat of Bajazet, the Emperor of the Turks, then at
the zenith of their power, opened Europe to the march of his
desolating hordes, and could his life have been extended a few
years longer, it is quite possible that he would have accomplished what seems to have been the object of Attila, and subjected the European as well as the Asiatic world to his terrible sway. As it was, he invaded and conquered India as well
as Egypt, and the master of, or wearer of twenty-eight crowns,
he reigned over the whole of Asia to the borders of China,
except the Turkish dominions, and even here he was the recognized master though he gave back the empire to the sons
of Bajazet. The character of his conquests—the death and
desolation that marked his path—was the most terrible as well
as the most extensive ever witnessed before or since, and many
of the largest and most powerful empires of Asia were as
utterly blotted from the earth as if it had opened and swallowed
them up. He himself was of pure Caucasian extraction, and
doubtless his generals and chiefs were the same, and the Caucasian Tartars formed a very considerable portion of his forces.
There was doubtless also a large mixed or mongrel element,

for of the throngs of female captives taken in these Mongolian invasions, few ever returned to their homes, but becoming the wives of Mongolian chiefs, those numerous and often powerful dynasties which have ruled over the Asiatic populations had their origin. Nevertheless a vast majority of these almost countless hordes led by Tamerlane were unmixed Mongolian, and, therefore, though the leader was himself a Caucasian or white man, the bloody and desolating character of his conquests were stamped by the cruelty and ferocity of that race. Perhaps no better illustration of the Caucasian and Mongolian character could be presented than the contrast between Alexander's invasion of Persia and India and similar invasions of Tamerlane. The first, though a "Pagan" several centuries before the Christian era, was humane and merciful to the conquered, and except in battle shed no blood, while the latter not content with the enforcement of the Moslem rule of tribute or death or the religion of the Prophet, slaughtered whole populations after the battle was over, and for the gratification of his ferocious hordes. His conquest of Bagdad and his pyramid of ninety thousand heads is one of those terrible things that historians are generally puzzled with, for not only is there nothing resembling it in history, but there seems to be no motive or sufficient cause for it. It was the result, the offspring of Mongol ferocity and apathetic cruelty, such as we now witness in India and China, and springs as much, perhaps, from a low grade of sensibility or incapacity to feel or sympathize with suffering, as from a sentiment of cruelty.

The Hindoos or East Indians, like the Chinese, also pretend to trace back their history to a time long anterior to our own historic era. Their claim, in this respect, is doubtless better founded than that of the former, but it, too, is absurd and valueless. The Hindoos were originally Caucasian, who, at some remote period, invaded and conquered India, and stamped their civilization and religion on the whole peninsula. It is quite likely, indeed it is certain, that India had been invaded and conquered by numerous nations or tribes of Caucasians long anterior to the Hindoo conquest. There are in our day too many traces of this, too many evidences of the former existence of the great master race of mankind in India, to permit us to doubt. The vast debris spread all over India, indeed the sixty or seventy dialects of Sanscrit proves that India must have been long subject to the dominion of the Caucasian. It is believed by many that *Hindoo Koosh*, or the high table land of Thibet, was the cradle of the race, and it is rational to suppose that long anterior to our own historic era white men may have formed the principal portion of the Indian population. They doubtless thus spread themselves over the peninsula; or if that was the birth-place of the Mongolian, then it is certain that restless and energetic Caucasian tribes at a very early day invaded and conquered the country. Even now there is a large Caucasian element in India. The Affghans are pure Caucasian, while the Sikhs, the Rajpoots, and a large portion of the people of Oude are doubtless of predominating Caucasian blood. That caste which English writers have so much to say about, and the good people of Exeter Hall desire so much to "abolish," is, to a great extent, mere mongrelism, and that which is not mongrelism is simply what England itself suffers from to a greater extent than any other country or people. The Normans invaded the latter country, took possession of their lands, and reduced the conquered Anglo-Saxons to slavery, where they have remained ever since, and though the Norman blood has long since disappeared, the theory or system remains, for a few cunning and adroit "Anglo-Saxons," claiming to be the descendants of Norman Conquerors, *now* monopolize the land and rule the great body of the people as absolutely as the real Normans did in their day.

The early invaders of India grasped everything, as did the
Normans in England, but they amalgamated with the conquered, and thus enfeebling themselves, fell a victim to fresh
invasions of pure Caucasians. They, in their turn, underwent
the same fate, and thus, from time immemorial there grew up
those multitudinous dynasties, each of which had its own character, and which became a caste, often, doubtless, as a means for
governing the people, and preserved by the conquerors as carefully as that which they in their turn imposed on the country.
The Normans and Saxons were of the same race, and the
greater the admixture of blood, the more energetic the population, while the admixture of the conquering Caucasian with
the conquered Mongolian, has rendered the modern Hindoo
powerless and contemptible in comparison with the English or
European invader of our times. The general subject of the
human races has been so little studied, and our actual knowledge of these great Asiatic populations is so limited and so
imperfect, that it is difficult to determine their present character, let alone their former history, and it is quite possible that
the present native of India is specifically different from the
Chinese. It has been the custom of writers on this subject to
assume that the Caucasian and Mongolian, with their often
extensive affiliations, constitute the sole population of the
Asiatic continent, and that the differences which are actually
presented are those produced alone by climate and external
influences. The writer has adopted this view, but without
assenting to it in fact, for the actual differences between
Nena Sahib or an Indian prince, and the true Mongol of
the Chinese model, are certainly as distinct as those separating the former from a modern Englishman, and therefore he
thinks it quite probable that further investigation will show a
race or species of men, mainly to be found in India, that are
yet to be known and to take their place in the great human

family, midway between the Caucasian and Mongolian. Be
this as it may, however, it is certain that our own race alone
has a history or is capable of those mental manifestations
which constitute the materials of history. The Mongolic element, though often invading and temporarily conquering large
portions of territory occupied by Caucasian populations, has
receded almost as rapidly as it advanced, and therefore their
actual centre of existence remains substantially the same at all
times. There is, however, a trace of Mongolian blood now
found outside of its own proper centre, but probably there is a
much larger Caucasian element among Mongolic nations. The
Caucasian Tartars invaded and conquered China a few centuries ago, and though doubtless mixed up with and mainly Mongol at this time, they are the ruling dynasty. The instincts
of this race naturally impelled it to escape from contact or collision with the superior race; thus, the great wall of China was
a vain attempt to keep out a race it fears and hates, and
which its instincts assure it must rule over itself wherever
they exist in juxtaposition. Many persons fancy that our trea-
ties with Japan and China will bring these vast populations
within the circle of modern civilization, and open up to ourselves a fancied Asiatic commerce, which, through California
and a Pacific railroad, we shall mainly monopolize. Of course
these notions originate in utter ignorance of what China is in
reality, and except in degree do not differ from that of the
Abolitionists in respect to negroes and negro "slavery." The
Mongol never will, as indeed he never can, become an element
in the modern or Christian civilization of our times and of our
race, and though there may be a certain trade carried on between us and China, it is not l kely to vary to any considerable
extent from that existing now, while any attempt to establish
a diplomatic intercourse or equality is simply absurd, and must
end in nothing.

This, then, is the history of the Mongolian race—the race nearest our own—all the history we have of it, and indeed all the history there is of it, for however brief or imperfect our own knowledge of the race, it is doubtless better and more reliable than is its own pretended history of itself. As has been said, unlike the Negro, whose capacities cannot go beyond the living or actual generation, and with whom millions of generations are the same as a single one, the Mongolian mind may perhaps, with more or less correctness, grasp the life of a few generations, but in no proper sense is it capable of acting, and consequently of writing history.

CHAPTER V.

ANATOMISTS and physiologists have labored very earnestly to account for or to show the "cause" of color, not of the Negro alone, but in the case of our own race. They have generally supposed that the pigmentum nigrum, a substance lying immediately beneath the outward skin, or cuticle, constituted that cause, and therefore the complexion was fair or dark, blonde or brunette, just as the "coloring" matter might happen to be dark or otherwise. This, in a sense, is doubtless true, but to speak of it as a cause is an abuse of terms, for it is simply a fact, and no more a cause than it is an effect. Cause and causes in natural phenomena are known only to Omnipotence, and why the Caucasian color is white or the Mongol yellow, or the Negro black, is as absolutely hidden from us as the cause of their existence at all—as wholly beyond the scope of human intelligence, and therefore of rational inquiry, as the cause of the return of the seasons, or why men and animals at a certain time arrive at maturity or finally decay and die. The divine wisdom and perfect fitness of the fact itself, however, are clearly appreciable, and we are able to see, not only its transcendent importance, but the utter impossibility of its being otherwise. There is in all the works of God perfect harmony, as well as perfect wisdom, and, therefore, such a monstrosity as a "colored man"—or a being like ourselves in all except the color of the negro—is not merely absurd, but as impossible in fact, though not so palpable to a superficial intelligence, as a white body with a negro head on its shoulders, or indeed as a dog with the head of any other animal or form of being.

The face of the Caucasian reflects the character, the emotions, the instincts, to a certain extent the intellectual forces, and even the acquired habits, the virtues or vices of the individual. This, to a certain extent, depends on the mobility of the facial muscles, and the general anatomical structure and outline of the features; but without our color, the expression would be very imperfect, and the face wholly incapable of expressing the inner nature and specific character of the race. For example: What is there at the same time so charming and so indicative of inner purity and innocence as the blush of maiden modesty? For an instant the face is scarlet, then, perhaps, paler than ever in its delicate transparency; and these physical changes, beautiful as they may be to the eye, are rendered a thousand times more so by our consciousness that they reflect moral emotions infinitely more beautiful. Can any one suppose such a thing possible to a black face? that these sudden and startling alternations of color, which reflect the moral perceptions and elevated nature of the white woman, are possible to the negress? And if the latter cannot reflect these things in her face—if her features are utterly incapable of expressing emotions so elevated and beautiful, is it not certain that she is without them—that they have no existence in her inner being, are no portion of her moral nature? To suppose otherwise is not only absurd, but impious; it is to suppose that the Almighty Creator would endow a being with moral wants and capacities that could have no development—with an inner nature denied any external reflection or manifestation of its wants or of itself. Of course, it is not intended to say that the negress has not a moral nature; it is only intended to demonstrate the fact that she has not *the* moral nature of the

white woman; and, therefore, those who would endow her
inner nature with these qualities, must necessarily charge the
Creator with the gross injustice of withholding from her any
expression of qualities so essential to her own happiness, as
well as to our conception of the dignity and beauty of womanhood. This same illustration is extensively diversified in regard to the other sex. It is seen every day in our social life,
and confronts us at every step. The white man is flushed with
anger, or livid with fear, or pale with grief. He is at one
moment so charged with the darker passions as to be almost
black, and the next so softened by sorrow or stricken by grief
that the face is bloodless and absolutely white. All these outward manifestations of the inner nature—of the moral being
with which God has endowed us—are familiar to every one.
They form a portion of our daily experience, and constitute an
essential part of our social life.

There are great differences among our people in regard to
the general expression of the features. Some reflect in their
faces all the emotions by which they are moved, while others
are so stolid, or they have acquired such a control over themselves in these respects, as to appear impenetrable. But this
has no connection with color, or any relation to that great
fundamental and specific fact by which and through which the
Almighty has adapted the character and revealed the relative
conditions of the several human races. Like all the other great
facts involved, color is the standard and exact admeasurement
of the specific character. The Caucasian is white, the Negro
is black; the first is the most superior, the latter the most inferior—and between these extremes of humanity are the inter-
mediate races, approximating to the former or approaching the
latter, just as the Almighty, in His boundless wisdom and
ineffable beneficence, has seen fit to order it. Color is no more
radical or universal, or no more a difference between white
men and negroes, than any other fact out of the countless mil-

lions of facts that separate them. It is more palpable to the
sense, more unavoidable, but no more universal or invariable
than the difference in the hair, the voice, the features, the form
of the limbs, the single globule of blood, or the myriads
and millions of things that constitute the Negro being. It
would seem that the Almighty Creator, when stamping this
palpable distinction on the very surface, had designed to guard
His work from any possible desecration, and therefore had
marked it so legibly, that human ignorance, fraud, folly, or
wickedness, could by no possibility mistake it. And indeed
it is not mistaken, for those perverse creatures among us who
clamor so loudly for negro equality, or that the negro shall be
treated as if he were a white man, only desire to force their
hideous theories on others, and would rather have their own
families utterly perish from the earth than to practice or live
up to their doctrine in this respect. The term "colored man,"
or "colored person," though natural enough to Europeans, or
to those who had never seen negroes, or different races from
themselves, could never have originated in a community having negroes in its midst, for it is not only a misnomer but an
absurdity as gross as to say a colored fish or a colored bird.
Finally, as color is the standard and the test of the specific
character, revealing the inner nature and actual capabilities of
the race, so, too, is it the test and standard of the normal
physical condition of the individual. The highest health of
the white man is distinguished by a pure and transparent skin,
and exactly as he departs from this, his color is clouded and
sallow; while that of the negro is marked by perfect black-
ness, and the departure from this is to dirty brown, almost ash-
color—thus, as in everything else, revealing the eternal truth
that life and well-being, social as well as individual, are identical with an exact recognition of these extremes, and that it is
only when disease and unnatural conditions prevail, that a certain approximation to color or to equality become possible.

CHAPTER VI.

To consider and properly contrast the attitude or the general outline of the negro form with that of the Caucasian, needs a large space to do the subject justice. But a few brief points are sufficient to grasp its essential features and enable every one to add or to fill up the details from his own experience. Cuvier, the great French zoologist, it is said might pick up a bone of any kind, however minute, in the deserts of Arabia, and from this alone determine the species, genus, and class to which it belonged. This at first seems almost incredible, but a moment's reflection shows not only its practicability, but the ease and certainty with which it may be accomplished. Indeed we have recently witnessed a still more remarkable instance of this tracing the life and defining the relations of organized beings from a minute and remote point. Agassiz has been able, from a single scale of a fish, to determine the specific character of fishes, and those, too, which he had never before seen! A bone is picked up at random by the zoologist; he soon discovers that it is a bone of the thigh of some animal, and this necessarily leads to the fact that it belonged to a quadruped, and it, in its turn, leads to other facts equally connected and dependent on each other, for that great fundamental and eternal law of harmony or adaptation which God has stamped on the organic and material universe permits of no incongruities or contradictions to mar its beauty or deface its grandeur. Thus an anatomist, who had given a certain amount of attention to the subject, might select the smallest bone, a carpal or bone of the finger, for example, and de- termine from among millions of similar ones, whether it was that of a white man or of a negro, with perfect certainty and the greatest ease. He would know that such bone formed part of a hand with a limited flexibility—that the bony struc- ture was in accord with the tendons and muscles that moved it, and gave it, compared with that of the Caucasian, a re- stricted capacity of action, of susceptibility, etc., and he would necessarily connect this hand with an arm of corresponding structure, and going on multiplying the connections and rela- tions, he would be led to the final result, and without possibil- ity of mistake, that the bone in question belonged to a negro. But while the analysis of a single bone or of a single feature of the negro being is thus sufficient to demonstrate the spe- cific character or to show the diversity of race, that great fact is still more obviously and with equal certainty revealed in the form, attitude, and other external qualities. The negro is inca- pable of an erect or direct perpendicular posture. The general structure of his limbs, the form of the pelvis, the spine, the way the head is set on the shoulders, in short, the *tout ensem- ble* of the anatomical formation, forbids an erect position. But while the whole structure is thus adapted to a slightly stooping posture, the head would seem to be the most impor- tant agency, for with any other head or the head of any other race, it would be impossible to retain an upright position at all.

The form or figure of the Caucasian is perfectly erect, with the eyes on a plane with the horizon, and the broad forehead, distinct features and full and flowing beard, stamp him with a superiority and even majesty denied to all other creatures, and relatively to all other races of men. On the contrary, the narrow and longitudinal head of the negro projecting posteri-

ally, places his eyes at an angle with the horizon, and thus alone
enables him to approximate to an erect position. Of course,
we are not to speculate on what is impossible or to suggest
what might happen if the negro head had resembled that of the
Caucasian, for the slightest change of an elementary atom in
the negro structure would render him an impossible monstrosity. But with the broad forehead and small cerebellum of the
white man, it is perfectly obvious that the negro would no
longer possess a centre of gravity, and therefore those philan-
thropic people who would "éducate" him into intellectual
equality or change the mental organism of the negro, would
simply render him incapable of standing on his feet or of an
upright position on any terms. Every one must have remarked
this peculiarity in the form and attitude of the negro. His head
is thrown upwards and backwards, showing a certain though
remote approximation to the quadruped both in its actual
formation and the manner in which it is set on his shoulders.
The narrow forehead and small cerebrum—the centre of the
intellectual powers—and the projection of the posterior portion
—the centre of the animal functions—render the negro head
radically and widely different from that of the white man. This
every one knows, because every one sees it every day, and the
universal and all pervading law of adaptation which God has
eternally stamped upon the structure of all His creatures enables the negro to thus preserve a centre of gravity and comparatively an upright posture. But were it true that men can
make themselves, can push aside the Almighty Creator Himself, as taught by certain "reformers" of the day, and vastly
improve the "breed" and, as the "friends of humanity" hold,
that the negro can be made to conform in his intellectual
qualities to those of the white man, then it is certain that their
difficulties would become greater than ever. That the cerebrum or anterior portion of the brain is the centre, the seat,

the organism,in fact, of the intellectual nature, is as certain as
that the eye is the organ of sight, and that in proportion to its
size relatively with the cerebellum—the centre of the animal
instincts—is there mental capacity, however latent it may be
in the case of individuals, is equally certain. And should these
would-be reformers of the work of the Almighty change the
intellectual nature of the negro, they would necessarily change
the organism through which, and by which, that nature is
manifested, and thus enlarging the anterior and diminishing
the posterior portion of the brain into correspondence with
their own, it is perfectly evident that they would destroy the
harmony which exists between the negro head and the negro
body, and instead of a black-white man, or a being with the
same intellectual nature as ours, they would render him as utterly incapable of locomotion or of an upright position at all
as if they had cut off his head, instead of re-creating it on the
model of their own! The whole anatomical structure, the feet,
the hands, the limbs, the size and form of the head, the features, the hair, the color, the *tout ensemble* of the negro being,
as it is revealed to the sense, embodies the negro inferiority
when compared with other races ; and as regards the white
man or Caucasian, it presents a contrast so striking and an interval so broad and unmistakable that it seems impossible any
one's senses could be so blunted, or his perceptions so perverted as to be rendered incapable of perceiving it. The flexi-
ble grace of the limbs, the straight lines of the figure, the
expressive features, the broad forehead and transparent color,
and flowing beard, all combine to give a grace and majesty to
the Caucasian that stamps him undisputed master of all living
beings, and even the creatures of the animal world perceive
and acknowledge this supremacy. It is not an uncommon
thing in India for a tiger, rendered desperate by hunger, to
suddenly leap into a crowd and to carry off a man, but instead

of a European he invariably selects a native, and while such a
thing as the seizure of a white man is unknown, the negroes
in Sierra Leone are frequently carried off and eaten by lions.
The instinct of the animal leads it to attack the inferior, and
therefore feebler being, as even our domestic animals are far
more likely to attack children than adults. The negro actually has nothing in common with the animal world that other
races have not, but those things common to men and animals
are much more prominent in him. Thus, while there is an
impassable and perpetual chasm between them, there is a certain resemblance between the negro and the ourang-outang.
The latter is the most advanced species of the simiadæ or ape
family, while the negro is the lowest in the scale of the human
creation, and the approximation to each other, though of
course eternally incomplete, is certainly striking. As stated
elsewhere, the author does not belong to that gloomy and forbidding school of materialism which would make the faculties
and even our moral emotions the mere result of organism.
But there is an inseparable connection which necessarily renders them the exact admeasurement of each other, and though
neither cause nor result, and their ultimate relation eternally
hidden from the finite mind, they are, in this existence at least,
inextricably bound up together. The approximation, therefore, of the negro to the ourang-outang, while there is a boundless space within the circle of which there can be no resemblence—for the negro is absolutely and entirely human—and
within which it is not proposed to enter, is exactly revealed in
the outward form and attitude. The negro, from the structure of his limbs, his head, etc., has a decided inclination to
the quadruped posture, while the ourang-outang has an equal
tendency to the upright human form. The latter often walks
partially erect, and sometimes even carries a club, while the
typical negro in Africa or Cuba, or anywhere in his natural

state, is quite as likely to squat on his hams as to stand on his feet. Thus, an anatomist with the negro and ourang-outang before him, after a careful comparison, would say, perhaps, that nature herself had been puzzled where to place them, and had finally compromised the matter by giving them an exactly equal inclination to the form and attitude of each other.

5

CHAPTER VII.

NEXT to color, there is nothing so palpable to the sense as the hair, or nothing that reveals the specific difference of race so unmistakably as the natural covering of the head. The hair of the Caucasian is a graceful and imposing feature or quality, of course in perfect harmony with everything else, but sometimes, and especially in the case of females, it is an attribute of physical beauty more striking and attractive than any other. Its color, golden or sunny brown, and the dazzling hues of black, purple, and auburn tresses, has been the theme of poets from time immemorial, while its luxuriance, and silky softness, and graceful length will continue to be the pride of one sex and the admiration of the other as long as the perception of beauty remains.

In the Mongol, Malay, or Indian, as well as the Negro, it remains the same through all the stages of life, and it is only in extreme old age that it becomes gray or silvery white, or even falls off from any portion of the head. The coarse, stiff, black hair of the Indian child is that also of its parents—and a gray-headed or bald-headed Indian, except in some cases of extreme old age, is as rare perhaps as that of a bald-headed negro. But the child of the Caucasian, with perfectly white or flaxen hair, expands into the maiden with clustering ringlets of auburn or perhaps raven black, to be threaded with silver, in middle life perhaps, and though less common than with the other sex, a few years later it becomes again, as in early child·

hood, perfectly white. But there are no exceptions to the
uniform color of the hair in other races. Such a thing as a
flaxen-haired or a light-haired negro child never existed.
There may be sometimes a slight approximation in this respect
among Mongols, but the hair of the negro, except in some
cases of extreme old age, remains absolutely the same at all
periods, from the cradle to the grave. The elementary structure, as shown by the elaborate microscopical observations of
Mr. Peter A. Browne, of Philadelphia, differs as widely as the
external or superficial modifications. The popular notion that
it is wool instead of hair that covers the negro head is like
many others, founded on a mere external resemblance, without
any actual correspondence. It is hair, but *sui generis*, or
rather specific and common to the negro alone, and however
widely different from that of white people, it is no more so
than any other quality or feature of the negro nature. The
variations of this feature in the white race are almost unlimited.
Hair dressing even has been elevated to the respectability of
an art, if not to the dignity of a science. For many generations the kings of France kept *artistes* of this character, who
often received a salary equal to the ministers of the crown, and
one of them, Oliver Le Dain, became in fact, if not in form,
the actual ruler of the kingdom. But it was the princesses
and ladies of the court that exalted this "art" to its highest
pitch of extravagance and display. Marie Antoinette—one of
the most unhappy women that ever lived—made it an important part of every day's employment, and exacted the same
labor from her attendants. Even in our own more sensible
times, the Empress Eugenie changes the fashions in this respect almost every month, and the styles or modes of dressing
their hair is an extravagant though amiable weakness of our
own fair countrywomen. There is in fact no mere physical
quality of the female so attractive, or that is capable of being

rendered so charming, as the hair, and the elaborate dressings, the time and labor spent on its decoration, proceed as much perhaps from that delicate perception of the beautiful innate in woman as it does from female vanity or the love of display. But with this " wealth of beauty" of the Caucasian woman, what an immeasurable interval separates her from the negress! Is it possible for any who sees the latter, with her short, stiff, uncombable fleece of seeming wool, to endow her with the attribute of beauty or comeliness? And though somewhat less palpable in the other sex, the hair is an essential element of manly beauty as well as dignity, and the " love locks" of the cavaliers and even the "soap locks" of more modern times, are identified with certain conceptions of manly grace. Can any one form such conceptions in respect to the hair of the negro? Can he identify any of these things with the crisp, stiff, seeming wool that covers the head of that race? Can the sentiment of beauty, grace or dignity, or indeed any idea whatever —except as a necessary provision of nature for covering the negro head—attach to the hair of the negro? This is all that is possible to the mind of a white person in actual juxtaposition with the negro, and therefore while the European Abolitionist may fancy his head adorned by "ambrosial curls," our own native Abolitionists are wholly unable to conceive of any use or purpose whatever for that dense mat of wiry and twisted hair which covers the negro head, except as a provision of nature for its protection. The protection of the head, or rather of the brain, is the purpose or the function of the hair in all races, but while that, in our race, is identified with elevated and striking qualities, it is the sole purpose in the case of the negro. The short, crisp, dense mass that covers the negro head, like every other quality or attribute of the negro nature, is in perfect harmony with the climatic and external circumstances with which God has surrounded him. The popular notion that the

negro skull is much thicker than that of the white man originated from this peculiarity of the covering of the negro head.
The hair is so dense, so curled and twisted together, and forms
such a complete mat or net work as to be wholly impenetrable
to the rays of a vertical sun, and to furnish a vastly better
protection for the brain than the thickest felt hat does to that
of the white man. Thus, though negroes on our southern
plantations, with the imitative instincts of their race, copy
after the whites and wear hats, it is merely a "fashionable
folly," and dictated by no natural want, nor in the slightest
degree adds to their happiness. And beside the protection
from the fierce heats of the tropics, the hair of the negro pro-
teets his head in other respects. It is so hard and wiry, and
in fact triangular in form, that a blow from the hand of a master would doubtless injure the latter vastly more than it would
the head of the negro, and the common practice among them
of butting each other with their heads, though knocking them
off their feet, and the concussion heard at considerable dis-
tances, never results in injury, for the dense mat of semi-wool
that covers the head protects it from mischief. The negro
hair is then designed solely for the protection of the negro
head, and not only differs widely from that of the Caucasian,
but from that of all other races, for the negro is a tropical race,
and the hair, like all other attributes of the negro being, physical and moral, is adapted to a tropical clime, and in perfect
accord with the physical wants and moral necessities of the race.

But the mere covering of the head, or the mere protection
of the brain, is not all that distinguishes the different races
in these respects. The beard is equally radical and universal, though not so palpable a specialty as color, and in some
respects it may be said to be a more important one. The
Caucasian alone has a beard, for though all others approximate
to it in this respect, it is the only bearded race, and some

writers on ethnology have been so impressed with this imposing and striking distinction that they have sought to make it
the basis of a classification of races. And there certainly is no
physical or outward quality that so imposingly impresses itself
on the senses as a mark of superiority, or evidence of supre
macy, as a full and flowing beard. Color, when in repose, or
when it does not give expression to the inner nature, does not,
in reality, constitute a distinction at all, but the beard is an
evidence of superiority, that, however varied the action or
whatever the circumstances, is equally distinct and universal
as an attribute of supremacy. This is sufficiently illustrated
in our own race and our every day experience. The youth is
beardless, and *pari passu* as he approaches to the maturity of
manhood there is a corresponding development of beard. The
intellect—the mental strength—the moral beauty, all the qualities of the inner being, as well as those outward attributes
tangible to the sense, harmonize perfectly with the growth of
the beard, and when that has reached its full development, it
is both the signal and the proof of mature manhood—an exact
admeasurement and absolute proof of the maturity of the individual as well as the type and standard of the race. This is
equally true when applied to different races. The Caucasian
is the only bearded race, but all others approximate in this
respect, and the negro is furthest removed of all, for the tropical woolly haired African or negro, except a little tuft on the
chin and sometimes on the upper lip, has nothing that can be
confounded with a beard. People sometimes see negroes with
considerable hair on their faces, and hence conclude that they
are as likely to have beards as white men ; but they forget
that all in our society who are not whites are considered negroes,
and therefore those bearded negroes have a large infusion, and
doubtless sometimes a vastly predominating infusion of Caucasian blood. The beard symbolizes our highest conceptions of

manhood—it is the outward evidence of mature development —of complete growth, mental as well as physical—of strength, wisdom and manly grace, and the full, flowing, and majestic beard of the Caucasian, in contrast with the negro or other subordinate races, is as striking and imposing as the mane of the lion when compared with the meaner beasts of the animal world. Like color or any other of the great fundamental facts separating races, the beard is sufficient to determine their specific character and their specific relations to each other, and we have only to apply our every day experience as regards this outward symbol of inner manhood to measure the relative inferiority of the negro. The Abolitionists demand that the "equal manhood" of the negro shall be recognized, and complain bitterly of a government that refuses to respond to their wishes in this respect, but if this "equal manhood" was actually revealed to them in the person of the negro as it is in the persons of white men, and as God has alone provided and ordained or permitted it to be revealed, they would be overwhelmed with astonishment or convulsed with laughter. A negro with a full and flowing beard, with this symbol of perfeet manhood or with this outward manifestation of the inner (Caucasian) being, would be a ludicrous monstrosity, as impossible, of course, as the Caliban of Shakespeare; but if such a supernatural being should suddenly make his appearance in an Abolition conventicle, the "friends of humanity" would be as much astonished as if an inhabitant of another world had come among them. A youth, with the majestic and flowing beard of adult life, if the monstrosity did not shock and disgust us, would be irresistibly comical, and equally so in the case of the childish and romping negro. Thus, were the leaders of the "anti-slavery enterprise" busily engaged in discussing the "equal manhood" of the negro, and in earnestly denouncing those who, unable to see it, decline to admit such a thing, and

a negro should enter the room with the actual proof of its existence—with the full, flowing beard of the Caucasian, and
therefore the outward symbol of an " equal manhood," as the
hand of the Eternal has revealed it in the person of the former—
the whole Abolition congregation, if not paralyzed with horror, would burst into uncontrolable laughter.   The wrongs of
the " slave," the cruelties of the master, the " hopes of humanity," the most doleful stories and the saddest tales of the
suffering " bondmen," would be interrupted by screams of
laughter at such a ludicrous spectacle as a negro with the
majestic and flowing beard of the white man.   This outward
symbol of complete manhood, or this external indication which
typifies the high nature and lofty qualities of the Caucasian,
is no more impossible, however, to the negro than that " equal
manhood" which is demanded for him, and therefore were the
" friends of humanity" to vary their programme and demand
an " equal" beard, or that we shall grant the negro the full
and flowing beard of the Caucasian, they would render their
performances more interesting without giving up any of their
" principles," as the absurdity is exactly the same in either
case.

CHAPTER VIII.

THE FEATURES.

THE features reflect the inner nature, the faculties or specific qualities, and they are distinct or indistinct, developed or undeveloped, as we ascend or descend in the scale of being. In the simpler forms of animal existence, there is close resemblence to vegetable life in this respect; but ascending to the vertebrata, and especially the mammalia, there is a broad distinction between the head and body, and instead of an undefined uniformity pervading the whole exterior surface, the face becomes a centre in which the essential character of the creature is written by the hand of Nature. It is true, that the general form of the body is significant of the grosser qualities. The muscular and motive forces of the horse are evidently designed for swiftness; those of the lion, and the felinæ generally, are designed both for strength and swiftness; while that of the ox and other mammalia is adapted to a negative kind of strength which results from a combination of all the physical forces, and not, as in the former case, from an excessive muscular development. But the higher qualities, even in animals, are legibly written in the face or features. In the human creation, of course, this external reflection of the inner nature in the features becomes vastly more distinct and real, and in our own race not unfrequently does the face become a very window of the soul, where may be read the sweetest and most exquisite emotions of a sensitive and delicate nature, or, as sometimes happens, the gross and sensual thoughts of a depraved and perverted one. There are, indeed, countless and innumerable variations in our own race in this respect. The white or Caucasian men of Asia, of Africa, Europe, and America, are so modified by climate, habits, government, religion, etc., that those ethnologists who are not anatomists have sometimes confounded them, and classed them as distinct species. Even on the same continent, in the same country, sometimes the same family, these variations are so marked that they always seem to belong to different species. The globular head, broad forehead, oval cheeks, straight nose, and distinct, well defined lips and mouth, however, whatever may be the expression, always remain the same, and can never be confounded with any other race of men. And these modifications in the Caucasian are not confined to the face, but pervade the whole surface. White, black, and red hair, white skin and brown ones, blondes and brunettes, are often found in the same family. It is even so in regard to size—some are short and others tall—some pigmies while others are giants—and not unfrequently in the same household, while the same nation exhibits every possible variety in this respect. The Caucasian race alone presents these variations—the other races great uniformity; and the negro, lowest in the scale, presents an almost absolute resemblance to each other. Of all the millions that have existed on the earth, their hair not only in color but in form has been absolutely the same, and such a being as a different-colored or straight-haired, or long-haired negro never existed. On visiting a plantation at the South, one sees a thousand negroes so nearly alike, that except where wide differences of age exist, they are all alike, and even in size rarely depart from that standard uniformity that nature has stamped upon the race. The entire external surface, as well as his interior organism, differs radically from the Caucasian. His muscles, the form of the limbs, his feet, hands, pelvis, skeleton, all the organs of locomotion, give him an outward attitude that, while radically different from the Caucasian, approaches an almost absolute uniformity of character in the negro. His longitudinal head, narrow and receding forehead, flat nose, enormous lips and protuberant jaws, in short, his flat, shapeless and indistinct features strikingly approximate to the animal creation, and they are as utterly incapable of reflecting certain emotions as so much flesh and blood of any other portion of his body. The Almighty and All-Wise Creator has made all things perfect, and adapted the negro features, as well as those of the white man, to the inner nature, but if it were true that the negro had certain qualities with which ignorance and delusion would endow him, then it would be quite evident that the Almighty Creator had made a fatal blunder in this case, for it is clearly a matter of physical demonstration that the negro features cannot reflect these qualities. The features of the animal are made to express its wants, to reflect the nature God has given it. We witness this every day among our domestic animals—the cat, the dog, the horse, all exhibit their qualities, their wants, their moods, at different times their anger, suffering, and affection, all that their natures are capable of, are reflected in their faces, and we understand them. In our own race, the transparent skin, the deeply cut and distinct features become often a perfect mirror of the inner nature, and reflect the nicest shades of feeling as well as the deepest emotions of the soul. Envy, anger, pride, shame, scowling hate and malignant fear, as well as gentle affection and the most exalted love, are written as legibly in the face as if they were things of physical form, and their innumerable modifications and variations are witnessed all about us, and every day of our lives. How grandly this is displayed in the case of the orator! This must have been apparent to those who heard Mr. Clay in the Senate, and saw those wonderful changes of feature—one moment convulsed with anger, then lit up with genius, or with pride and pomp of conscious power, and in another reflecting, perhaps, all a woman's sweetness or a child's gentleness. Color, of course, is essential to this, for a display of the passions and emotions on the dark ground-work of the negro skin would be as impossible as a rainbow at midnight, but without the deeply cut and distinctly marked features of the Caucasian, color would be comparatively useless in reflecting the grander emotions of the soul. Any one referring to his own experience for a moment will see how impossible, as a mere physical matter, that the negro face can reflect the qualities attributed to him by those who are ignorant of his real nature. The narrow and receding forehead, the shallow eyes, flat nose, almost on a level with the cheeks, the protruding and enormous lips,—the only thing that really can be said to be distinct in the negro face,—the *tout ensemble* without form or meaning when contrasted with the white man, is, in connection with the color, the dark ground of the negro skin, clearly incapable of reflecting certain qualities of our own race. The negro has, of course, moral emotions, as have all human creatures, and his face, like that of the Caucasian, is capable of reflecting all *his* wants, his likes and dislikes, his hopes and fears, but every one who has seen him must *know* that the higher qualities of the Caucasian cannot find expression in the negro features, and therefore he does not possess those qualities, or, as has been said, the All-Wise and Almighty Creator of all has committed a fatal mistake, and unjustly endowed him with qualities which he is forever forbidden to express!

CHAPTER IX.

A FEW years since, an eminent historian, in a public lecture, discussed the probabilities of a universal language as an instrument of universal history, and as means for the universal civilization of mankind! Another public lecturer discussing this subject, and on a professedly scientific basis, held that language had a miraculous origin, though the period when this supernatural gift was conferred on man was left wholly to the imagination of his audience. Others, and among them Buffon, Pritchard, and even several ethnologists, have scarcely risen above this nonsense, while their uses or application of this faculty have been vastly more injurious to science than even their original misconceptions on the general subject.

Language is naturally divided into two distinct and widely separated portions, having no necessary connection, though at certain points or stages uniting and combining together. First, is that universal capacity of expressing itself—its wants, its sufferings, and its enjoyments—which God has given to all His creatures, from the insect at our feet to the Caucasian man standing at the head of this vast and innumerable host of living beings. In the second place, in its structure and arrangement into parts or portions of speech; in short, its grammatical construction. With the former it is alone or mainly proposed to deal in this place, though it will be necessary occasionally to refer to the latter. As has been said, all living or rather all animal beings have the faculty of expressing their wants, and they have a vocal organism in exact correspondence with these wants and the purposes for which they are designed by the common Creator of all. Except to a few laborious and enthusiastic students of natural history, the vast world of insect life is a *terra incognita*, but each one of these myriad of beings is adapted to some specific purpose and beneficently designed by the Almighty Master of Life for the same universal enjoyment which is so distinctly revealed as the end of their existence in the more elaborately organized and higher endowed classes of animal being. And millions of these minute and often unseen creatures are daily and hourly singing praises to the Almighty Creator for His infinite goodness, rendering the fields and forests vocal with the music of their gratitude and the exuberance of their enjoyment. As we ascend in the scale of animated existence, the vocal faculty or language becomes still more distinctly revealed, with a vocal apparatus or organism in exact correspondence with the function or faculty that God has given to the being in question. The pigeon, of course, cannot give us the notes of the canary bird, nor the owl sing the songs of the nightingale. The serpent cannot exchange his hiss for the growl of the tiger, nor the ass abandon its uncouth utterances for the mighty roar or the majestic voice of the lion. Each is permitted to express its wants, its sufferings, and its joys, and each is provided with a vocal organism specific and peculiar to itself and to its kind, and in accord with the universal law of adaptation which inseparably unites organism with function. This, then, in its elementary form, is language—a faculty common to the animal world, and a necessity of animal existence. It differs in no essential respect in regard to human beings, or it varies no more from that of the animal world than other functions or faculties of the human being. There is, it is true, a point of departure or divergence where the analogies of the animal

world are no longer applicable to human beings, or where animal beings cannot furnish parallels for those endowed with a
moral nature and destined for immortality; but a vocal organism with its corresponding faculty or function is essentially the
same thing in both, and differs only in form and degree among
the innumerable beings that compose or are comprised within
the vast world of animated existence. While language, therefore, the voice or faculty by which animals as well as human
beings express their wants, is universal and only varied as the
structure and nature are varied, and while the vocal organism
is in exact harmony with the faculty or function in all cases
and in every phase of animated existence, there is also, and of
necessity, a specific modification of this faculty in the case of
the several human races or species. The vocal organs of the
negro differ widely from those of the white man, and of course
there is a corresponding difference in the language. The specific or the most essential feature of the negro nature is his
imitative instincts, or his capacity for imitating the qualities
and for acquiring the habitudes of the white man. This, of
course, is limited to his actual juxtaposition with the superior
race, for aside from that organic necessity which utterly forbids its being otherwise, there is no historical fact better
attested than that which shows him invariably relapsing into
savageism whenever he is left without the restraining support
of the former. But for wise and beneficent purposes, God has
endowed him with a capacity of imitation, and he is enabled
to apply it to such an extent that those ignorant of the negro
nature actually offer it as a proof of his equal capacity! But
with all his power to thus imitate the habits and to copy the
language of the white man, it is not possible that a single
example can be furnished of his success in regard to the latter.
With us, and especially at the North, all are negroes who are
tainted with negro blood, and thus many persons will imagine

that they have seen negroes who were as competent to speak our language as white men themselves. But no actual or typical negro will be able—no matter what pains have been taken to " educate" him—to speak the language of the white man with absolute correctness. European ethnologists have, notwithstanding, sought to make language the means for trac- ing the history and determining the character of races, the worthlessness and indeed the absurdity of which only needs a single illustration to expose it. The negroes of Hayti have imitated or copied the language of their former masters, the French, therefore they are of the same race, and the future ethnologists would pronounce them Frenchmen! As the negro cannot preserve anything that he copies from the Caucasian beyond a certain period, the negroes of that island are rapidly losing all that they obtained from their former masters, and though the educated portion on the coasts, and especially the mongrels, yet retain the French language, those in the interior are rapidly relapsing into their native African tongue. And a century or two hence, when the French is entirely extinct and the existing negro population speak an African dialect, or what is far more probable, speak our own, the ethnological enquirer would decide that those led by Touissant and Chris- tophe in the war of "Independence" were Frenchmen instead of Negroes, because, forsooth, the public documents of the time showed they spoke the French language! Thus, while language is an important means for tracing nationalities or varieties of our own race, as, for example, the modern Spanish, French, Italian, etc., in connection with the great Latin family of southern Europe, it is simply absurd to apply it to distinct species like Caucasians and negroes. Each race or each spe- cies, as each and every other form of life, is in perfect har- mony with itself, and therefore the voice of the negro, both in its tones and its structure, varies just as widely from that of

LANGUAGE. 113

the white man as any other feature or faculty of the negro being. Any one accustomed to negroes would distinguish the
negro voice at night among any number of those of white
men by its tones alone, and without regard to his peculiar
utterances. Tones or mere sounds are of course indescribable,
and therefore no comparison in this respect is possible, but all
those familiar with the tones of the negro voice know that it
is never musical or capable of those soft and sweet inflections
or modulations common to our own race. Music is to the
negro an impossible art, and therefore such a thing as a negro
singer is unknown. It is true that, a few years since, certain
amiable people, both at the North and in England, believed
for a time that they had secured a prodigy of this kind in the
person of the " Black Swan," but after a careful and patient
trial, it was found to be a mistake. She was not even a negress, though perhaps of predominating negro blood, and was
aided and encouraged by every possible means, especially in
England, where she was actually placed under the care of
Queen Victoria's music master, but without avail—Nature was
superior to art—the laws of God more potent than those of
human invention—and the " Black Swan" finally disappeared
from public view. The negro is fond of music, as are all other
beings, and indeed all animal beings of the more elevated
classes, but music is to him merely a thing of the senses. With
the white race music is perceived as well as felt—an intellectual as well as sensuous thing—and though it by no
means follows that intellectual persons, with minds above
the common average, should also have musical powers, that
sensitive and exquisite organization which is necessary to a
musical genius must be united with a brain of corresponding
complexity. The brain and the nerves constitute a whole—a
system—however widely portions of the latter may diverge in
their especial functions, and it is as impossible that the musical

temperament, or that the elaborate and exquisitely sensuous system of the Caucasian could be united with the brain of the negro, as it would be to unite the color of the former with the negro structure. The negro, therefore, neither perceives nor can he give expression to music—he has neither the brain nor the delicacy of nerve nor the vocal organism that is essential to this faculty—all that is possible to him is a certain approximation through his wonderful powers of imitation, but which is less available to him in this respect perhaps than any other. His brain is much smaller, but his nerves are much larger, and his senses are consequently much more acute, and here is the cause of that "musical power" with which ignorant and mistaken persons have endowed him. Music is felt by the nerves rather than perceived by the brain, in his feet as much as in his head, and with an intensity unknown and unfelt by whites. His imitative instinct enables him to rapidly acquire the language of his master, but he also loses it with similar rapidity. The negroes imported to the West India Islands, though living on large plantations, soon acquired the language of the few whites, so far as words were concerned, but an organic necessity compelled them to retain the structure of their original tongue. Thus, those in British islands spoke English, in French islands, French, etc., but the general structure remained the same in all, and now, when the external force applied by the several European governments has removed the control and guidance of the superior race, they are rapidly losing the words of their former masters, and in this as well as every other respect returning to their native Africanism. In Hayti, where the imitative capacity has little or nothing to stimulate it, this process is very rapid indeed, and could they be entirely isolated, the utter extinction of the French language would doubtless occur within the present century.

CHAPTER X.

THE senses are those special organisms that connect us with the outer world through which external impressions are received and transmitted to the brain—the great sensorium or centre of the nervous system. They are popularly designated as sight, hearing, smelling, touch, and taste, each having its own peculiar organism; some, as sight, exceedingly elaborate, and others, like taste, quite simple, being little more than a delicate expansion of nervous matter spread upon the tongue and lining the inner surface of the mouth. The nervous system includes the brain and the nerves, but is, in fact, an indivisible whole, of which the brain forms the centre, and the nerves the circumference, in exact proportion as we ascend in the scale of being. The centre of the nervous system is increased and the circumference diminished as the brain becomes larger and the nerves smaller. Among quadrupeds—the horse, for example—the nerves are enormously large in comparison with the brain of that animal; and this holds good throughout, so that an intelligent physiologist might determine the possible capabilities of any of the higher order of animals by a simple comparison of the brain and nerves. And in the human creation a single skull of a Mongol, or Malay, or Negro, and especially of the latter, should be quite sufficient to enable a physiologist to comprehend the essential character of the race to which it belonged. True, he might, as has often happened, mistake it for an abnormal specimen of the Caucasian,

and thus display a vast amount of learned nonsense of the Gall-
Spurzheim order, but if he knew it to be an actual negro
skull, and then compared it with that of the Caucasian, he should
be able not only to determine the intellectual inferiority, but
the vastly preponderating sensualism of the former. He would
see that the relatively small cerebrum, and the large cerebellum, must be united with a corresponding development of the
senses, and a comparatively dominating sensualism. The mere
organism of the senses, of sight, hearing, etc., though of course
differing widely from those of the Caucasian, it is not necessary to describe, for even in animals of the higher class there
is a certain resemblance, and the student of anatomy studies
the mechanism of the eye in the ox or horse as satisfactorily
as in that of the human creature.

The organisms while thus, in a sense, similar—of the eye, for
example—in whites and negroes, is more elaborately and delicately constituted in the case of the former, and therefore it is
also vastly more liable to disease, to congenital defects, to
strabismus, etc., and especially short-sightedness. The negro,
on the contrary, rarely suffers from these things, or even from
inflammation of the eyes, so common among white people, and
though, in keeping with the imitative instinct of the race, the
negro " preacher" dons spectacles as well as white neck-cloth,
it may be doubted if there ever was a case of near-sightedness
in the typical negro. Though in extreme old age they doubtless lose the power of vision common to their youth, it is rare
that negroes need spectacles at any age. The organism is
supplied with a larger portion of nervous matter than in the
case of the whites, and the function or sense is thus endowed
with a strength and acuteness vastly greater than are the
senses of the Caucasian. Travelers and others mingling among
savages, Indians, negroes, etc., have observed the extraordinary power and acuteness of the external senses, and have

supposed that this was a result of their savage condition, which, calling for a constant exercise of these faculties, gave them an extraordinary development. And Pritchard, carrying this theory or notion to an extreme, inferred that men were originally created negroes, for the exigencies of savage life demanded, as he supposed, a black color as well as acuteness of the senses! Doubtless the civilized negro of America ordinarily displays less strength and acuteness of sense than his wild brother of Africa, but he is born with the same faculties, and were the surrounding circumstances changed so as to call them into more active exercise, he would exhibit similar characteristics.

The Almighty Creator, with infinite wisdom, has adapted all His creatures to the ends or purposes of their creation. The Caucasian or white man, with his large brain and elevated reasoning powers, is thus provided with all that is necessary to guard his safety and to increase his happiness. Inferior races, with smaller brains and feebler mental powers are endowed with strength and acuteness of the external senses which enable them to contend specifically with surrounding circumstances and to provide for their safety. This is strikingly manifest in the North American Indian who marks or makes a trail in the forest which he follows with unerring confidence, though the eye of the white man sees nothing whatever. The descriptions of Indian character in Cooper's novels are in these respects perfectly correct and true to nature, as are all those of the Indianized white man, Leather-Stocking, Hawkeye, etc. The one depends upon his senses—his sight, hearing, etc., the other on his powers of reasoning or reflection, which in the end enable him to " sarcumvent" his Huron enemies and to win the victory. Each, according to his " gifts," is able to fulfil the purposes of his creation, and while the superior intelligence of the Caucasian is spreading that race, with

its benign and civilizing consequences, over the whole northern continent, the strength and acuteness of his senses have
enabled the Indian to resist to a degree all these mighty forces
for three hundred years.

Some historians have advanced the notion that Rome was
overrun by northern barbarians, similar to our North American Indians, but if the mighty hordes led by Alaric and
Genseric to the conquest of Italy, had been Indians, not one
would have escaped to tell the tale of their destruction. A
high civilization, rotten at heart, falls an easy conquest to
ruder and more simple communities of the same race—thus,
the effete and corrupt Roman aristocracy fell before the simple and rude populations of Northern Europe, as the polished
and scholastic Greeks had succumbed to the Romans, when
the latter practised the simple and hardy virtues of their earlier history.   In our own times we have seen Spain, long
ruled over by an effete and worn-out aristocracy, sink from a
first class to a fourth rate power, while France, relieved from
the dead weight of "nobility," has in half a century become
the leading power of the world.   And if the English masses
have not sufficient vitality to cast off the mighty pressure of a
diseased and effete aristocracy by an internal reform like that
which the French passed through in 1789, then it is certain
that, at no distant day, the nation will fall a conquest to some
external power that has greater vitality than itself, however
deficient it may be in wealth and learning, and those refine-
ments that pass for high civilization.   But while nations ruled
over by privileged classes thus carry within them the seeds of
their own destruction, and sooner or later fall a conquest to
ruder and simpler societies, the intellectual superiority of the
white man always enables him to conquer inferior races, whatever may be the disparity of numbers, and Clive with three
thousand Europeans, attacking the Hindoo horde of one hun-

dred thousand, or Cortez invading Mexico with five hundred
followers, amply illustrates the natural supremacy of the Caucasian race. But, on the contrary, if the Aztecs had had the
intellectual capacity of the Caucasian superadded to their own
specific qualities—the strength and acuteness of the senses—
common to the native race, not alone would Cortéz have failed
to conquer them, but it may be doubted if all Europe, combined together for that purpose, could have accomplished it.

There are no examples for testing the capabilities of negroes
in these respects, for there is no instance in history where they
have contested the supremacy of the white man, the insurrection in Hayti having been the work of the "colored people"
and mulattoes, and the negroes only forced into it by their fears
after the outbreak was complete. But we have the actual
physical facts as well as our every-day experience of the negro
qualities, and therefore can arrive at positive truth when comparing him with the superior race. The large distribution of
nervous matter to the organs of sense and consequent dominating sensualism (not mere animalism), is the direct cause of
that extreme sloth and indolence universal with the race. The
small brain and limited reasoning power of the negro render
him incapable of comprehending the wants of the future, while
the sloth dependent on the dominating sensualism, together
with strong animal appetites impelling him always to gross
self-indulgence, render a master guide or protector essential to
his own welfare. Indeed it may be matter of doubt which is
the paramount cause of the negro's inability to provide for
future necessities—his limited reasoning power or his indolence—his small brain or his dominating sensualism. It is a
statistical *fact* that "free" negroes do not produce sufficient
for their support, and consequently that they tend perpetually
to extinction, and when it is remembered that the small brain
and feeble intellectual power render them incapable of reason-

ing on the future rewards of self-denial, and that the large
distribution of nervous matter in the organs of sense, and
the consequent sensualism impels them to gross indulgence
of the present, and moreover that they are in juxtaposition,
and must contend with white people, then it is plain enough
to see that it could not be otherwise, and that the total extinction of these unfortunate beings is necessarily a question
of time alone.

But it is not the mere predominance of the senses, or the
strength and acuteness of the sense which so broadly and radically separates whites and negroes. They are entirely different in the manifestations of these qualities. As has been
observed, there are few if any near-sighted negroes, or negroes
with other defects of vision, and the sense of smell in negroes
permits them to discriminate and to indicate the presence of
the rattle snake, or other venomous serpents. And in respect
to the sense of touch or feeling, the peculiarity of the negro
nature is perhaps most remarkable of all. This sense in the
white person, though universal of course, is mainly located in
the hand and fingers. Sir Charles Bell, an eminent English
surgeon, has written an interesting work—one of the Bridge-
water treatises—on the flexibility and adaptation of the human
hand, and other volumes might be given to the world without
exhausting the subject. The universal law of adaptation,
indeed, demands that the sense of touch, the flexibility of the
hand, the delicacy of the fingers, should be in accord with the
large brain and commanding intellect, otherwise the world
itself would long since have come to a stand-still, and human
invention ended with the antediluvians. It is true the structure—the arrangement of the bones, muscles, tendons, etc., in
short, the mere mechanism of the hand, is essential, but without the sense of feeling, or that delicacy of touch found only

in the fingers of the Caucasian, the mechanical perfections of the hand would be comparatively useless.

All the nice manipulations in surgery, in the arts, in painting, statuary, and the thousands of delicate fabrics seen every day and all about us, demand both intellect and delicacy of hand, and these, too, in that complete perfection found alone in the Caucasian. The sense of touch, on the contrary, in the negro is not in the hand or fingers, or only partially so, but spreads all over the surface and envelops the entire person. The hand itself, in its mere mechanism, is incompatible with delicate manipulation. The coarse, blunt, webbed fingers of the negress, for example, even if we could imagine delicacy of touch and intellect to direct, could not in any length of time or millions of years be brought to produce those delicate fabrics or work those exquisite embroideries which constitute the pursuits or make up the amusements of the Caucasian female. The mechanism of the negro hand, the absence or rather the obtuseness of the sense of touch in the fingers, and the limited negro intellect, therefore, utterly forbid that negroes shall be mechanics, except it be in those grosser trades, such as coopers, blacksmiths, etc., which need little more than muscular strength and industry to practice them. But the sense of touch, though feeble in the hand or fingers, is none the less largely developed as are the other senses of the negro, and spreads over the whole surface of the body. This is witnessed every day at the South, where whipping, as with Northern children, is the ordinary punishment of negroes. As in all other foolish notions that spring from the one great misconception—that negroes have the same nature as white people, the " anti-slavery" people of the North and of Europe labor under a ludicrous mistake in respect to this matter. They take their notions of flogging from the practice of the British army and the Russian knout, where strong men are cut to pieces by the "cat" or beaten to death by clubs, and they suppose that precisely similar barbarity is practiced on the "poor slave." And the runaway negro has doubtless added to these notions, perhaps, without meaning it. At Abolition conventicles he is expected, of course, to horrify the crowd with awful tales of his sufferings, but having always had plenty to eat and never overworked, he has really nothing to fall back on but the "cruel whippings," which the imaginations of the former readily transform into their own notions, but which, in fact, correspond to that which they deal out to their own children without a moment's compunction. The sensibility of the negro skin closely resembles that of childhood, and while there are doubtless cases of great barbarity in these respects, as we all know there are in cases of children, the ordinary flogging of negroes is much the same as that which parents, guardians, teachers, etc., deal out to white children, and the "terrible lash" so dolefully gloated over by the ignorant and deluded usually dwindles down into a petty switch in reality. But it is painful to the negro, perhaps more so than hanging would be, for while the local susceptibility of the skin makes him feel the slightest punishment in this respect, the obtuse sensibility of the brain and nervous system generally would enable him, as is often manifest, to bear hanging very well. Those who can remember being flogged in childhood will also remember the great pain that it gave them, though now in their adult age they would laugh at such a thing. The negro is a child forever, a child in many respects in his physical as well as his mental nature, and the flogging of the negro of fifty does not differ much, if any, from the flogging of a child of ten, and while the British soldier or Russian would receive his three hundred lashes without wincing, the big burly negro will yell more furiously than a school-boy when he receives a dozen cuts with an ordinary switch.

CHAPTER XI.

THE BRAIN.

THE brain is the seat or the centre of the intellect, in short, the mental organism. The " school men" believed that mind, intellect, the reasoning faculty, whatever we may term it, had no locality or organism, but, on the contrary, was some impalpable, shadowy, unfixed principle that existed as much in the feet or hands as in any other portion of the body. And even Locke and Bacon, while they promulgated the great truths of inductive philosophy, were not sufficiently grounded in its elementary principles to understand clearly the foundation of their own doctrines. Nor did Dugald Stuart, Dr. Brown, or even the great Kant, of more modern times, understand any better the fixed truths on which rest the vast and imperfect systems of philosophy which they labored so assiduously to build up in their day. It remained for Gall, Spurzheim, and their followers to do this—to demonstrate certain great elementary truths which form a foundation, eternal as time itself —for the mental phenomena to rest upon, and whatever advance may be made hereafter in the study of these phenomena, its basis is immovable. Metaphysicians were wont to shut themselves up in their libraries and to analyze their own emotions, etc., which when noted down, became afterwards the material for ponderous lectures or the still more ponderous volumes inflicted on society. Rarely, perhaps, were these speculations connected with the brain—indeed it is a rare thing to find a physiologist indulging in metaphysical speculation, while the most famous among the "philosophers" were profoundly ignorant of that organ, though they fancied they knew all about its functions! The man that should undertake to write a treatise on respiration, and at the same time was utterly ignorant of the structure of the lungs, or to give a lecture on the circulation, while he knew nothing of the blood vessels, would certainly be laughed at, and yet innumerable volumes have been written, and continue to be written, on the functions of the brain or on "moral and mental philosophy," by men who never saw a human brain in all their lives! Gall and Spurzheim did, therefore, a great good to the world when they began their investigations of the laws of the mind, by the study of the brain itself as the first and absolutely essential step to be taken in these investigations. It is true, they, and especially their followers, sought to set up a fancy science under the name of Phrenology, and the former thus, to a great extent, neutralized a reputation which otherwise would have secured the respect of the scientific world. And it is also true that others before them had recognized the same truths with more or less distinctness, but it is certain that Gall and Spurzheim demonstrated and placed beyond doubt the great, vital, and essential truth that the brain is the organ of the mind, and that the mental capacity, other things being equal, is in exact proportion to the size of the brain relatively with the body. This truth holds good throughout the animal world, and the intelligence of any given animal or species of animal, is always in keeping with the size of the brain when compared with the size of the body.

The brain is composed of anterior and posterior portions— of the cerebrum and the cerebellum—the first the centre of intelligence, the latter of sensation, or the first the seat of the intellect, and the latter of the animal instincts, and the proportions they bear to each other determines the character. As the

anterior portion is enlarged and the posterior diminished the
creature ascends, or as the anterior portion is diminished and
the posterior portion enlarged it descends, in the scale of being.
These are the general laws governing men and animals. There
is intelligence in proportion to the size of the brain compared
with that of the body, and in the former there is intellectual
capacity—latent or real—in proportion to the enlarged cerebrum and diminished cerebellum. It is true we see every day
seeming contradictions to the laws in question, but they are
not so, not even exceptions, for they are not general but universal. Every day we meet people with small heads and great
intelligence, with large heads and large stupidities, but a closer
examination may disclose the truth that the seemingly small
head is all brain, all cerebrum, all in front of the ears, while
the large one is all behind, and only reveals a largely developed
animalism. And even when this is not sufficient to explain
the seeming anomaly, there is a vast and inexhaustible field
for conjecture—of accident—where misapplied or undeveloped
powers have been the sport of circumstances. A man may
have a large brain, great natural powers, in truth, genius of
the most glorious kind, and the world remain in total ignorance of the fact, and among the countless millions of Europe
doomed generation after generation to a profound animalism,
there doubtless have been many "mute inglorious Miltons,"
who have lived and died and made no sign of the Divinity
within. On the contrary, there have been men of much distinction—of great usefulness to their fellows and to the generations after them, who, naturally considered, were ·on the
dead level of the race, but by their industry, perseverance, and
energy have left undying names to posterity. Then, again,
circumstances have made men great. An epoch in the annals
of a nation—great and stirring events in the life of-a people—
stimulate and call into exercise qualities and capacities that

make men famous, who otherwise would not be heard of. Our
own great revolutionary period furnished examples of this, and
still later, we have Jackson, Webster, Clay, Calhoun, and their
senatorial cotemporaries, who many doubtless think will
never be equalled, though their equals in fact are in the senate
now, and only need similar circumstances to manifest that
equality.

The organism of the race—the species—whether human or
animal, never changes or varies from that eternal type fixed
from the beginning by the hand of God; and men, therefore,
are now, in their natural capacities what they always have
been and always will be, whatever the external circumstances
that may control or modify the development of these capacities. And the brain being the organ or organism of the mind,
as the eye is of the sight or the ear of the sense of hearing, it
may be measured and tested, and its capabilities determined,
with as entire accuracy as any other function or faculty. Not,
it is true, as the phrenologists or craniologists contend, that the
brain reveals the character of individuals of the same species,
but the character of the species itself, and its relative capabilities when contrasted with other races or species of men.
This is beyond doubt or question, or will be beyond doubt or
question with all those who understand it, and taking the
Caucasian as the standard or test, the capabilities of the Mongol, the Malay, the Aboriginal American, or negro, may be
determined with as absolute certainty as the color of their
skins or any other mere physical quality. The brain of the
Caucasian averages ninety-two cubic inches, that of the negro
seventy-five to eighty-five inches, while the bodily proportions
can scarcely be said to vary. There are great variations among
whites as to size—there are giants as well as dwarfs, and
quite as great variety in the form,—from the "lean and
hungry Cassius," to the rounded proportions of a Falstaff or

Daniel Lambert. But on a Southern plantation of a thousand negroes, sex and age are the only difference or the principal difference that one sees, and a stranger would find some trouble to recognize any other, or at all events to distinguish faces. The brain of the negro corresponds in this respect with the body, and though there are doubtless cases where there is some slight difference, there seems to be none of those wide departures witnessed in these respects among whites.

The material, the fibre or texture of the brain itself is little understood, and though it is quite likely that what we call genius is attended by a corresponding delicacy or fineness of texture in the nervous mass, and future exploration in this abstruse matter may reveal to us important truths, at this time little is known in regard to the brain except the great fundamental and universal law that, in proportion to its size relatively with that of the body is there intellectual power, actual or latent. Many, doubtless, fancy that there are immense differences in men in this respect—that a Webster, or Clay, or Bonaparte are vastly superior to common men—but they have only to remember that the brain is the organ of the intellect, to see its fallacy. The notion has sprung from the habitudes of European society, where a man clothed in the pomp and parade of high rank is supposed to be vastly and immeasurably superior to his fellows, while, in truth, most of these, or, at all events many of these are absolutely (naturally) inferior to the base multitudes that prostrate themselves in the dust at their feet. Nevertheless, there are striking differences in these respects; not more so, however, than in strength of body, beauty of features, difference of hair, complexion, etc. But in the case of the negro there is an eternal sameness, a perpetual oneness, the same color, the same hair, the same features, same size of the body, and the same volume of brain. All the physical and moral facts that make up the negro being irresistibly

lead to the conclusion that the Almighty Creator designed
him for juxtaposition with the superior white man, and therefore such a thing as a negro-genius—a poet, inventor, or one
having any originality of any kind whatever—is totally unnecessary, as they are totally unknown in the experience of
mankind. Some, with more or less white blood, have exhibited more or less talent, possibly even have shown eccentric
indications of genius, but among a million of adult typical
negroes, there probably would not be a single brain that would
vary from the others sufficiently to be detected by the eye,
and therefore not an individual negro whose natural capacities
were so much greater than those of his fellows as to be recognized by the reason.

Such are briefly the leading and fundamental facts that constitute the mental organism and distinguish the intellectual
character of races, that separate white men and negroes by an
interval broader and deeper than in any other forms of humanity, and render an attempted social equality not merely a great
folly but a gross impiety. As has been stated, in exact proportion to the volume of brain, relatively with the size of body
in men and animals, there is intelligence, and as the cerebrum
or anterior portion predominates over the cerebellum or posterior portion, there is a corresponding predominance of intellectualism over animalism in the human races. The negro
brain in its totality is ten to fifteen per cent. less than that of
the Caucasian, while in its relations—the relatively large cerebellum and small cerebrum—the inferiority of the mental
organism is still more decided; thus, while in mere volume,
and therefore in the sum total of mental power, the negro is
vastly inferior to the white man, the relative proportion of the
brain and of the animal and intellectual natures adds still more
to the Caucasian superiority, while it opens up before us abun-
dant explanations of the diversified forms in which that supe-

riority is continually manifested. There are no terms or mere words that enable us to express the absolute scientific superiority of the white man. We can only measure it, or indeed comprehend it, by comparison, but this will be sufficiently intelligible when it is said that the past history and present condition of both races correspond exactly with the size and form of the brain in each. The science, the literature, the progress, enlightenment and intellectual grandeur of the Caucasian from the beginning of authentic history to this moment, and which have accompanied him from the banks of the Nile to those of the Mississippi, are all fitting revelations of the Caucasian brain, while the utter absence of all these things— the long night of darkness that enshrouds the negro being, and which is only broken in upon when in juxtaposition and permitted to imitate his master, is the result or necessity of his mental organism.

There being nothing superior to the Caucasian, it may be said that he is endowed with unlimited powers; that is, while the mental organism remains the same, his powers of acquisition and the increase of his knowledge have no limit. A generation in the exercise of its faculties acquires a certain amount of knowledge; this is transmitted to the next; it, in turn, adds its proportion, and so on, each generation in its turn accepting the knowledge of its progenitors and transmitting with its own acquisitions the sum total to its successors. This is called civilization, and we can suppose no limit to it, except it be in the destruction of the existing order and a new creation. On the contrary, the negro brain is incapable of grasping ideas, or what we call abstract truths, as absolutely so as the white child, indeed as necessarily incapable of such a thing as for a person to see without eyes, or hear without ears. In contact with, and permitted to imitate the white man, the negro learns to read, to write, to make speeches, to preach, to edit newspapers, etc.,

6*

but all this is like that of the boy of ten or twelve who debates
à la Webster or declaims from Demosthenes. People ignorant of the negro mistake this borrowed for real knowledge, as
one ignorant of metals may have a brass watch imposed on
him for a golden one. The negro is therefore incapable of
progress, a single generation being capable of all that millions
of generations are, and those populations in Africa isolated
from white men are exactly now as they were when the Hebrews escaped from Egypt, and where they must be millions
of years hence, if left to themselves. Of course this is no mere
opinion or conjecture of the author. It is a necessity of the
negro being—a consequence of the negro structure—a fixed
and eternally inseparable result of the mental organism, which
without a re-creation—another brain—could no more be otherwise than water could run up hill, or a reversal of the law of
gravitation in any respect could be possible. But people,
ignorant of the elementary principles of science as well as of
the nature of the negro, fancy that this is quite possible ; that,
however inferior the organism of the negro in these respects,
it is the result of many centuries of savagery and "slavery,"
and therefore if he were made "free," given the same rights
with the same chances for mental cultivation, that the brain
might gradually alter and become like that of the white man!
This involves gross impiety, if it were not the offspring of
ignorance and folly, for it supposes that chance and human
forces are more potent than the Almighty Creator, whose
work is thus the sport of circumstances. They would seek by
stimulating the mind to add ten per cent. to the negro brain—
then to add to the cerebrum while they diminished the cerebellum—certainly a work of much greater magnitude than
changing the color of the negro skin ; but even the most ignorant or the most impious among these people would scarcely
undertake the latter operation. If reason could at all enter

into the matter, it would surely be more reasonable to suppose
that mind might be changed by acting on matter, rather than
the reverse, and therefore it would be better to change the
color of the skin, as the first, as it would also be the most prac-
ticable, step to be taken in this grand undertaking of setting
aside the Creator and re-creating the negro. But, after all,
their labors would fail—after they had changed the color, after
they had increased the volume of the brain and duly modified
its relations as well as altered its texture—in short, when they
had turned him into a white man, then all would be in vain,
for such a brain could no more be born of a negress than an
elephant could be!

CHAPTER XII.

In the several preceding chapters, those outward characteristics that specifically distinguish the negro have been briefly
considered. It has been shown that color, the hair, the figure,
the brain, etc., are simply facts out of many millions of facts
that separate the races; that each and all of them are original,
invariable, and everlasting, and the exception, or the absence
of any of them, or of any of the associated facts not enumerated, at any time, in the case of a single individual or any generation, or under any possible circumstances of time, climate, or
external agencies whatever, is, or would be, necessarily impossible. Nature is always true to herself, and even in those
abnormal specimens sometimes presented to our observation—
those so-called monstrosities—there is, properly speaking, no
departure from her original designs, or from those fixed and
eternal laws that govern organic life. We sometimes see
Albinos, but except a certain tinge to the color, itself totally
unlike any color in other races, the absolute negro, that is the
millions of facts that constitute the negro being, are untouched. We witness all kinds of abnormal development in
our own race, in animals, in the vegetable world, in all the
innumerable beings and things that surround us. For example
—let any one spend an autumn day in the forest, and turn his
attention to the strange and often ludicrous sights that surround him. It often seems as if nature delighted herself in
treating odd and uncouth shapes, as if intended for relaxation

and relief from her graver and grander labors. But even here there is no violation of the higher law—the order of nature though very often interrupted by accident, is never contradicted—the abnormal development, the most uncouth and monstrous consequences are still pervaded by the eternal decree stamped upon the whole universe, that forbids forever any change in the minutest atom of this mighty mass of life. The Albino, the deformed or monstrous Negro, the seemingly wide departure from the normal standard, still obeys the higher law. All the peculiarities that distinguish him from his race are *sui generis*, without any approximation or resemblance to the white man. So, too, with the latter, and so, too, with all monstrosities in the lower animals. The things that constitute the monstrosity, that separate the creature, or seem to do so, from his own kind, separate him also from other species, whether of men or animals. The eternal gulf, the impassable barrier, the decreed limits fixed by the Creator himself, are never passed. A negro, with the color, or the hair, or the language, or the brain, or the sense of touch, or taste, or sight of the Caucasian, would not be a monstrosity but an impossibility. He might differ very widely from his own race in any one of these things, as we actually witness in the case of Albinos, in fact might retain scarcely any outward resemblance to his kind, and yet exist; but none has ever had, or ever will have, an existence that has any thing in common with the white man, for that would contradict the universal order of God himself.

Such being the fact, all that is external or tangible to the sense being thus widely, immeasurably, and indestructibly different from the Caucasian or white man, it is obvious that, in all beyond the outer surface, the same relative differences must exist. It was originally intended to demonstrate this in detail—to show the actual anatomical facts and structural dif-

ferences in the organs, the tissues, the systems, down to the
minutest atom of the bodily structure. It was designed to
present the reader with numerous plates, showing all this—
the minutest particle, the single globule of blood, even,
painted after the employment of the microscope, being sufficiently palpable to the sense, to show that the primordial
atoms of the negro structure are as specifically, and relatively
as widely, different from the white man's as the color, the hair,
or any of those outward qualities that confront us daily in the
streets. But this would have added so much to the expense
of the work, as to often place it out of the reach of the day
laborer and working man, those who alone, or mainly, need to
understand the great " anti-slavery" imposture of our times,
and the world-wide conspiracy against their freedom, manhood and happiness, which has so long held them in abject
submission to its clamorous pretences of philanthropy and humanity. Nor is it at all essential. A moment's reflection or
consideration is quite sufficient to convince any rational mind
that the outward differences must have their counterpart in
the entire structure. Of course any thing exceptional—a blem-
ish, a congenital deformity on the surface—has no corresponding relation with the interior, but that which is specific, uniform, and invariable, as the color, the hair, the features, etc.,
must of necessity pervade the *tout ensemble* of being, whether
human, animal, or vegetable. The apple, pear, peach, etc.,
have their own specific features externally, and their corresponding qualities internally. The shad differs from the salmon
in its absolute structure equally with its outward appearance.
The whole anatomical arrangement of the horse differs as
widely from that of the ass as the outward features vary,
And the entire bodily structure of the negro, down to the minutest atom of elementary matter, differs just as widely, of
course, as the color of the skin or other external qualities, from

those of the white man. It is equally palpable to the reason that the nature of the negro, his instincts, all the faculties of his mind, and all the functions of his body, are pervaded by the same or by relative differences from those of the Caucasian. To suppose otherwise is not to suppose a monstrosity, for, as has been remarked, monstrosities, however wide the departure from the normal standard, are *sui generis*, without any approximation to different beings—but such things are simply impossible. As it is plainly impossible that any being could exist half like or half unlike any other creature, so, too, it is obvious that beings with different structures could not possess the same qualities or manifest the same nature. Can any one imagine an apple with the qualities of the pear or peach, or even of another apple that differed from it in its material structure? Can it be supposed that a lion could ever have the nature of the tiger, or panther, or cat, or of any of the felina? Can it be believed that a bull-dog ever manifested the nature of a hound, or that the mastiff or spaniel could be made to exhibit the specific qualities of either? No, indeed. Nature makes no mistakes, nor does the Almighty Master of life permit His creatures to violate or transcend His eternal decrees.

It being, therefore, an invariable, indestructible, and eternal law, that the outward qualities are exactly harmonized with the interior structure down to the minutest atom of elementary particles and equally invariable and everlasting that the organism is in harmonious correspondence with the functions, the instincts, in a word, the nature, we are able to understand, with absolute certainty, the *specific* qualities, and to approach with tolerable certainty the relative differences and actual interval that separate the white and black races. The figures of the plate in the opening of this work indicate these vital and all-important truths.

The first figure exhibits the typical Caucasian, not the cultivated man of our time, but the "barbarian," the Oriental—the cotemporary with David, Solomon, Cyrus, and others of remote antiquity. The second figure is the Negro of the same period, as found on the monuments, and, at the present time, in all those portions of Africa where the negro is isolated, and there are no *débris* of other races existing among them. By himself he never changes in his outward manifestations. One generation is as a million of generations, and therefore the thousands now annually imported into Cuba are seen to be just as this figure represents him four thousand years ago.

Nor is the figure of the Caucasian changed, for though the American of to-day is at an immeasurable distance in knowledge, the actual physical and intellectual man remains the same as this figure represents him four thousand years ago. Both figures have the same color, and yet the *specific* differences are none the less palpable—the Caucasian and Negro type being equally distinct and widely different.

The third figure is an American—a white man of to-day—whose intellectual development, refinement of mind and manners, costume and habitudes are widely different; nevertheless, the physical qualities and specific capabilities are the same as those of his Oriental ancestors of by-gone generations.

The fourth figure is an American Negro, but a typical Negro without taint or admixture with other races. His features, moulded and softened by juxtaposition with the Caucasian, present a great improvement, certainly, over the isolated or African type, but the organism, the actual physical and mental nature remains the same.

The white man is least and the negro most affected by external agents, such as climate, time, systems of government, etc. The fourth figure in contrast with the isolated negro of Africa, exhibits a certain degree of improvement, progress, or advance that illustrates the actual capabilities of the race when placed under circumstances favorable to its development. The size of the brain, the actual organism and absolute nature, of course, remains unaltered, just as all these things remain unchanged and unchangeable in the uneducated white laborer of our own times; but the negro, in juxtaposition with the superior race, becomes educated, and all his latent capabilities fully developed. Thus, while the color, the hair, the entire organism is just what it was thousands of years ago, and what it must be forever, or as long as the present order of creation continues, there is a certain modification in the features and still greater changes in the expression. The uncouth and uneducated European laborer contrasted with the educated classes, or with the generality of Americans, exhibits a wide difference, not so much in the features as in the expression; and though the negro in Africa is in a far more natural position, relatively considered, than the European laborer, the negro in our midst exhibits, perhaps, even a greater difference over his isolated brother. And if we suppose, for a moment, that the masses of English laborers were educated, fed on the same fare, and subject to the same circumstances as the English nobles, then we may form a reasonable estimate of the relative advance of the American over the African negro. The former would differ in no respect whatever from the privileged and educated class, and if all the negroes of Africa were brought here or were placed in juxtaposition and natural relation with the superior race, they would exhibit the same characteristics common to our so-called slaves, and the fourth figure in this plate would doubtless present a typical illustration of them. A good many people, ignorant of the laws of organism, suppose that our negro population have made a great advance over the wild and barbarous tribes of Africa, and, as shown by the second and fourth figures in the plate, this is so, but it is only in the outward expression, while the essential nature is ever

the same. The negro infant, for example, broug.t from
Africa and placed under existing circumstances in Mississippi,
would be represented by the fourth figure, while the infant
born here and carried to Africa to grow up with the wild
tribes of the interior, would, on the contrary, be illustrated by
the second figure of the plate.

There are a multitude of moral considerations involved, of
course, and that cannot be measured or tested by material
illustrations, but we may form a reasonable estimate of the
superiority of condition and of the greater happiness of the
negro over his African brethren, by a simple comparison
of these figures. As has been observed, it corresponds with
the difference between the educated and non-educated white
man, but it is greater, for the negro is more affected by
external circumstances, and therefore while the actual size and
relations of the negro brain and the specific nature of the
negro are unalterable, the outward form of his head as well as
the expression of his face is strikingly improved over that of
the typical African.

In general terms, it may be said, that the " American slave"
is educated and the isolated African negro is not; that the
former is civilized and the latter a barbarian; that, though in
a sense in a natural position (for he multiplies in Africa), he is
in his normal condition only when in juxtaposition and natural
relation to the superior white man. It is sometimes supposed
that the negro is incapable of progress, and so, of course, he
is when isolated from the superior race, but when placed in
his normal condition, and his imitative capacities called into
action, he is capable of progress to a certain extent. God,
while endowing him with widely different and vastly inferior
faculties, has gifted him with imitative capacities so admirable,
that those who are ignorant of his real nature mistake them
for those of the white man. Like children, like the inferioɪ

animals, and like all other inferior races, he naturally imitates the superior being; but beyond this general tendency common to all subordinate creatures, there is a peculiar capacity in the negro in this respect, which, more than anything else, warrants us in terming it the *specific* feature of the race. Placed in his normal condition, he becomes intelligent, civilized, pious, industrious, and if his master is a man of refined mind and dainty habits, the negro becomes so, even more than children who imitate the habitudes of their parents. Thus, it will be seen on Southern plantations generally, that they correspond with their masters, and if the habits and practices of the former are moral and Christian-like, the negroes approximate to the same standard. On the contrary, if they are under the guidance of coarse and brutal masters, or are left with nothing to imitate but the habits of a gross and tyrannical overseer, then they become idle, vicious, and thieving; and take every chance that offers to run away from their homes.

In speaking of negro education, of course no such meaning as that applied to white people is intended. Reading, writing, arithmetic, etc., have no relation or connection with the development of the negro powers. He simply needs to be in a position where the imitative capacity with which God has so beneficently endowed him is most completely called into action, and, as has been observed, he then becomes an industrious, moral, and well-behaved creature, or he is idle, sensual, vicious and worthless, just as the master or overseer pleases to make him. There are doubtless exceptional instances, but with all the wide-spread and boundless effort of the ignorant and deluded people in England and America to seduce them from their homes, there are probably but few negroes—real negroes —who ever abandoned their masters, unless their education had been neglected. The instinct of the negro is obedience to his master, and the strongest affection of his nature—far above that for his wife or offspring—is for the master who feeds, guides, and cares for him, indeed is his Providence; and his utter horror of migration, unless it be with his master, these qualities, so dominant in the negro, would be or might be made a barrier of protection against outside seductions, were they properly understood and appreciated by those having them in charge. This negro education, civilization, progress in fact, which the negro is capable of when in his normal condition, and his imitative capacities are permitted a healthy development, of course is rapidly lost when isolated from the white man. If the four millions now in our midst were suddenly left to themselves, but a few years—probably within fifty—everything that now distinguishes them—that is, all that they have imitated from the superior race—would become extinct.

Leaving out of the consideration mulattoes and mongrels, and taking into view simply the negro—the four millions of negroes of untainted blood which now exist in our midst—it is reasonable to say that, fifty years hence, there would not be one that would speak his present language, that would be a Christian, that would retain his name, or any other thing whatever which he now possesses and has imitated from his masters. This may seem a startling declaration to many who live in daily contact with these people, while by those ignorant and deplorably deluded parties who fancy that they are engaged in a work of humanity when seeking to undo the work of the Almighty Creator, by turning black into white and the negro into a Caucasian, it will scarcely be understood; but it involves a truth that may be easily and plainly illustrated. A very large portion of our negroes are the children and grandchildren of those brought from Africa, and not a few, perhaps, were themselves brought in by the "slave trade," which it will be remembered was continued down to 1808.

Now of all these there probably is not one that can speak the language of his progenitors, not one that retains his African religion or the slightest relic of African history or tradition, not one with even an African name, and if they have thus rapidly lost all that they possessed of their own, that was original and specific, of course, if isolated from their masters, they would still more rapidly lose that which they have imitated from a superior race.

Such, then, is the negro—the lowest in the scale as the Caucasian is the most elevated in the human creation—a creature not degraded—for none of God's creatures are degraded—but that is widely different and vastly subordinate to the elaborately organized and highly endowed white man. The *specific* qualities are not matters of opinion but of fact, that appeal to our senses at every step, but the specific differences and actual intervals that separate races, though often susceptible of successful illustrations, must to a great extent be determined by experience. The author has attempted to define these differences in some essential respects, and believes he has succeeded with sufficient exactitude to warrant correct conclusions in respect to the almost innumerable things that could not be discussed nor even alluded to in a work of this kind. We have this race among us—they or their descendants must remain an element of our population forever. It is doubtless the design of the Almighty that the Caucasian and negro, under certain circumstances which will be considered elsewhere, should exist in juxtaposition, and therefore a specific knowledge of this race, and its true relations to our own, is the most vital and indeed transcendent question or consideration that was ever presented to a civilized and Christian people. Nor can this be delayed or pushed aside, for even now the nation is rapidly drifting into serious difficulties and possibly terrible calamities, in consequence of that wide-spread ignorance and misconception prevalent in regard to the negro's nature and his true relations to the white man. The blind and stupid warfare waged so long upon the domestic institutions of the South, has doubtless thus far injured the negro most, and it may be demonstrated with ease that the worst and most brutal master ever known could not inflict so much misery on the negro as the so-called friend of freedom, who, in utter ignorance of the negro nature, would force him to live out the life of a widely different being. But the time has come when this ignorance and delusion threatens to involve the whole framework of American society, and nothing but the simple truth—the recognition of the actual and unchangeable facts fixed eternally by the hand of God, can save the nation from dire calamities.

PART II.

CHAPTER XIII.

MULATTOISM AND MONGRELISM.

ALL the generic and specific forms of life are governed by their own peculiar laws of interunion, and hybridism or hybridity is therefore a phenomenon of varying character, having, it is true, certain resemblances in those instances which approach each other, but absolutely different in all cases. Naturalists have sometimes made great blunders in this respect, for they have assumed that hybridism was governed by the same laws in all cases, and therefore sought its application or inferred its presence in instances the most remote and contradictory. The most extraordinary, and, indeed, inexcusable instance of the kind has been seen in the efforts made to confound the distinctions of race, and to pervert truth into the most shameful and what would seem to be the most palpable falsehoods. It has been assumed by naturalists of high character that different genera never produce offspring, that the *offspring* of different species are incapable of reproduction, and that varieties are unlimited in their powers of virility. If, therefore, there were doubt in respect to the character of certain (supposed) genera, and it was found that offspring followed a conjunction of sexes, in this particular instance, it was inferred that they were merely different species. And if the product or progeny of these *species* were found to be equally virile, then it was inferred that they were all originally of the same species, and nothing but varieties. This test, so simple that it can hardly be mistaken, serves with sufficient accuracy to determine the real character, and when the naturalist properly applies the laws of hybridity, that is, admits a modification of these laws in all cases or in all the different genera subjected to his examination, then he is armed with sufficient data to render his labors accurate and effective. But however pains-taking or correct in other particulars, when he assumes that hybridity is a unit, and rigidly applies this in all cases, or to families widely remote in other respects, his labors, from this defect, must be comparatively valueless.

The instance already referred to, where hybridity was thus presented, was as follows:—The mule, as is well-known, is the offspring of the horse and ass. It does not, in its turn, reproduce itself, therefore the horse and ass were different species. Prichard and others applied this test, or marked this test, in the case of human beings, of whites and negroes, and proved by it that they were of the same species. It was seen that white men cohabited with negro women, and the offspring in turn, reproduced itself, and consequently that the parents were of the same species. Or, as this has passed as current coin hitherto, and seemed perfectly satisfactory, indeed wholly unanswerable to naturalists and men of science as well as others, it is best, perhaps, to place it in distinct and categorical terms before the reader. 1st. It is universally admitted by naturalists that incapacity in the offspring to reproduce itself demonstrates the different species of the progenitors, while, on the contrary, a capacity in the offspring to beget offspring in its turn demonstrates similarity of species in the progenitors. 2d. The mule, or the offspring of the horse and ass, does not reproduce itself, therefore the horse and ass are different species. 3d. The mulatto offspring of the white man and negro woman does beget offspring, therefore the white man and negro woman are of the same species.

This was the assumption and the reasoning of Prichard and other European ethnologists, and if hybridity were a unit, or principle of rigid and uniform character in all cases, in human beings as in animals and vegetables, in the case of the white man and negress, exactly as in that of the horse and ass—then, indeed, would the inference seem unavoidable that whites and negroes constituted in fact a single species. But they were guilty of two fundamental errors in this matter—an error of fact, and an error of reasoning, or perhaps it would be more correct to say that both were errors of fact. At all events, *facts* that demonstrate difference of species in whites and negroes beyond possibility of doubt were distorted into proofs which seemed to demonstrate sameness or similarity of species with equal certainty.

Hybridity, as has been said, is not a unit, is not a fixed, uniform law or principle. A moment's consideration is sufficient to convince any intelligent mind of this truth. Each form of life has necessarily its own character, its own specific qualities, and the laws governing its reproductive powers must be in correspondence, and just as differently manifested as any of its specific qualities. To suppose that the laws of the phe-nomena governing the reproductive functions of the horse and ass are exactly similar to those manifested in the case of human beings, is as absurd as to suppose that the term of ges-tation, the length of life, the mode of their locomotion, or any other qualities—should be exactly the same in both cases. But nothing more need be said. It is perfectly obvious that the laws of reproduction must be radically different in the human creatures, and therefore the inference of Pritchard and others, that whites and negroes were of the same species, because the mulatto, unlike the *mule*, did reproduce itself, is simply absurd.

7

But they were still further and still more vitally mistaken in respect to their assumptions of fact. The mulatto, literally speaking, or in the ordinary sense, does beget offspring, but mulattoism is as positively sterile as muleism. The phenomenon of hybridity is manifested, as has been stated, in conformity with the nature of the beings concerned, and as the human creatures are separated by an almost measureless as well as impassable distance from the horse and ass, the laws of hybridity are, of course, correspondingly different. Instead of a single generation, as in the animals referred to, sterility in the human creatures is embraced within four generations, where a boundary is arrived at as absolutely fixed and impassable as the single generation in the case of the former.

But in order to understand the matter clearly, it is proposed to present the reader with the preliminary principles or facts, and inductive facts, that lead to this vital and all-important conclusion. It is all-important, not as demonstrating beyond doubt the vital and fundamental truth of distinct species, for that is a self-evident and indeed unavoidable truth that meets us at every step, and confronts our senses almost every hour or day of our lives. But mulattoism is a subject of stupendous importance in itself, and as the public are generally, and the "anti-slavery" writers especially, profoundly ignorant of it, and of all the laws that govern it, it is proposed to present the elementary principles or basis on which the whole subject rests.*

1st. In the case of the white man cohabiting with the negress, or "married" to a negro female, there will be a more limited progeny than if she were married to one of her own race.

* The author has devoted much time and labor to this interesting subject, and, together with his own and the observations of friends and correspondents, covering several thousand cases of the mixed blood, is able to deduce the general laws as stated in the text, and with entire confidence in their essential accuracy.

2d. The mulatto offspring of this connection intermarrying with other hybrids, will exhibit still less virility.

3d. The offspring of the former again intermarrying with hybrids equally removed from the original parentage, shows a yet greater diminution of virile power.

4th. By still intermarrying with hybrids, and of a corresponding remove, virility is correspondingly decreased.

5th. Finally, the fourth generation of mulattoism is as absolutely sterile as muleism, and though there may be, at rare intervals, a possible exception, yet, in every practical sense, and for all the purposes of philosophic inquiry, it may be assumed as the natural and impassable barrier of this abnormal and exceptional form of being. Of the essential correctness of these laws, or their data, almost every one living in the South, or perhaps in the larger cities of the Middle States, will be able to satisfy himself, if he will take the trouble to investigate the matter. He need not pursue the subject to its ultimate end, or to an extent necessary to arrive at all the results here presented, but he may, with comparatively trifling attention to it, satisfy himself of the *tendencies involved, and that there is somewhere at least approximating to these laws a fixed and absolute barrier beyond which mulattoism can not exist.* All the dealers in "slaves" and many "slave owners" know this from observation and individual experience, and while entirely ignorant of any thing like the scientific formulæ here presented, not a few among the former have actually stated it to the author in total unconsciousness that either he or any one else had ever thus formalized the essential character of mulattoism. But there is a very important feature of this matter, which, not understood or overlooked, may lead astray those who undertake its investigation. As has been said, hybridity is a phenomenon to be tested and determined by the nature of the beings involved, and as it must be wholly different in the human creatures from that manifested in animals, and life is limited to four generations in the case of mulattoes, while the mule is confined to a single generation, so, too, must the mere quality or capacity of offspring be taken into consideration. The mule is remarkable for its powers of endurance—the mulatto for its fragility and incapacity to endure hardships. A northern climate is fatal to the negro, but the same climate is still more fatal to the hybrid, for his approximation to the Caucasian, and therefore capacity for a northern clime, is more than balanced by his constitutional tendencies to fragility and decay. Thus, of the ten thousand free negroes in Massachusetts, whom, "freedom" and climate together, were there no more external additions, must finally exterminate, the last man among them would be a typical negro, or, at all events, approximating nearest to the typical standard.

But it is in the female hybrid that this tendency to decay, or this vice of constitutional formation, is most apparent. Many of them are incapable of nourishing or taking care of their offspring, and, together with miscarriages and the numerous forms of disease connected with maternity, they are often found to have had a large number of children, not one of whom reached maturity. In taking into view, therefore, the sterility of mulattoism, we must have regard to its vices of formation as well as its limited virility, and that nature completes her processes, whether of growth or decay, through many different forms ; and while mulattoism is as absolutely confined to four generations as mules are to a single-generation, the former result is worked out through constitutional fragility and limited longevity as much, perhaps, as by an imperfect reproductive capacity.

It is seen, therefore, that Prichard and the European ethnologists made a radical mistake in this matter, and the very proofs which they relied on to establish their single-race theory, or that whites and negroes were of the same species, actually prove the precisely opposite fact, that they are of different species. Not only is the phenomenon of hybridity different in human beings, from that peculiar to animals, but it differs in the different races of the former. The author's inquiries on this subject have been limited to the white and negro races or species, but the evidence presented to his observation, during the war with Mexico, was sufficiently authentic to warrant the conclusion that hybrids have greater tenacity of life, when the offspring of whites and aborigines, than in the case of whites and negroes. The former approximate closer to our own race, and it is only reasonable to suppose that, in precise proportion to this fact, or to this starting point, is the hybrid offspring endowed with vitality ; and the same rule may be applied with equal certainty to all the other species of men.

The sexual instinct, or the instinct of reproduction, is universal in animal existence. It is that which multiplies its kind, that peoples the earth and fills the world with innumerable tribes of beings and endless processions of generations, each after its kind exhibiting the same qualities and subject to the same laws as the original types, without the slightest atom of change, though countless generations intervene between them. In respect to human beings endowed with reason and moral feeling, it is evidently designed by the Almighty Creator of all that the instinct of reproduction should be held in subjection to those higher qualities. Nevertheless, instinct in respect to the sexual functions is strikingly manifest in the lower races of mankind.

When white men—travelers and explorers—suddenly make their appearance in African villages, where they were never before seen, the females run and hide themselves from their sight; and among the multitude of white prisoners captured by the aborigines of this continent, there has probably never been an instance of the violation of their persons by their savage captors. In respect to the so-called insurrection of negroes in Hayti or San Domingo, where, though all of the white blood, men, women, and children in their nurses' a-ms were remorselessly butchered by the terror-stricken blacks, there are no authenticated instances of the violation of white females.

A negro insurrection—that is, a revolt of the negro from the rule of the white man, to obtain the liberty of the latter— is simply nonsensical: as entirely so as to suppose an insurrection to obtain the complexion or any other physical attribute of the superior race; but should some white miscreant, as attempted lately at Harper's Ferry, delude " slaves" to slaughter the families of their masters, there need be little or no apprehension in respect to that hideous and monstrous idea so prominent in abolition writings—the violation of the persons of white females.   It is true, hybrids and mongrels might perpetrate such monstrous crimes, but the negro—the typical, pure-blooded negro—driven on by his fears and dread of the master race, would only seek its extermination, never the indulgence to *him* of such unnatural propensities.

The instinct of reproduction in animals is governed by fixed laws; but, as has been said, designed by the common Creator to be ruled by the reason and subjected to the moral affections in the higher human nature; nevertheless, the ignorance and corruption of our social life have perverted these designs, and covered society with blotches and ulcers horrible to contemplate.   In this city alone there are said to be ten thousand prostitutes—lost creatures, so lost that nature denies them offspring, to reproduce themselves, to form a link or have a place in the mighty processions of their kind, that stand out distinct and accursed, dead though alive.   And yet each of these blasted ones was created with capacities of love, of affection, of receiv-

ing and conferring happiness boundless and mensureless. God
made them pure and beautiful, and man has transformed them
into beings so vile, that their very existence must not be recognized by the pure and virtuous! God created them but a
little lower than the angels—man has perverted them into
something scarcely better than devils!

What an awful perversion of the instincts of reproduction—
of that great vital and fundamental law which animals obey
without any violation of it, but which we, in our lofty nature
and God-given powers, have thus transformed into such hideous
shapes and worked into such sickening and diseased results!
The sexes are equal in numbers, and therefore nature designs
that all men should marry—that one man should be united to
one woman—that they should always be attracted to each
other by the affections, and, in their love and companionship,
their care for their offspring, for their home and its sweet
enjoyments, it offers them rewards the purest, the most exalted, as well as the most rational, that our being is capable of
feeling.   And yet the sad spectacle is presented every day and
all about us, that that which God designed should be the source
of our greatest happiness is perverted into the most loathsome
and most hideous of social miseries!   What may be the causes
or the principal causes (for there are doubtless many) of this
hideous ulcer at the very heart of modern society, it is need-
less to inquire—the actual or proximate cause is the perversion
of the sexual laws—the violation of the instincts of reproduction wholly unknown among animals and comparatively unknown among the subordinate races of mankind.   It is the
proud Caucasian—the large-brained and gloriously endowed
Caucasian—who mostly exhibits this terrible crime against the
higher law, and who thus awfully sins against God and his
own nature.   Such a thing as *prostitution* is unknown among
negroes—among the aborigines of this continent, and scarcely

perceptible among Mongols or Chinese. There are, it is true, great vices, shocking indecencies and beastly practices among the Mongols and other subordinate races, but prostitution—the indiscriminate sale of the bodies as well as the desecration of the souls of women for money, as practiced openly in all the great centres of Christendom, is peculiar to the Caucasian alone—to that exalted and highly endowed race which God has so gifted and placed at the head of all other races of mankind.

Mulattoism is to the South what prostitution is to the North —that is, those depraved persons who give themselves up to a wicked perversion of the sexual instincts, resort to the mongrel or "colored women" instead of houses of ill-fame, as in the former case. Such a thing as love, or natural affection, never has nor can attract persons of different races, and therefore all the cohabitations of white men and negro women are abnormal—a perversion of the instincts of reproduction. This " original sin," as it may well be termed, carries with it, by inevitable necesssity, certain consequences, and the declaration of Holy Writ, that the children are punished to the third and fourth generation for the sins of their fathers, is literally true in a physiological sense. The precise laws governing the generation of mulattoism have been already stated, and need not be repeated in this place, but it may be well to remember that the offspring constantly diminishes when hybrids intermarry with hybrids of the same remove, until, reaching the fourth generation, it loses all generative capacity as absolutely as the mule. With this radical and fundamental vice of organization, it will be readily seen that mongrelism can never become an important or dangerous element of population. Mr. Clay once advanced the opinion that the mixed blood of the South was rapidly increasing, and therefore a time would probably come when the negro blood would be absorbed by the whites, and the negro life be utterly extinct. The ignorant abolition writers have made much of this opinion of Mr. Clay, but whatever the general intellectual superiority of that distinguished gentleman, any common sense person must know that his ignorance of the laws of organization renders his opinion on this subject of no value whatever. Two hundred or one hundred years ago, the proportion of the sexes among the white people was doubtless less equal than now, and therefore those abnormal cohabitations of white men with negro women were more frequent than at present. But after a certain amount or number of the mixed blood these cohabitations would take that direction, and, as at present, would be mainly confined to the hybrid and " colored" women. And in view of the fragility, sterility, and almost universal tendency to disease and disorganization in this mixed and mongrel element, it is seen at a glance how impossible it is that it should ever be of sufficient amount to threaten the safety or even to disturb the peace of Southern society. In proportion to the normal population or to the pure blood, it is doubtless less than it was fifty years ago, and it may even become less in the future, but it is wholly and absolutely impossible that it can ever exist in larger proportion than at present.

This vicious intercourse with the mongrel women at the South, of course, has no resemblance or relation to amalgamation ; but it is ignorantly or wilfully thus confounded by the abolition writers of the day. Amalgamation is reciprocal union of the sexes, such as that between the Normans and the Anglo-Saxons in England—that occurs constantly between the natives of this country and those who have migrated here from Europe, and indeed as occurred in Mexico and other Spanish provinces, where the Spanish conquerors, who brought few Spanish females with them, sought wives among the natives or Indian races. The white blood of the South, like

7*

that of the North, is pure and untainted, and a white woman so lost and degraded as to mate with a negro, would not be permitted to even live among negroes in a Southern community. Occasionally a monstrous indecency of this kind does occur at the North, but they are usually English or other foreign-born persons, and unless there was some moral or physical cause—some disease of body or mind which rendered her incapable of self-guidance,. it can hardly be supposed that an American-born woman ever committed such an indecent outrage upon her own womanhood, and sin against God, as to mate with a negro. At the South, as has been said, such a thing is altogether impossible, for the woman would not alone be driven from the society of her own race, as at the North, but she would not be permitted (if known) to live even among negroes! Amalgamation can never occur at the South, and scarcely needs an exposition in this place ; but as it is now actually taking place in Jamaica and other islands, and, to a certain extent in Cuba, and, moreover, such a monstrous social cataclysm is necessarily involved in the theory or idea of the abolition of " slavery," it is well enough, perhaps, to give it an explanation.

There are about four millions of negroes in this country, and if, for the purposes of illustration, we may suppose the theory of anti-slaveryism to be finally reduced to practice, the following results must or would occur:—Four millions of whites would form marital unions with these negroes—the men taking negresses to wife, and the females negroes for husbands, ending with the next generation, of course, in mulattoes and the extinction of negroes. The third generation would absorb the mulattoes and end in quadroons; the fourth generation would manifest a corresponding diminution, and a time come when every atom of negro blood would disappear as utterly as if there had never been a negro on this continent. The popular notion would be, perhaps, like that of Mr. Clay, that amalgamation of the races would absorb the negro blood, it being the smaller element, and this would remain forever floating in the veins of posterity. But this could not be: it would die out, and in time become totally extinct.

If, for example, one hundred of the leading and influential Abolitionists of the day should practically live out their own doctrines—should be placed on some island in the Pacific Ocean, each with a negress as wife, and utterly excluded from intercourse of any kind with the rest of mankind, they and their posterity would, after a certain time, utterly perish from existence. In the second generation whites and negroes alike would be extinct—that which the hand of the Eternal had fashioned, fixed, and designed for His glory and the happiness of His creatures would be blotched, deformed, and transformed by their own wickedness into mulattoes, and could no more exist beyond a given period than any other physical degeneration, no more than tumors, cancers, or other abnormal growths or physical disease can become permanent conditions. The fourth generation, as stated elsewhere, with diminished and diminishing vitality, would impart such feeble glimmerings of life, that their immediate progeny would be as absolutely limited in their powers of virility as mules, and the whole mass of disease and corruption would disappear from the earth, which God has forbidden it to desecrate any longer by its foul and disgusting presence.*   But contemplating the subject

* Royalism, or a Hereditary Aristocracy, or class that attempts to create a permanent superiority over the great body of the people by incestuous intermarriage with its own members, is punished with similar results as those that attend the violation of the sexual relations of different Races. And the idiotic, impotent, and diseased offspring of hereditary kings has always a certain physiological resemblance to the effete and sterile mulatto. Both are violations of the normal order, and both are limited to a determinate existence, just as any other diseased conditions which nature forbids to live.

in mass, or practical abolitionism, as it would work itself out among the millions, if we are permitted, for the purposes of illustration, to suppose such, a monstrous and stupendous crime against God and our own being as the actual and prac- tical development of the theory, widely different results would naturally follow. As has been said, four millions of our own white race would be involved in this monstrous maelstrom of amalgamation with the subject race, while the remaining twenty millions would be left untouched and unpol- luted by the physical degradation that must needs follow such a stupendous sin as practical abolitionism. But they would not escape the moral deterioration, and the nation, weighed down by mulattoism, by such an ulcer on the body politic, by such a frightful mass of disease and death, would doubtless fall a conquest to some other nation or variety of the master race, and again become English provinces or dependencies of some other European power!

Nations are punished in this life, however it may be with in- dividuals, and a sin so enormous, a crime and impiety against God so awful, an outrage on their own nature so boundless and bottomless as practical abolitionism, or the actual living out of the abolition theory, would drag after it, as an inex- orable necessity, a corresponding punishment.

History is pregnant with examples of this inevitable law. Nations after nations have risen, flourished, decayed, and died on the African continent; millions upon millions of white Chris- tian men have existed in the valley of the Nile alone; three hundred Christian bishops have met in convention on the site of ancient Carthage, when London was unknown and Rome itself the seat of the heathen Cæsars; and now, of the five hundred millions of Caucasians known to have existed on that continent since the Christian era began, there are probably not one million of typical white men left to tell the tale of their destruction, or to mourn over the desolation brought upon them by the crimes and sins of their progenitors. The vastly preponderating white element would doubtless save us from similar consequences, should we ever commit such a hideous crime as that involved in the practical application of the abolition theory; but, as has been said, we would most likely fall a conquest to some European power. But should this fate not overtake us, should we be left to struggle with the load of sin and disease thus brought upon ourselves by our crimes against reason and the ordinances of the Eternal, the nation would in time slough off mulattoism, and finally recover from the foul and horrible contamination of admixture with the blood of the negro. The twenty-millions of pure and untainted blood would increase so rapidly over the diseased portion, that finally every trace, atom, and drop or globule of the latter would be utterly extinct, and though the time for this process to work itself out, or for the white race to recover its healthy and natural condition, cannot be estimated with any certainty, such would needs be the final result. This same process, though the parties are directly reversed, is now in active operation in Mexico, and all the Spanish-American States. The Spanish conquerors brought few countrywomen with them, and therefore sought wives among the natives or aboriginal race, and amalgamation became universal in all the Spanish provinces, the result of which has been the generation of a vast and wide-spread mongrelism. The Spanish dominion usually embodied in the pure blood, not from any prejudice against the mixed element, but from jealousy of the native born, preserved order and general prosperity. But the overthrow of this dominion brought the mongrel element into power, for though Iturbide, Santa Anna, Bravo, Bustamente, Parades, all or nearly all the chiefs of Independence were of pure Castilian blood, it was the mongrel element that over-

threw the Spanish power and established the republic. Spaniards were constantly migrating to the American possessions
of the Spanish crown, but, with the overthrow of the Spanish
dominion, this supply of white blood was cut off, and instead
of the generation of mongrelism, from that instant the reparatory process began, which can only end in sloughing off the
mixed blood, and the restoration of the aboriginal race to its
natural and healthy condition, as it was before the Spanish
conquest and the admixture of the white element. This
mixed or mongrel element is found in the cities, but it is rapidly declining. Mexico had, at the era of Independence, two
hundred thousand inhabitants. It has now little over one
hundred thousand people. Puebla, Perote, Jalapa, all the
cities of Mexico decline in similar proportion, while the rural
population—the pure, untainted, aboriginal element—though
placed under great and striking disadvantages, holds its own,
and were it guided and cared for, as it was one hundred years
ago, would doubtless rapidly increase in number. Nor is it
alone the fragility, feebleness, the vicious organization and imperfect vitality of mulattoism, or of the mongrel element, that
is thus rapidly diminishing the population in Mexican cities.
The *morale* of mongrelism partakes of the physical deformity,
and the vices of the mind are as striking and constant as the
defects of the body. A creature with half the nature and
wants of the white man united in the same existence with
those of the Indian, is confronted with another, perhaps three-
fourths white, while on the other side of him is one who has
three-fourths Indian blood, and a population made up of such
materials is necessarily and perpetually at war with itself.
Hence in all the revolutions of Mexico there is no design, no
common object that unite men in common purposes, no sense,
reason, or common impulse whatever, except to destroy, to
overturn, to seize power to-day without any purpose for to-

morrow. And this goes on, and must go on until nature re-
pairs the outrages inflicted on her, until mongrelism dies out
and the aboriginal or Indian element is restored to its pristine
condition, until every atom of the white blood is extinct and
the Indian race is again what it was at the time of the Spanish
conquest.

The subject opens up questions of mighty import to us,
and possibly, as Mr. Calhoun believed, great dangers to our
people and the future of civilization; but if understood—if
American legislators and statesmen comprehend the real character of these vast populations south of us, known as the
Spanish-American republics, and apply to them the true principles of social and political economy, when the time comes to
deal with them, there need be little or no apprehension in regard to the results. Meanwhile, the solution of these problems
is every day becoming simpler and more easily understood.
The mixed blood is rapidly dying out; a time must come when
it will be wholly extinct, and then the white American will
stand face to face with the native, a race which, whatever may
be our experience of it in the North, is easily governed, and as
has been said, if understood, there need be little or no apprehension of danger or difficulty in regard to it.

The same process is going on in Jamaica and other islands,
though here it is the negro instead of the Indian that is in
issue. An idea or assumption was set up in England that the
negroes of these islands were *black* white men—men like themselves, except in color—and therefore naturally entitled to the
same rights; and a party sprung up that at last induced the
British Parliament to "abolish" the existing relations of the
whites and negroes, and to place them on the same political
and legal level. The white people protested against this
wrong and outrage on reason and common sense, but it was
of no avail. Their cry for mercy was unheard—at all events,

disregarded—and the helpless and outraged whites are new in process of utter extinction by amalgamation.

The same political and legal *status* leads, of course, to the same social level, and it, in turn, to the general admixture of blood. A white woman is not likely, even under these unnatural circumstances, to desecrate her womanhood by mating with a negro, though public sentiment forces her to associate with them. But this woman marries a man with one-eighth or one-fourth of negro blood, without hesitation, and the woman of this shade readily mates with a mulatto, and the latter with the typical negro. Thus, while natural instinct shrinks from such a crime against nature and such an impiety toward God as the marriage or mating of the pure types, the outward force of legal and political systems impels all shades of mongrelism in the direction of the preponderating element; and a time must come when the white blood, becoming extinct, the negro will relapse, of course, into his native Africanism.

The outward presence of a foreign government impels the unhappy white people of these fertile and beautiful islands into this monstrous violation of the laws of organization, and certain ultimate social destruction; but the power of the government also restrains the negro element from a rapid collapse into its native Africanism. In Hayti, where all external or governmental influence is withdrawn, the negro nature already strongly manifests its normal savagery, when no longer restrained by the master race, and the worship of Obi or Feticism, and even the native African dialect, is becoming common to many districts in that island. In general terms, it may be said that the exact moment when the white blood becomes extinct is also the instant when Africanism is perfectly restored, but the outward presence of the British government on the islands, and of the Colonization Society in Liberia, will prevent the complete development of this otherwise natural and necessary law. That the white blood of Jamaica must be absorbed, or rather must die out, is a necessity, an effect, a fate that is unavoidable—the final end being alone a question of time. A foreign government, as has been said, regardless of the protests and the cry for mercy of its unfortunate people, forcibly changed their relations to the subordinate race. It declared the negroes the legal and political equals of the whites ; this necessarily led to social equality—that, in its turn, to the marriage of whites and quadroons—quadroons with mulattoes, and mulattoes with negroes ; thus the process, beginning with the act of the British Parliament abolishing " slavery," ends naturally and necessarily in the social immolation and final extinction of the white people of that island.

All the links in the chain are continuous—all the series of events dependent on each other—all the steps of the process naturally united ; the emancipation, the legal equality, the social level, the admixture of blood, and the ultimate extinction, are part and parcel of the same awful crime against nature and against God, against the laws of organization and against the decrees of the Eternal. The *end*, therefore, of these things must be the restoration of the pure Indian type on the main land and that of the negro in the islands ; and, as has been said, though the time needed for the completion of this reparatory process—for such it is, physiologically considered—may not be determined with certainty, it can not be very distant, and were white men to stand aloof and permit the process to work itself out, without interference, it is quite probable that a hundred, or, at most, a hundred and fifty years hence, there would not be a drop of white blood found south of our own limits.

Mulattoism is an abnormalism—a disease—a result that brings suffering unspeakable as well as extinction—that is unavoidable ; and, in view of this fate brought upon them by a

foreign government, who can doubt but that the total slaughter of the white people of Jamaica would have been merciful,
in comparison to that forced upon them by the abolition of
" slavery," and equality with negroes? Or will any one sufficiently informed on this subject, who understands the physical
and moral suffering involved or inseparably linked with the
mixed blood, doubt for a moment that, as a question of
humanity, it would be vastly more humane to slaughter all the
negroes in our midst, rather than apply to them the abolition
theory, or rather than doom them to legal equality, to amalgamation, to mulattoism, mongrelism, and that final unavoidable
extinction that necessarily attends the minor element under
these circumstances? But in addition to the physical suffering attending the process of extinction in Jamaica, it was, or
is, or must be, the annihilation of Caucasian intelligence, of
civilization, of all that God has bestowed upon His creatures
that is exalted and glorious, and therefore the crime perpetrated,
however blindly or well-intentioned, must stand out in future
ages the most awful and impious ever known in human annals.

Such is a brief outline of the physiological laws governing
mulattoism and mongrelism—that abnormal or diseased condition which results from admixture of the blood of separate
races or species of men. Its mental and moral features are
equally distinct and discordant, though less susceptible of explanation or of being classified, as in the case of the merely
physical qualities. As a general principle the mongrel has
intellectual ability in proportion as he approximates to the superior race. This is a necessary truth; there is mental capacity
or intelligence, latent or actual, in exact proportion to the size
of the brain, in animals, indeed, as well as human beings, as certainly and invariably as there is muscular power in proportion
to the size and form of the muscles; but this principle is hardly
a guide or test in respect to the moral qualities of the mixed

blood. There is scarcely anything or any phase of the general
subject that has so blinded and led astray " anti-slavery" writers
as this subject of mulattoism ; for they were not only ignorant
of it, but never dreamed for a moment that there was any such
thing in existence, and constantly assumed in their reasonings
(?) that the mulatto was a negro, and therefore presented him,
and even the quadroon, as an evidence of the mental capacity
of that race. One of these people would find his way to England or the North, was educated, became an editor, physician,
priest, sometimes even an author, on a small scale perhaps, at
all events a public lecturer, to whom white men and women
listened with the utmost gravity, and perfectly satisfied themselves of the mental equality of the races, for here was a negro
who talked the same language, had the same ideas, and was
quite as eloquent as the general average among white men.
Even the Abbé Gregoire labored under this very absurd and
very general misconception, and wrote a book giving the biography of fifteen negroes to prove the mental equality of the
races, not one of whom was a negro at all ! Some mules are
doubtless superior to some horses, but no mule was ever equal
to the average horse ; and doubtless some mulattoes have been
superior to some white men, but no mulatto ever did nor ever
can reach the intellectual standard of the Caucasian. What
nonsense it would be to point out a favorite mule to show that
asses were the equals of horses ; yet this nonsense, or similar
nonsense, is practised every day by those who rely upon
mongrels and hybrids to prove the mental capacity of the
negro ! Indeed, quadroons, and even mongrels, with only
one-eighth of negro blood, like Roberts, the President of Liberia, have been quoted as illustrations of negro character and
accepted as perfectly satisfactory by the blind followers of
the equally blind teachers of Abolitionism. The fact that
such a thing as an " educated" mulatto exists at all among us,

as long as we have uneducated white men, is a disgrace to the nation, to our institutions, to our social development; and in England it-serves as a test of social wrong and wickedness frightful to contemplate. As has been said, no mule was ever equal to the average horse, so no mulatto was ever created equal to the standard white man; yet in England there are eight millions unable to read or write, and through human institutions rendered inferior to the "educated" mulatto! The moral qualities of the mixed element are less definite, but every one's observations, as well as history and statistics, tend to the same general conclusion—the greater viciousness of the mulatto when compared with either of the original types or typical races. This essential truth, common to all exceptional and abnormal conditions, is universally manifested among "slaves" at the South, "free" negroes at the North, mestizoes in Mexico, or the whilom hybrids of Hayti. The mongrels of Mexico—the so-called Leperos—are thieves, ladrones, robbers, and assassins, not like the Italian bravos of a former age, who, to a certain extent, redeemed their horrible crimes by a kind of chivalrous daring which gave their victims some chance for life, but secret, crouching, and cowardly assassins, who never attack where there is the slightest danger to themselves. They crouch, concealed in the shadow of a wall or door-way, enveloped in huge cloaks, with the exception of the arm that wields the keen, narrow-bladed, and double-edged knife, which is plunged in the back of the hapless victim, and then they invariably run away, unless supported by their vile companions. In the field they never face white men except when their numbers are overwhelming, and they give no quarter; but if themselves defeated, their cry for mercy is so intolerable in its groveling clamor, that the victor is disposed to dispatch them at once to get rid of it. With diminished vitality, and less hold on existence than the pure blood, the mongrel, while utterly reckless of life in respect to others, clings to it himself and shrinks from death with an abject terror rarely or never witnessed in the original races. The typical negro, for example, though brave enough when led by his master, shrinks in terror from the face of the lordly Caucasian when not thus supported, and a score or two of the latter in the open field would doubtless drive a thousand negroes before them like sheep to the slaughter. But a negro condemned to die, to be hanged, to be burned even, rarely manifests dread or apprehension of any kind. His imperfect innervation, his sluggish brain, and low grade of sensibility, render him incapable of anticipating that terrible physical suffering from which the elaborate and exquisitely organized Caucasian suffers under these circumstances. So, too, the Indian—"the stoic of the woods—the man without a tear," as the poet Campbell, and others ignorant of his nature, have represented him—a creature, according to their absurd fancies, fashioned on the Roman model, with the self-poised and philosophical indifference to outward things of a Seneca, and the calm contempt of physical suffering of a Cato, but who, all this time, in his grosser organization, has none of the white man's perceptions of physical pain, and therefore sings his death-song in total unconsciousness of that which to us is the extreme, or supposed extreme, of physical suffering.

This organic insensibility of the lower races to physical pain, which renders them indifferent to the approach of death, is sometimes equalled, and perhaps surpassed, as regards the outward expression, by the dominating moral forces in the case of the higher organized Caucasian. Lamartine has said that the mistress of Louis XV., the notorious Duchess Du Barry, was the only person sent to the guillotine during the reign of terror that asked for mercy, or shrank with terror from the approach of death. Not men alone, but women, even delicately nurtured young girls, who, under ordinary circumstances, would faint on witnessing the death of a sparrow, ascended the steps of the guillotine without a tear or the quiver of a muscle. They died for an idea, and a false one at that, but they believed it true and immutable as heaven itself, and the exaltation of the mind over the body, the dominating moral forces over the laws of the physical being, enabled them to meet death without a murmur, and, as regards the outward expression, to seem as indifferent to the physical pain involved, as the Indian or the negro, whose lower organization is incapable of such suffering.

But the mulatto or mongrel has neither the physical insensibility of the inferior nor the moral force of the superior race, and the instinctive consciousness of his feeble vitality renders him the most cowardly of human beings. The generals and leaders of the mixed blood in Spanish-America, as well as those of Hayti, have been as much distinguished for their monstrous vices, their treachery, cowardice, sensuality, and ferocity, as for any special ability they may have displayed. The cruel and despotic government of Spain, when desirous to crush the revolutionists, invariably trusted the bloody work to mongrel chiefs, who just as invariably exceeded their orders, and when directed to decimate a town or village, often massacred the entire population.

The mongrel generals of Hayti were even more ferocious and bloody, if not surpassing in treachery and cowardice the Indian mongrels of the Continent. Rigaud, the most distinguished of the Haytien chiefs, was also the most repulsive in his enormous and beastly vices. Christophe and Dessalines were negroes, and they simply acted out the negro instinct under those unnatural circumstances. They remorselessly slaughtered all the white men, women, and children of the island that they could find, for when the negro rises against his master, it is not to conquer but to exterminate the dreaded race; and the helpless infant or its frightened and despairing mother touches no chord of mercy in the souls of these frantic and terror-stricken wretches when forced or betrayed into resistance to their masters. But the mongrel leaders, and especially Rigaud, were mere moral monsters, whose deeds of slaughter were alternated with scenes of beastly debauchery and unnatural and devilish revelry, such as could neither originate in the simple animalism of the negro nor with the most sensual, perverse, and fiendish among white men.

But we have this viciousness of the mongrel displayed continually before us at the North as well as at the South. Ninetenths of the crime committed by so-called negroes is the work of the mongrel—the females almost all being as lewd and lascivious as the males are idle, sensual, and dishonest. The strange and disgusting delusion that has fastened itself on so many minds at the North seeks to cast an air of romance over these mongrel women—these " girls almost white"—and in negro novels and on the stage represent them as " victims of caste," and often doomed to a fate worse than death to gratify the " vices of the whites." And a diseased sentimentality, as indecent as it is nonsensical, is indulged by certain "pious ladies" in respect to these "interesting" quadroons, etc., who are almost always essentially vicious, while their own white sisters falling every hour from the ranks of pure womanhood, are unheeded, and their terrible miseries totally disregarded.

Finally, it scarcely need be repeated that mongrelism is a diseased condition—a penalty that nature imposes for the violation of her laws—a punishment that, by an inexorable necessity, is inflicted on the offspring of those who, in total disregard of her ordinances, of instinct, of natural affection, and of reason, form sexual interunions with persons of different races, but which, like all other abnormal conditions, is confined within fixed limits and mercifully doomed to final extinction.

CHAPTER XIV.

THE "SLAVE TRADE," OR THE IMPORTATION OF NEGROES.

IN the preceding chapters of this work it has been shown that the human family, like all other forms of being, is composed of a certain number of species, all having a general resemblance, but each specifically different from the other - that the Caucasian and Negro are placed by the will of the Almighty Creator at the two extremes of humanity—the former being the most superior and the latter the most inferior of all the known human races; that the physical structure or organization is always and necessarily connected with corresponding faculties or functions, and therefore the more prominent physical qualities of the negro have been presented, in order to illustrate his mental and moral nature. It has also been shown that the all-powerful instinct (prejudice) which revolts at the commingling of the blood of different races (stronger even with the negro than our own race) springs from a fundamental organic necessity, impelling us to preserve our structural integrity, and if disregarded and violated, it carries with it a corresponding penalty, and the miserable progeny, like all other abnormal conditions, is limited to a determinate existence; that that which the Eternal hand has moulded and fashioned is also eternal, and beyond the power, caprice, ignorance, or wickedness of His creatures, to change or modify; and therefore all the departures from the typical standard—all forms and degrees of the mongrel or mixed blood—are doomed to final extinction. Here we have, then, four millions of a

widely different race in our midst, and though we of the present generation may not be responsible for their presence among
us, and are only called upon to deal with the fact itself, without regard to its origin, the subject is of profound interest, and
however current or unanimous the opinion may now be against
the original " slave trade," it is believed that a larger knowledge and a more extended acquaintance with the facts embraced in that subject will finally result in a total change of
popular (American) opinion. And what American will not
rejoice at such a result, if, when all the facts are known and
tested by reason and conscience and the dictates of a true
humanity, it is found that, however censurable the means employed may sometimes have been, the " slave trade," the original importation of African negroes by our ancestors, was
right? The negro, as has been shown, from the necessities of
his organism—the size and form of his brain—is, perforce,
when isolated and by himself, a savage—an idle, non-advancing, and non-producing savage, and history, ancient and modern, in a word, all human experience, confirms this physiological
and material *fact*. African travelers, finding occasionally the
débris of Caucasian populations and the remains of Mahometan
civilization, have told fanciful tales about negro industry,
thrift, and morality, while dreamers at home have indulged in
even more absurd fancies still in regard to the future of Africa.
But why go to Africa to theorize about the negro, when we
have him here, and subject to our senses as well as our reason?
Why speculate on impossible assumptions, when the negro
brain may be seen any day at a medical college, and its
incapacity—its organic and inherent incapacity—to be any
thing else, or to ever manifest any thing else, but just that
which all human experience confirms and assures us must be,
as it always has been, the destiny of this race, when left to
itself? To talk of the civilization of the negro of Africa is like

8

talking of the change of color of the negro, for it involves the same absurdities, the same impossibilities ; and were not those who indulge in it utterly ignorant of the subject, one might say the same impieties, for the assumption that they can change the intellectual nature which God has given the negro, is as grossly impious as if they were to undertake his physical re-creation.

The negro, therefore, isolated in Africa, as has been said, must be in the future what he has been in the past, and without a supernatural interposition, must remain forever a simple, non-producing, and non-advancing savage. Can this have been the design of the Almighty ? There are some things we are not permitted to know, that it is impious as well as foolish to seek to know, that the Almighty, in His infinite beneficence as well as wisdom forbids us to inquire into, or rather to attempt to inquire into ; but in all that is necessary to our happiness and for the well-being of the innumerable creatures that surround us, we may know, indirectly, it is true, but none the less certainly, the design of the Almighty Creator.

All things are obviously designed for use—all the innumerable hosts of living creatures for specific purposes ; the natures of many are known to us now ; every day is adding to our knowledge, and a time will assuredly come when the nature and purposes of the most ferocious of wild animals and the most venomous of serpents will be clearly understood and applied to their proper uses. It is, therefore, the obvious design of the Creator that the negro should be useful, should labor, should be a producer, and as his organism forbids this, if left to himself, it is evidently intended that he should be in juxta-position with the superior Caucasian. It is equally obvious that the tropical latitudes endowed with such exuberant fertility were designed for cultivation, for use, for the growth and production of those indigenous products found nowhere else except within the tropics and tropicoid regions of the earth. The organization of the Caucasian utterly forbids physical labor under a tropical sun. He may live there, enjoy life, longevity, the full and healthy spring of all his faculties, without lassitude or any of that weight upon his energies which ill-informed persons have supposed followed a residence in these climes, but he can not cultivate the earth or grow the products of the soil by his own labor. The negro organism, on the contrary, is adapted to this production, and the rays of a vertical sun stimulate and quicken his energies, instead of prostrating them, as in the case of the former. In another place this subject will be fully discussed, and therefore it will be sufficient in this place to simply state the fact, that the labor of the negro can alone grow the indigenous products of the tropics, and without this labor the great tropical centre of the American continent must consequently remain a barren waste.

The introduction of negroes into the Spanish islands of the West Indies can, therefore, hardly be called an accident. Negro servants were introduced into Spain by the Arabian and Moorish conquerors. From time immemorial negro "slaves" were the favorite household servants of the oriental Caucasians —not alone because they were the most docile and submissive of human beings, but because they were the most faithful and absolutely incapable of betraying their masters, and scarcely a Moorish family of consideration entered Spain without being accompanied by some of these trusty and favorite servants. The recent Portuguese discoveries and conquests on the African coasts had also brought many negroes into the Peninsula, and when Columbus and the Spaniards began their settlements in the New World, there were negroes to be found in almost every town in Spain. The conquest of the miserable natives of Hispaniola and Cuba, and their partition among the Spanish adventurers, failed to gratify their fierce desire for wealth, and from the brutality of their masters, the still lurking desire of these poor creatures for their former condition, or, it may have been, as declared by the Spanish writers, their original feebleness of constitution, they rapidly faded away in the mines and on the plantations, and more vigorous laborers became an abso-lute necessity, if cultivation, progress, and civilization were to be carried on in these islands. It was thus a material and in-dustrial necessity, rather than any fancied humanity on the part of Las Casas and his friends in behalf of the Indians, that carried negroes into the Spanish islands. Some accompanied the earliest adventurers; they were seen to be safe, and to re-main perfectly healthy when Spaniards themselves were con-stantly smitten down by the fierce suns and deadly malaria of the tropics, while instead of the drooping and listless air that distinguished the natives, these negroes were the most joyous and contented of human beings.

The interests of civilization and of a true humanity were, therefore, united with the humane desires of Las Casas and his friends in respect to the natives, and negroes soon became the sole reliance of the planters and others to whom lands had been assigned by the Spanish princes. Modern writers—Helps, Prescott, and others—laboring under the world-wide miscon-ceptions of our times in regard to negroes, have expressed aston-ishment at the (to them) strange inconsistency of Las Casas, who, laboring so earnestly in behalf of the Indians, quite unconsciously aided in substituting the negro, and thus, as they suppose, laid the foundation or led the way to the enslavement of one race, while working for the freedom of another. But neither Las Casas, nor any one else, had any notion of freedom or slavery in connection with these negroes. Such a thing as a free negro was doubtless unknown in Spain or anywhere else, or, if known, it was simply because he had lost or strayed from his master. History does not, it is true, cast much light on the subject, but

it is certain that neither Las Casas nor any of his cotemporaries had any conception of negro freedom, or associated with
that race any other condition or social status than that which
modern writers have universally designated as negro slavery.

Nor was he laboring for the freedom of the Indians, as that
term is now understood. Many, perhaps most of those who
defended the natives from the oppressions of the Spaniards,
were prompted solely by religious zeal. These poor "heathens," they held, were entitled, not to freedom, to political or
social rights of any kind, but to the rights of religion, to participate in the Holy Sacraments, to enjoy the privileges which
the Church promised to all who would accept them, and as the
ferocity of the Spaniards constantly interfered with this, hunted
them down and slaughtered them without mercy, or rapidly
destroyed them by hard labor and the excessive burthens
heaped upon them when they no longer resisted their invaders,
the priests generally, and many others, sought to defend
them.

Las Casas, who seems to have been a generous and noble-
hearted man, devoted himself for many years, indeed a whole
life-time, to the cause of the natives, but at no time or in any
way was he laboring for their freedom or to secure to them
social or political rights of any kind. Other priests labored to
secure their spiritual welfare, or what they believed to be this,
while Las Casas, though a profoundly religious man, sought
their material preservation, and to save them from that direful
fate of total extinction which even then was threatened, and
which finally has been so complete, that at this moment there
is not one single descendant of these people left to tell the tale
of their destruction. The popular notion, therefore, that Las
Casas was the author or originator of the "slave trade," and
of American (negro) "slavery," in order to "free" the native
race, is altogether groundless.

It originated, as has been stated, in an industrial necessity—
and while he assented to it, with the humane belief, doubtless,
that it would tend to benefit the native race in relieving it
from the excessive and fatal burthens imposed by the Spaniards, his assent or dissent could have no influence whatever
on the subject. And as he was not laboring for the freedom
of the natives—for nothing whatever but their mere material
preservation—of course he could have no doubts or anxieties in
regard to negroes in that respect, and when he saw them resisting alike the deadly malaria of the climate and the brutality
of their masters, and contented and happy, he doubtless felt
that it was a wise and beneficent arrangement of Providence
that had thus adapted them to their condition and to the fulfilment of the great purposes of civilization and human progress.

The supply of negro labor in San Domingo, Cuba, and other
islands, was followed, however, by extensive importations for
the main land, and finally the trade, falling into the hands of
the Dutch and English, became a world-wide commerce, and
negroes were taken into every nook and corner of the New
World where there were found buyers, or where the traders
could dispose of their human cargoes. And here begins the
wrong side of the matter—the cruelties, injustice, outrages, and
inhumanities which, together with the false theories, morbid
philanthropy, and a certain amount of falsehood, have made the
term "slave trade" synonymous with everything that is di-
abolical and devilish that the imagination can conceive of.
The Spanish government of the day limited the introduction
of negroes, and provided for an equal number of females, and
encouraged the importation of children; indeed, while there is
no reason to suppose that they ever contemplated the negro as
abstractly entitled to the rights claimed for them in our times,
it is certain that both the governments of Charles V. and
Philip II. did regard them as human, and made every provi-

sion that was proper for their kind and humane treatment, both in regard to their passage from Africa and their treatment on the plantations. But when the physical adaptation of the negro had become so clearly demonstrated in the Spanish islands, the British and Dutch merchants began to import them in such multitudes, and the prices fell so low, that it would not pay to import women and children,(and then began that nameless and unspeakable outrage, not merely on human but on animal nature, which has distinguished this trade ever since, and, to the disgrace of all Christendom, which at this moment distinguishes it in the neighboring island of Cuba—the separation of the sexes and the violation of the rights of reproduction.) Instead of a simple supply of negro labor essential to tropical production, and which violated no instinct, want, or necessity of the negro nature, ships were now fitted out on speculation; cargoes of men, as mere work-animals, were obtained in Africa and carried to any port where there was a chance of a market, not in the tropics alone, but all over North America; and the British Provinces of New England, as well as Cuba and Porto Rico, became the marts for traffic in human beings. This accounts for the great mortality of these people in the islands. In general terms, it may be said the negro will work no more than he ought to work; that is, nature has so adapted him that he can not be forced in this respect; but when they could be purchased so cheaply, the master had little interest in their health, and together with the very small native increase going on, the mortality vastly preponderated. The New England as well as the Middle States were fully supplied with these cheap negroes, but they never were profitable, and the laws of industrial adaptation has steadily carried their descendants southward.

The "slave trade," after the first fifty years of its commencement, up to the American Revolution, may be said to

have been in the hands of the British mainly, of the merchants
of Bristol and Liverpool. These traders, as has been said,
made it a mere matter of commerce, dealing in it just as they
did in any other article of commerce, and many of the largest
fortunes in England are believed to have had their foundations
laid in this traffic. So far as the colonists participated in it,
they approached somewhat to the earliest Spaniards, and
though there were more males imported than there were females, the horrible practice of the islands, which forbade these
people to fulfill the command of the Almighty, and multiply
their kind, did not prevail to any considerable extent. Nature
always recovers from the outrages committed on her laws, and
though no legislation or human means has sought to remedy
the disproportions of the sexes, they are now probably equal,
though of the imported progenitors of our negroes probably
two-thirds at least were males, and though even a larger proportion than this were imported into Northern ports, there
are now scarcely a quarter of a million in the Northern States,
while the descendants of those imported into the North have
expanded into four millions at the South! What a lesson
these facts present to the blind and infatuated "friends of freedom" in Kansas, and the equally blind believers in the ordinance of 1787. The negro, by a higher law than human enact-
ments, goes where he is needed, and *permanently* no where
else. A broad and liberal survey of the whole ground—the
nature of the negro, his utter uselessness when isolated or separated from the white man—his organic adaptation to tropical
production—the wonderful fertility of tropical soils—the vast
importance of their peculiar products to civilization and human
well-being—demonstrates, beyond doupt the right and justice
of the original "slave trade," or the original importation of
African negroes into America. The abuses that finally attended
it have been made to overshadow the thing itself, in the popular

estimation, but despite all these, and all other drawbacks, it is certain that the introduction of these negroes has resulted in a vastly preponderating good to our race, while the four millions of Christianized and enlightened negroes in our midst, when compared with any similar number of their race in Africa, are in a condition so immeasurably happy and desirable, that we can find no terms that will sufficiently express it.)

The frightful tales invented of their cruel treatment on the passage from Africa may be dismissed with the single remark that it was the highest interest of the traders to take the utmost care of them, and if that be not sufficient, with the simple but pregnant fact that the average mortality, when the trade was legal, was only eleven per cent., while the illegal trade, the efforts to put it down, the false philanthropy, and mistaken interference, have raised the mortality to something like forty per cent. !

There were but two mistakes, wrongs, inhumanities, outrages on nature, whatever we may term them, involved in the "slave trade," so far as we were concerned: 1st, the importation mainly of males, and the consequent violation of the laws of reproduction—of that fundamental and universal command of the Almighty to multiply their kind and to replenish the earth; and, 2d, their importation into northern latitudes, unsuited to the physical and industrial nature of the negro. But, as has been said, nature, sooner or later, recovers from every outrage upon her laws, and while we, in our ignorance and folly, have been disputing over our petty theories in respect to this subject, her reparatory processes have silently and steadily gone on and corrected our mistakes, and, therefore, both of the real *wrongs* connected with the "slave trade" are now substantially *righted*.

It is, however, discreditable to our intelligence that the statute book of the nation is disfigured by our laws and legis-

8*

lation on this subject. England has waged a war upon the
distinctions of nature and the natural relations of races, ever
since we threw off her dominion, and set up a new system of
government founded on the fixed and unchangeable laws of
nature. The preservation of her own system—the rule of
classes and of artificial distinctions among men of the same
race—impels her by a blind instinct quite as much, perhaps, as
reason, to pursue this policy, and therefore, under the pretense
of putting down the " slave trade," she has constantly labored
to obliterate the distinctions of race, and force or corrupt the
white men of America into affiliation and equality with negroes.
The war upon the " slave trade" was simply the means for
accomplishing her ends—the equalization of races in the New
World, and in Canada, the West Indies, in all her American
possessions, she has succeeded. Negroes, whites, Indians, and
mongrels are all alike her *subjects*, and the distinctions of society, as in Europe, are wholly artificial, while those of race,
of nature, that are fixed by the hand of the Eternal, are impiously disregarded. And we have been her tools, her miserable
dupes, and ourselves labored for our own degradation, to accomplish her objects and obliterate the distinctions of races.
The question of importing more negroes—to keep open or to
prohibit the " slave trade"—was and is a question of expedi-
ency, that our government should decide for itself, without
regard to the opinions or policy of any other people. But to
blindly follow England in her nefarious and impious efforts to
break down the distinctions of race, to pronounce the conduct
of our own ancestors infamous and worthy of death because
English opinion and monarchical influences and exigencies demand it, is a disgrace to the manhood of our people and the
intelligence of our statesmen that should not be permitted to
disgrace our government any longer; and it is to be hoped
that the time is not distant when this disgraceful legislation
will be swept from our statute book.'

CHAPTER XV.

THERE are now between four and five millions of negroes in
the United States. They or their descendants must remain
forever—for good or evil—an element of our population.
What are their natural relations to the whites?—what their
normal condition?

The Almighty has obviously designed all His creatures—
animal as well as human—for wise, beneficent, and useful purposes. In our ignorance of the animal world, we have only
domesticated or applied to useful purposes a very small number, the horse, the ox, ass, dog, etc.; but these we practically
understand, so that even the most ignorant will not abuse
them or violate their instincts. The most ignorant farmer or
laborer would never attempt to force the dog to perform the
domestic *rôle* of the cat, or the ox that of the horse, or the
sheep that of the ass, etc. He knows the natures of these animals—their relations to himself and to each other, and governs
them accordingly.

The natural relations of parent and offspring, of brothers
and sisters, of husbands and wives, are also measurably understood by the most ignorant, for natural instinct quite as much
as reason guides us in these things. The father knows that
the child should obey him, and the latter feels instinctively
that this obedience is a sacred duty. The same instinct prompts
the brother to love his sister, and it may be said that all the
relations of consanguinity, and the duties that spring from

them, are regulated more by instinct than by reason. There are innumerable books written on this subject, to teach the duties of parents and offspring, husbands and wives, etc., but with a proper cultivation of the intellect and of the affections, just perceptions of the duties involved follow intuitively.

Passing beyond these domestic and family relations—the relations of individuals—of one man to another, and to the State or general citizenship, are less understood, for here nature must be led by reason, and though there are certain great and fixed facts that serve as landmarks for our guidance, we must mainly rely upon our reason.

It is true, Christianity indicated these relations two thousand years ago; nevertheless, they are almost totally disregarded in the Old World; but though too often misunderstood and misapplied among ourselves, they are sufficiently comprehended to constitute the foundation of our social order.

Another advance, and we arrive at the relations of races—of white men and negroes—and of other races that may chance to be in juxtaposition, and of which the whole world may be said to be profoundly ignorant in theory, while one-half of our people have justly and truly solved them in practice. The social order of the South—the social and legal *status* of the negro—reposes on the natural relations of the white and black races, and, as has been observed, while the world is ignorant of these relations, the people of the South, indeed it may be said the American people, have practically solved them, and to the mutual benefit of all concerned. But before we can enter on a discussion of the natural relations and social adaptations of races, we must first clearly understand the relations that we bear to each other as individuals, and to the State or aggregate of individuals.

All the individuals of a species, whether animal or human, of course have the same faculties, the same wants, in a word,

the same specialties. Occasionally chance—some accident, remote or immediate—deforms or blights individuals ; they may
be idiotic, insane, or otherwise incapable, but these are exceptional cases that do not disturb the great, fixed, and unchangeable equality, sameness, or uniformity of the race. The white
or Caucasian race, as has been observed, varies much more
than any other race. There are tall men and short men, giants
and pigmies, blondes and brunettes, red-haired and black-
haired, but the nature remains the same ; and if they were all
placed under the same circumstances of climate, government,
religion, etc., all would exhibit the same moral characteristics, and, to a certain extent, the same physical appearances.
This is sufficiently illustrated among ourselves every day.
Almost universally our people have sprung from the "lower
classes" of European society. The coarse skin, big hands and
feet, the broad teeth, pug nose, etc., of the Irish and German
laborer pass away in a generation or two, and their American
offspring have more delicate and classical features than even
the most favored and privileged European aristocracy. Having the same faculties, the same wants, etc., it is a self-evident
truth that they are entitled to the same rights, the same oppor-
tunities, to live out the nature with which God has endowed
them. The Divine Author of Christianity promulgated this
vital truth with great impressiveness. He selected his dis-
ciples from the lowest and most oppressed classes of the people,
and thundered his most terrible denunciations in the ears of
the sacerdotal aristocracy. The great body of the Jewish
people were mere beasts of burden to their brethren—the
priestly oligarchy—which governed the State and lived in idle
luxury on the toil, ignorance, superstition, and misery of the
people. Ou all occasions these oppressors were denounced,
and the great and everlasting truth that God was no respecter
of persons, and all men equally precious in His sight—even

the beggar Lazarus and the repentent Magdalene—were the daily teachings of Christ. And there can be no doubt that the persecution and final crucifixion of the Author of the Christian religion was intended, by the rulers of the Jews, to crush out the great doctrine of equality, and thus to preserve their ascendency over the minds and fortunes of the people. The Divine ordinance—to " do unto others as we would have them do unto us"—is a complete exposition of our natural relations to each other, and an indestructible rule of nature as well as a religious obligation. All men—that is, all who belong to the race or species—having the same nature and designed by the Creator for the same purposes, the same rights and the same duties, it is an obvious inference that all human governments should rest on this great fundamental truth. No man should be permitted, indeed no man should be base enough to claim privileges denied to his fellow, or to any class of his fellows, and the same great principle which Christ ordained should guide His followers in their personal relations, should be the only legitimate rule in their political relations. To do unto others as we would have them do to us—to recognize in all other men the rights we claim for ourselves—to admit those reciprocal obligations which, in truth, spring from the necessities of our being—in short, to demand equal rights for ourselves, and to admit the same rights on the part of our fellows, seems so obvious, so instinctive, so just, and indeed self-evident, that an intelligent and just mind wonders how it ever could be otherwise, or that systems of government can exist in our own enlightened times in utter contradiction to such simple and self-evident truths. Government, the State, the aggregate citizenship, based on the great fundamental truth of equality, becomes a simple, beneficent, and easily understood institution. It leaves all men where God and nature places them, in natural relation to each other. Its functions, however complicated the details, are simply protective, leaving individuals to ascend or descend in the social scale, just as their industry, cultivation, and moral worth may be appreciated by their fellow-citizens. It protects one man from the violence or injustice of another, and the aggregate citizenship or nation from foreign aggression.

It is a misnomer to speak of government conferring rights; it may (or the thing called government in other lands may) take away, suppress, or withhold rights; but rights, as declared by Mr. Jefferson, are inherent and in fact inseparable from individual existence. God has endowed every man with the capacity of self-government, and imposed this self-government as a duty as well as a right. He has given him certain wants instincts, desires, etc., and endowed him with reason to govern and guide these things. As a citizen, he of course does not, or can not surrender any of his natural rights or control over himself. The State protects him from wrong or injustice, but himself a portion of the citizenship, he still governs himself. It is a contradiction to suppose that one man can govern another better than he can govern himself—that is, under the same circumstances, and therefore it is palpably absurd to limit suffrage or to exclude a portion of the people from participation in the government. All being naturally equal—for though some men may have more mental capacity than others, as we sometimes see some have greater physical powers—they have all the same nature; and therefore govern themselves and fulfill the purposes of their creation when they all vote at elections and participate in the making of laws. For purposes of convenience, a limited number of the people are delegated to conduct the government, but the popular will, the desire of the people, the rule of the entire citizenship, is complete; every vote tells, every man's voice is heard, every one governs himself. And the government, limited or rather confined to its legitimate function of protection, leaves every one a complete and boundless liberty to do every thing or any thing that his instincts, wishes, caprices even, may prompt him to do, so long as he does not infringe upon the rights, interests, etc., of others.

Such, then, are the natural relations we bear to each other, and the social and governmental adaptations that spring from them. The mere conventional formula may be varied at times —the circle of individual action contracted or expanded as the public exigencies may demand, but the right and the duty of every man to an equal participation in the government, or in the creation of laws which govern all, is vital, and every man denied this is necessarily a slave, for he is then governed by the will of others and not by his own, as God and nature have ordained he should be.

There are no contradictions or discords in nature. All creatures, and the purposes God has assigned to them, are perfectly harmonious ; and all their relations to each other, and the duties that spring from them, are in perfect accord. It is our ignorance, and sometimes our caprices and vices, that interrupt this harmony ; but it is consoling to know, that happiness is inseparable from the due fulfilment of our duties, and therefore the wiser the world becomes, the better it will be. The man who loves his wife the most will also have the tenderest affection for his children ; those who are most careful to respect the rights of others will be the most secure in their own rights, and the government, or state, or nation based on the natural relations that men bear to each other, will be the most prosperous and powerful.

We are, it is true, at a great distance from the practical or complete development of our system, but in theory it is right, and most Americans recognize the truth and justice of its elementary principles. On the contrary, Europeans, and especially Englishmen, have scarcely a perception or glimpse of men's natural relations to each other, and their whole social and political system, if thus it may be called, is in direct conflict with these relations, with the vital principle of democracy, with reason and common sense. A woman is the chief of the nation, whose husband is her subject—thus violating the relations of the sexes—of husband and wife—and thrusting her from the normal position of woman as well as contradicting the relations and duties of citizenship. God created her, adapted her, and designed her, for a wife and mother, a help-mate to her husband and the teacher and guide of her children; He endowed her with corresponding instincts to love, venerate, and obey her husband and devote her life to the happiness and welfare of her offspring, and to trample on His laws—to smother these instincts and force this woman to be a queen, a chief of state, the ruler over millions of men, is as sinful as it is irrational, as great an outrage on herself—her womanhood—as it is on the people who suffer from it. The annual expenditure for royalty amounts to several millions, and requires probably that some thirty thousand people should be employed or compelled to devote their labor to this purpose. Thirty thousand men, women, and children, ignorant, abject, and miserable, with no chance whatever for education, for the cultivation of their faculties or the healthy development of their natures, are bound to lives of toil and a mere animal existence in order to furnish means for this one family, not of happiness, but of boundless folly, which is supposed to constitute royal dignity. God created this woman with the same faculties, endowed her with the same instincts, and designed her for the same purposes as all other women in England, but the human law, disregarding the evident designs of the Almighty, has impiously sought to make her a different and superior being, to reverse the natural relations of the sexes, to render her husband subject to her will, to place her above many millions of men, the head of the state, to even force this fragile, weak, and helpless female to be the commander-in-chief of their armies, and they crush and pervert thirty thousand other people out of the natural order, and doom them to a mere animal existence, in order to sustain this one family in "royal splendor." The two things are inseparable—the violation of the natural relation drags after it these frightful consequences. All these people thus doomed to ignorance and toil, to support the luxury and grandeur of royalty, would, under the same circumstances, be just as grand, majestic, and royal as the present royal family, and the wrong in the present instance may be measured or tested by the consideration that of these thirty thousand poor, ignorant, abject, and toiling creatures, whose labor, or the proceeds of whose labor is appropriated to the support of royalty, the majority would doubtless exhibit more capacity and refinement than those who rule over them, if, standing where nature placed them all in common, they were permitted to compete for superiority. The same unnatural order prevails on the Continent : the natural equality that God has stamped upon the race—for they are all white men—is disregarded, and though the people are ignorant, debased by poverty, excessive toil, and misery, the *status quo* is preserved alone by force. Nearly four millions of armed men are kept in constant readiness to repress and keep down the instinct of equality, while a " civil" force of perhaps a million more is constantly acting in conjunction with the former, in preserving that artificial and unnatural rule which the few—a mere fraction of the population—exercise over the many. And so instinctive and irrepressible is this sentiment—this innate and eternal law written by the finger of the Almighty on the soul and organism of the race— that if these armed forces were withdrawn, every government in Europe would be demolished within a week. Nor can the existing condition be preserved much longer. Those writers ignorant of the essential nature of the race, often indulge in absurd fancies in regard to the future of European society. They are good enough to say that democratic institutions may do for America, but that they will not suit the people of Europe, and therefore monarchy is to be a permanent institution. Democracy or equality is a fact rather than a principle. Beings who have the same nature, the same wants, and the same instincts will struggle, as they must struggle, for ever, to enjoy the same rights and to live out the same life. And though they are chained down by ignorance and misery as well as by the armed hordes of their tyrants, there can be no peace, no cessation of the conflict, no stopping-place short of the universal recognition of their natural relations to each other, and that fixed and eternal equality which the Almighty Creator has stamped upon the race and fixed for ever in its physical and mental structure.

If the natural relations that men bear to each other are thus misunderstood and disregarded in Europe, it may well be supposed that they are wholly ignorant of the natural relations of races, and without even the remotest conception of the relations that naturally exist between white men and negroes. It is therefore a subject never introduced or treated of—a *terra incognita* to the European mind,—and dependent as we are on European authority, the natural relation of races, and the normal condition of the negro, have only quite recently become a subject of American investigation.

But while our writers and men of science have been, and quite generally are even now, wholly ignorant of these relations, indeed, worse still, in slavish subserviency to European dictation, have accepted the absurd theories of the former in explanation of the phenomena constantly presented to their view, our people have practically solved their natural relations to the inferior race, and placed or rather retained the negro in his normal condition.

There are eight millions of white people and four millions of negroes in juxtaposition. The latter are, in domestic subordination and social adaptation, corresponding with their wants, their instincts, their faculties, the nature with which God has endowed them. They are different and subordinate creatures, and they are in a different and subordinate social position, harmonizing with their natural relations to the superior race, and therefore they are in their normal condition. This, if not exactly a self-evident, is certainly an unavoidable truth—a truth that no amount or extent of sophistry, self-deception, authoritative dictum, or perverted reasoning can gainsay a moment, for it rests upon *facts*, fixed forever by the hand of the Creator. The negro is different from, and inferior to the white man. He is in a different and inferior position, and therefore, of necessity, is in a normal condition. *That*, as a general proposition, is true beyond doubt, for there is no place or material for doubt. God has made him different—widely different, as has been shown; that difference is as unchangeable as are any of the works of the Almighty. *He* has therefore designed him, of course, for different purposes—for a different and subordinate social position whenever and wherever the races are in juxtaposition. It needs no argument to prove this truth, great and startling as it must be to those who have never before contemplated it. The *facts*—the simple, palpable, unchangeable facts—only need to be stated, and the inference, the inductive fact, the absolute truth, is unavoidable. God has made the negro different from, and inferior to the white man. They are in juxtaposition—the human law corresponds with the higher law of the Almighty; the negro is in a different and subordinate position, and therefore in a normal condition.

But it may be said by some that while this is so, or while the negro, in juxtaposition, *must* be subordinate, it does not follow that the actual condition of things at the South is essentially right, natural, and just. They would be mistaken, however, for the *facts* involved do not permit or admit of any such assertion. The white man *is* superior, the negro *is* inferior, and therefore the inference is unavoidable that the latter is in his normal condition whenever the social law or legal adaptation is in harmony with these natural relations of white men and negroes. It is true that a wide field for inquiry, for comparison, for arriving at relative truth, is here opened to our view, but the simple, precise, and unavoidable truth remains unaltered and unalterable—the different and inferior negro is in a different and inferior social position at the South, and therefore in harmony with the natural relations of the races, he is in a normal condition. If it were said that the existing condition were defective—that in some respects injustice were done the negro—that there was a wide field for improvement in the social habits of the South—in short, for the progress and improvement of Southern society, then there would be reason, perhaps, in such suggestions. But to say or to assert that the condition of the negro at the South was wrong or unjust in its essential character, would be altogether absurd, and an abuse of language that none but those wholly ignorant of the facts involved would ever, or could ever, indulge in. The simple statement of the facts lying at the base of Southern society, however false our perceptions of them, or whatever our ignorance of them, or whatever may be the perversity of those who will not seek to comprehend them, is sufficient, when clearly presented, to convince every rational mind that the negro is in his normal condition only when in social subordination to the white man.

But however obvious or irresistible this momentous truth,

when it is thus forced upon the mind as an inductive fact, it is
also demonstrable through processes of comparison, which, if
not quite so direct or palpable, are equally certain and reliable.
And the normal condition of the negro, or the social adaptation at the South, necessarily involves the protection as well as
the subordination of the inferior race. The two things are in
fact inseparable, as in the case of parents and children, or the
relations of husband and wife, or indeed any condition of
things resting on a basis of natural law.

Any one capable of reasoning at all must see that four millions of subordinate negroes in juxtaposition with eight millions of superior white men, must be in a subordinate social
position—that the instinct of self-preservation, the primal
law, obviously demands that the superior shall place the inferior in just such position as its own interests and safety may
need—that it may and should even destroy it, utterly obliterate it from the earth, if its own safety requires it—though
such instance never could happen unless some outside force or
intermeddling brought it about—that the mode or manner, or
special means are of secondary consideration, and to be determined or worked out according to circumstances, the habits,
progress, and condition of the master race. Contemplating,
therefore, the great existing fact—the juxtaposition of vast
masses of widely different social elements at the South—the
inference is unavoidable, that it is the right and the duty of the
dominant race to provide for the wants of such a population,
and that, for the common welfare and safety, they may and must
place the negro element just where their own reason and experience assure them is proper and desirable. This has been
done, and is done, but instead of the State or government providing directly for these things, individuals are left, to a great
extent at least, to provide for the wants of the subordinate
race. The motive of personal interest, therefore, is brought

into action—a motive often, doubtless, stronger than affection, and though, like the latter, it will not always save the weak and dependent from wrong and cruelty, it usually serves as a sufficient protection. The father loves his child, the being so inferior, so weak and dependent on his affection. He has absolute control over the actions, the labor, the time, habits, etc., of his son, may compel him to labor for him, or hire out or sell his services to another, and it is only on rare occasions that this natural affection of the father is not sufficient protection for the offspring, and the State is compelled to interpose its power to save the latter from the parent's cruelty. It is the utmost interest of the father to treat his offspring with kindness, and though affection is the dominant feeling, his real interests are always advanced by this treatment, so that it might be said that the man who loves his children most will have the most useful and the best children. And in the relation of husband and wife a similar result necessarily follows: the husband who loves his wife most tenderly will—other things being equal—always have the best wife, and the wife who loves her husband and children most devotedly will be rewarded by the greatest love and the greatest happiness in return.

In the case of the master and so-called slave, interest instead of affection is the dominant feeling; but even here they are inseparable as well as in the relations just referred to. It is the utmost interest of the master to treat his negro subject with the greatest kindness, and in exact proportion as he does so, he calls into action the affections of the latter. Every one who practically understands the negro, knows that the strongest affection his nature is capable of feeling is love for his master—that affection for wife, parents, or offspring, all sink into insignificance in comparison with the strong and devoted love he gives to the superior being who guides, cares, and provides for all his wants.

There is, then, this radical difference between parent and child, and master and "slave"—the first, prompted by affection, is rewarded by interest, while the latter, impelled by interest, is followed by affection ; and the grand result in both cases is happiness, well-being, the mutual benefit and common welfare of all concerned—that universal reward which God bestows on all His creatures, when, recognizing their natural relations to each, they adapt their domestic habits and social regulations to those relations.

The popular mind of the North, so deplorably ignorant of all the facts of Southern society, has a general conception, perhaps, of negro subordination at the South, but none whatever of the reciprocities of the social condition.   The negro—a different and inferior creature—must be in a social position harmonizing with this great, fundamental, and unchangeable fact ; but while he owes obedience, natural, organic, and spontaneous, he also-has the natural right of protection.   Or, in other words, while he owes obedience to his master, the latter owes him protection, care, guidance, and provision for all his wants, and he can not relieve himself of this duty or these duties without damaging himself.   For example : the master who overworked his people, or underfed them, or treated them cruelly in any way, would necessarily compromise his interests to the precise extent that he practiced, or sought to practice, these cruelties.   They would become feeble from over-exertion, or weak and prostrated from the want of healthy food ; while indifference to the master's interests, sullenness, perhaps sometimes fierce hate, would impel them to damage his property, and in any and every case their labor would be less valuable.   Furthermore, God has so adapted the negro that he can not be overworked ; and though the master or overseer may kill him in the effort, he can not, nor can any human power, force him beyond a given point, or compel him to that extreme exertion which the poor white laborer of Europe is often forced into. Subordination and protection, the obedience of the inferior and the care of the superior, the subjection of the negro and the guidance of the white man, are therefore inseparable, and when we outgrow and abandon the mental habits borrowed from Europe and designate the social condition where these elements exist, by a proper term or word, it should be a compound one that embodies both of these things.

Such, then, are the domestic habits and social adaptations at the South, or where widely different races are in juxtaposition, and which, in truth, spring from the necessities of social existence whenever they are found together. But, as already remarked, the truth, essential justice, beneficence, and necessity of this condition—this subordination on the one hand and protection on the other—while an obvious, and, indeed, unavoidable conclusion or inference from the great and unchangeable facts involved—are equally demonstrable by comparison with other conditions. Or, in other words, while the mere statement of existing facts, in their natural order and their true relations, irresistibly and unavoidably forces the mind to the conclusion that Southern society reposes on a basis of natural law and everlasting truth, its essential justice, naturalness, and beneficence may be made equally clear to the mind by comparing it with other conditions where these elements are found to exist. We absolutely know nothing of the negro of antiquity except that recently revealed on the Egyptian monuments, through the labors of Champolion and others, and possibly a glimpse occasionally of negro populations through Roman history. The ignorant Abolitionists, and the scarcely less ignorant European ethnologists, on this subject, fancy negro empires and grand civil-

9

izations long since extinct; and Livingstone and others, with
the false and nonsenical notion that there should be found
remains of these imaginary empires, of course succeeded in
finding them occasionally, or the interests of the "friends of
humanity" would languish, and perhaps subside altogether.
But the author desires to say to the reader that while, as an
anatomist, he *knows* that an isolated civilized negro is just as impossible as a straight-haired or white-skinned negro, he has also
consulted history, ancient and modern, European and Oriental, Pagan and Christian, and in the *tout ensemble* of the experience of mankind there is nothing written—book, pamphlet,
or manuscript—in the world that casts any light whatever on
this matter, or that authorizes the notion that populations,
where the negro element dominated, had a history. Since
the great "anti-slavery" imposture of modern times began,
there are many writers and lecturers who assume such things,
as that negro empires had often existed and exercised vast influ-
enees on the progress of mankind—that the rich and powerful
republic of Carthage was negro—that even Hannibal, the man
who so long contested the empire of the world with the grand
old Romans, was a negro—indeed, some of these ignorant and
impious people have assumed that Christ was a negro; but
it is repeated, there is no negro history, nothing whatever,
except what we now see on the Egyptian monuments, that
indicate the position of the negro or the condition of society
when in juxtaposition with white men.

As depicted on the monuments, the negro was then as he is
now at the South, in a position of subordination; while isolated, he was as he is now, a simple, unproductive, non-advancing savage. In this condition of isolation he multiplies himself, and therefore is in a natural condition. His acute and
powerful senses make amends for his limited intelligence, and
enable him to contend with the fiercer and more powerful crea-

tures of the animal creation, while the fervid suns and luxuriant soils of the tropics, where the earth may be said to produce spontaneously, enable him to live with little more exertion than simply to gather their rich and nutritious products. It is a natural condition, so far as it goes, for, as has been said, he increases and multiplies his kind; but it can not have been designed as the permanent condition of the race, for that involves the anomaly of waste, uselessness, a broad blank in the economy of the universe. But as that aspect of the subject will be discussed in another place, it need not be entered on here.

The condition of savagism, or whatever we may term it, where the negro is isolated and without any thing to call his wonderful powers of imitation into action, where he is simply a useless, non-advancing heathen, surely no one, however perverted his mind may be on this subject, will venture to say is a preferable condition to that which he enjoys at the South. It might suffice to say that he increases with more than double rapidity, to demonstrate the fact of his superiority of condition in the latter; but there are moral considerations that show this with still greater distinctness. It is true that we must not take our own standard to test this matter, or we must not assume that that which would constitute our own happiness would also secure the greatest happiness of the negro. Of course the white man never did and never could live such a life as the isolated negro; but, contemplating the negro in the South as he now exists, in comparison with the condition of the isolated negro in Africa, will any one or can any one doubt for an instant the immense superiority of the former condition? He is cared for in his childhood by his master as well as his mother, taken care of when ill, always supplied with an abundance of food and clothing, given every chance for the development of his imitative faculties, permitted to marry generally as he pleases, to feel always that he has a guide and protector, and a constant, peaceful home ; and in his old age will be cared for and decently buried with all the sanctions and comforts of the Christian religion. In Africa, a negro, isolated from the white man, rarely has a home, rarely knows his father, is left unprotected in his childhood to all the chances and uncertainties of savagism, sometimes nearly starved, at other times gorged with unwholesome food, without any possible chance for education or the development of his faculties, liable at any moment of his life, in some wild eruption of hostile tribes, to be carried off a slave, perhaps to be eaten by the victors, and after running the gauntlet of savagism, if he lives to old age, to be left to perish of hunger, if no longer able to seek food for himself. But it is quite unnecessary to multiply words on this point ; the condition of the negro in America, under the broad glare of American civilization and the beneficent influences of Christianity, is so vastly and indeed immeasurably superior to that of the African or isolated negro, that we have no terms in our language that can truly or fully express it. We ourselves, under our beneficent democratic institutions, doubtless enjoy an extent of happiness or well-being, over that of the masses of our race in the Old World, somewhat difficult to measure or express in words, and it is reasonable to say that the negro population of the South, relatively or comparatively, enjoy even greater happiness, when contrasted with African savagism. There is, in fact, no other condition to compare with, for freedom, the imaginary state that the Abolitionists have labored for so long, is not a condition, and has an existence in their imaginations alone, and not in the actual breathing and living world about us. They have a theory, or rather an abstract idea, that the negro is a *black*-white man, a black Caucasian, a creature like ourselves except in color, and therefore that, placed under the same circumstances—

that is, given the same rights and held to the same responsibilities—he will manifest the same qualities, etc. On this
foolish assumption legislatures and individuals have acted,
and both in the South and in the North considerable numbers of these people have been thrust from their normal condition into what? Why, into the condition of widely different
beings.

If any one were to propose to give the negro straight hair,
or a flowing beard, or transparent color, or to force on him
any other physical feature of the white man, everybody would
denounce the wrong as well as the folly of thus torturing the
poor creature with that which nature forbids to be done. It
has been shown that, in the mental qualities and instincts of
the negro, the differences between him and the white man are
exactly measured by the differences in the physical qualities,
and therefore the efforts of the Abolitionists to endow the
negro with freedom involve exactly the same impieties and
the same follies as if they sought to change the color of the
skin. Or if it was sought to force the child to live out the
life of the adult—or the woman that of the man, or to compel
our domestic animals to change their manifestations and to
contradict the nature God has given them, it would be
promptly denounced as cruel, impious, and foolish. All that
could be done would be to destroy them—to shorten the life
of the unhappy creatures; and this is exactly what has been
done, and is now done, in regard to negroes; but, owing to a
universal ignorance and wide-spread misconception, that which
should be denounced as the grossest wrong has been regarded
as the highest morality and philanthropy!

The negro is thrust from the care and protection of a master at the South, but he has none of the responsibilities of
society laid on him, and furthermore, there is no very pressing
competition for the means of subsistence. He has nothing of

what **are** called rights—that is, is not forced to live the life of
another being—and though he has no master to teach and
guide him, his powers of imitation are, to a certain extent,
called into action, for he is still in juxtaposition and subordination. But even under these favorable circumstances, he rapidly—
as contrasted with those under the care of masters—declines and
dies. There is, at this time, a large number of these people
in Maryland, Virginia and other transition States. Their condition is truly deplorable, and is every day getting worse, for
the increase of whites is every day adding to the pressure on
them, and rendering the means of subsistence more difficult to
obtain. It seems to many, doubtless, a great wrong to place
them again in a normal condition, and true relation to the
whites—which would be a wrong like that of the inebriate
forced back into temperance—a process, in truth, of great suffering, but desirable in the end. If the abnormal habit of
drunkenness continues, the man will die within a given time;
but if he reforms and recovers his normal state, he may live
many years.

There will be few, if any, more negroes " emancipated," as
forcing them out of a normal condition has been termed, in the
South, and therefore it is only a question of time when these
people, left as they are now, will become extinct. As a question of kindness and humanity, therefore, it is like that of the
drunkard : left as they are, they must perish ; but if restored
to a normal state, whatever their temporary suffering, they or
their descendants may live forever. Most unfortunately, however, there is another difficulty involved in the fortunes of
these poor people. They have a large infusion of white blood
—a very large portion, perhaps, are mulattoes, and therefore
while in the case of the typical negro there could be no doubt
where true humanity pointed us, in the case of these mongrels
there is room for doubt and difficulty. But in the more

Northern States, where it is sought to force the habitudes of white men on them, they perish rapidly. The mortality is greater in New England than in the Middle States, and greatest of all in Massachusetts where they are citizens, and the ignorant and misguided, however well-meaning, "friends of freedom" have their own way, and give full scope to their terrible kindness. The whole subject may be summed up thus:— The negro, in a normal condition, increases more rapidly than the whites—for the negress, if not more prolific, escapes by her lower sensibility the numerous chances of miscarriage, premature births, weakly children, etc., which ordinarily attend on the higher and more susceptible organization of the white female.

The "free" or abnormal negro of the Southern States tends to extinction—of the Middle States still more rapidly—and finally, most rapidly of all in New England. Or the actual laws governing this matter may may be summed up thus:—In precise proportion as the negro is thrust from his normal condition into that of the white man, he tends to extinction, or one might say, that precisely as the rights of the white man are forced on the negro, he is destroyed. All the negroes brought to this continent were in a normal condition. The monstrous assumption set up by British writers when the colonists began to throw off the British dominion, that negroes were *black*-white men, and, naturally considered, entitled to the same *status*, after nearly a hundred years, and an amount of wrong, falsehood, and suffering to these people that is beyond computation, has at last culminated. From this time forth, few, if any, will be "emancipated." Indeed, it is far more likely that the numbers restored to a normal condition will outnumber those thrust from their natural relations to white men. If all the legislation on the subject were suddenly blotted out, of course there would be no such thing as a "free negro" on this continent, and this is the point towards which the course of American society is now rapidly tending. It may be somewhat difficult to determine that period—for we know not what may be the action of many of the States that have a considerable population of this kind—but one can not err when saying that it can not be remote, and it is absolutely certain to arrive within the next hundred years. Indeed, it is most probable that from the culmination of the great " anti-slavery" imposture, or from the starting-point of the reaction, to the final period when such a social monstrosity as a " free" negro will be entirely extinct in the New World, the interval will be less than that of the strange and wide-spread delusion which has so long run riot .over the understanding, the common sense, the interests, and self-respect of our people.

Of course, no comparison proper can be made with so shadowy and intangible a thing as this. It is not a condition— it is only an attempt after that which neither has nor can have an existence. If it had been assumed simply that the *status* of the negro was wrong at the South, and that some other *status* was proper for him, then possibly an experiment would have been legitimate. But, as it was assumed that the negro was a Caucasian, whose color merely was different, and naturally entitled to the position of the white man, all these efforts were made to reduce the assumption to practice, and compel him to live out the life of the former. There could be and can be only a single end to such effort. God created him a negro, a different and inferior being, and of course no human power could alter or modify, to the millionth part of an atom, the work of the Eternal. That which destroys a creature, or under which he dies, can never be right, or even approach to that which is right. When nature is so outraged that she refuses to indorse the human action, or when she in mercy interposes her power to limit such action, then we can not possibly mistake the wrong we are doing, or attempting to do. It is an historical fact that slaves never propagated while in that condition, and the supply was constantly kept up by fresh wars and increased captives. It was such a stupendous outrage on the natural relations, that men of the same species bear to each other, or on that natural and unchangeable equality common to the race, that nature refused to propagate it, or to consent to its permanent existence. Nature also refuses offspring to prostitution—that terrible cancer so corrupting to Northern society, and who does not see her wisdom and beneficence in thus refusing a permanent existence to so foul a blot on the sexual relations? So, too, in the case of mulattoism, where a monstrous violation of the physical integrity of the races is involved, nature interposes and forbids it to live. And in incest—the violation of the laws of consanguinity, where relatives intermarry—nature appropriately punishes them, through the idiocy and impotency of their offspring, which is always forbidden to exist beyond a determinate period. Free negroism, therefore—the attempt to force a different and inferior being to live out the life of a different and superior being—is not a condition, and can not be compared with that which is, or that which the higher law of nature grants, a fixed order of life. There are, then, only two possible conditions for the negro—isolation or juxtaposition with the white man—African heathenism or subordination to a master—a blank in the economy of the universe, or the social order of the South, where he is an important element in the civilization, progress, and general welfare of both races. It is not in the scope of this work to treat of the natural relations or social adaptations of other races. They must be determined by experience, though the starting point—the fundamental truth—that when in juxtaposition they must occupy a subordinate social position, corresponding with the degree of inferiority to the white man, may be said to be self-evident, or, at all events, an unavoidable truth.

In conclusion, it may be well to repeat the great leading truths that underlie the subject discussed in this chapter.

All of God's creatures, animal as well as human, have a right to live out the life—the specific nature—that He has endowed them with, and we have comprehended this great, vital, and fundamental law in respect to our domestic animals, and generally conform to it. The natural relations of the sexes—of parents and offspring—are also understood, and generally lived up to in our daily life. The natural relations of men to each other are less understood, but the natural order, the equality of rights, and equality of duties, based on an equality of wants, is a vital principle of Christianity, and however far we may be from living it out in practice, our political system, and the whole superstructure of our civil and legal institutions, repose upon this fundamental law of nature.

This natural order is generally disregarded in the Old World, though even there, with all their numerous false traditions, relics of barbarism, and ancient wrongs, as well as modern corruptions, they are forced, to a certain extent, in their legal and civil institutions, to recognize it. Nature absolutely forbids any change or any violation of her laws, or, in other words, the work of the Almighty can not be altered by human force or accident. The millions of Europe are, therefore, unchanged in their essential natures, and the few who rule and wrong them are only able to prevent the development of their specific and latent capabilities by their systems of repression. But the natural order—the natural relations they bear to each other—the inherent and eternal equality that God has stamped forever on the organism of the race, is perpetually struggling to manifest itself; and though buried in a profound animalism, though deluded by false theories and corrupted by innumerable lies, and steeped in poverty and misery fathomless and measureless, they are only temporarily kept from asserting the natural order and specific nature of the race by four millions of bayonets.

The natural relations of races, and especially of the white man and negro, have been wholly misunderstood, for, ignorant of the nature and specific wants of the negro, it necessarily followed that it should be so. But while in theory we have been ignorant of these relations, the people of the South have solved them in practice. Their actual experience of the negro nature, of its wants, its capacities, its industrial adaptations, perhaps we may say, the instinctive necessities of a society where widely different social elements are in juxtaposition, have developed a social order in practical harmony with the best interests and highest happiness of both races. That society rests on the same basis as that of the North, with the superadded negro element, which, in social subordination corresponding with its natural inferiority and natural relations to the white man, is immovable and everlasting, so long as the foundations of the world remain unaltered and unalterable. Ignorance and impiety may beat against it; folly, delusion, and madness may waste their wild energies in blind warfare on it; European kings and nobles, all those who live and flourish for a time on the perversion of the natural order and the degradation of so many millions of their kind—their natural equals—may combine to overthrow it; dupes, instruments, open foes and secret traitors may aid them, and the great ignorant and deluded masses for a time may be blindly impelled in this direction, but all in vain; the social order—the supremacy of the master and the obedience of the " slave"—will remain forever, for it is based on the higher law of the Almighty, the natural relations of the races, the organic and eternal superiority of the white man and the organic and everlasting inferiority of the negro.

CHAPTER XVI.

CHATTELISM.

THE common European notion (and the American, borrowed from it), regards the American "slave" as a chattel—a thing sold like a horse or dog, and equally the absolute property of his master. Lord Brougham and others have denounced this barbarism, as they have called it, with great bitterness, and the former has declared that it is immoral, abhorrent, and even illegal "for man to hold property in man"—a declaration that might be true enough, perhaps, if negroes were black-white men, as supposed, but which, in view of the actual facts involved, is simply absurd. They suppose that negroes in America are held by the same tenure that the Romans and other nations of antiquity held their slaves. But there is no resemblance whatever, and, in truth, it would be difficult to find anywhere in history conditions so absolutely and so widely different. All the so-called heathen nations had slaves, or rather they had captives taken in war, whose lives were forfeited, and who thus became the property of their conquerors. The rule or custom seems to have been universal, and it was only after the introduction of Christianity that it became obsolete. A Roman army invaded Gaul or Germany—a great battle or series of battles occurred—those captured on the field became the property of the victors, while the nation or country became a Roman province, and ever after paid tribute to the Roman civil officers. Gaul, Britain, most of Germany, indeed, nearly all the then known world, were thus overrun

by the Roman armies, and the vast multitudes that were defeated in battle were carried off to Italy to cultivate the lands
of the Roman nobility. There was no question of freedom or
slavery, or of rights of any kind involved—the man risked his
life, and if defeated, this life was forfeited to the victor. The
latter might or might not slay him the next morning, or the
next week, or the next year, or twenty years after, just as he
pleased. He might send him to work on his lands in Italy,
keep him as a domestic in his household, compel him to enter
the arena and combat as a gladiator for the popular amuse-
ment, or direct him to be crucified or given to feed his fishes, or
he might sell him to others, who, of course, had the same control
over him; or, finally, by one supreme act of generosity, he might
give him back his forfeited life, when, as a freedman—not
freeman—he entered the ranks of ordinary citizenship and was
lost in the mighty mass of Romans that made up the population of the great city. Freedom or slavery, or what, in modern times, is called such, had nothing to do with the matter.
It was a question of life and death rather than of freedom and
slavery. The life, the actual physical existence was forfeited
—the man had no right to live, and only did live by the suffer-
ance of the captor or master, and therefore all subordinate
considerations were lost in this one great, all-dominating fact.
Many wise, learned, and accomplished men were slaves or
were of this unfortunate class, and remained thus through life,
subject often, doubtless, to the caprices and cruelty of illiterate and brutal owners, who at any moment could put them to
the torture or to a cruel death. The rule was universal among
all the ancient nations, except the Hebrews, who, in some respects, or as regarded their own people, made some humane
modifications. It was entirely personal—the state or government having nothing to do with the matter either as regarded
the original forfeit or the cancelling of the bonds and the

restoration to liberty, or rather to life, of the unfortunate cap-
tive.

There was a certain social prejudice in respect to freedmen,
or the children of those who had been slaves, but there does
not appear to have been any legal or political disability. They
had forfeited their lives—they became absolutely dead in law,
mere things, chattels, or property of their owners, of which
the government or state took no more account than of horses
or oxen, or any other property; but the moment that their
lives were restored to them, then they at once entered the
ranks of citizenship with all the rights and privileges common
in those days, and in those relatively barbarous times.

There were some incidental features or phases of this terrible condition that are too marked to pass over without notice,
as they tend to show, in a very striking manner, the wide and
indeed unapproachable distance between it and that which, in
our own times, has been so generally confounded with it.
Servile wars were almost constantly occurring events. Opinion, even in the rudest times, has always, to a certain extent,
governed the world, and the universal custom of enslaving
those defeated in battle was submitted to in the first instance
without a murmur. It was the fortune of war, and no one disputed the inexorable rule which doomed them to become the
absolute chattels or property of the victor; but when their
numbers increased to any considerable extent in any locality,
the natural instinct which told them they were the equals, and
very often the superiors of those who owned them, could not
be restrained, and the long and terrible servile wars almost
always raging within the bosom of the Roman Empire probably weakened and more than any other thing prepared it for
that awful overthrow which finally overtook the Roman
colossus. Another equally striking feature distinguished this
condition. The slave population never increased itself in the

regular and natural order. Most of them were adult males, originally, and the small number of females may sufficiently account for the constant tendency to extinction; but beyond this, the abnormal condition, the terrible and transcendent wrong of forcing beings like themselves, with the same wants and the same instincts as their masters, to lives in absolute and abject subjection to the wills of others, was necessarily incompatible with a permanent existence.

This universal custom prevailed—all men, even the wisest and best, in their profound ignorance of their own nature, believed slavery to be right, just as many good men in our own times believe that the European condition, which dooms the millions to subjection to the few, is right; but it was so utterly in conflict with natural instinct that the servile population tended constantly to extinction, and therefore, as observed, it soon died out when the spirit of Christianity modified the customs of war, and the conquered became prisoners to be exchanged, instead of slaves subject to the caprices and cruelties of creatures like themselves. Some superficial writers, ignorant of the underlying facts, have supposed that Greece and Rome were great and prosperous because they had slaves, a process of reasoning quite equal to saying that a man enjoyed good health because he had a fever-sore on one of his legs! These nations and all other nations have been prosperous and powerful in precise proportion to the number of free men, and weak and contemptible in exact proportion to the multiplicity of slaves—a truth as evident at this day as in any other, and rendered more palpable in our own history and condition than ever before. Greece and Rome were great and powerful, in contrast with the great Oriental empires—Persian, Babylonian, Egyptian, etc.—because there was a large free population in the former, while in the latter they were all slaves, or the slaves of slaves. Of course no such condition could exist in

our times, and the most ignorant and abject portion of the
European population could not be placed or kept in such position a single hour. The Oriental populations still practice it,
to a certain extent, perhaps. The Turks, when they invaded
the lower empire and captured Constantinople, made slaves
of their prisoners, and long trains of unhappy beings, wealthy
matrons and delicately nurtured young girls, chained by the
wrists to their own servants, or to rude soldiers and uncouth
peasants, were marched off to become the abject and miserable
slaves of still more gross and brutal masters. The sale of Cir-
cassian girls for Turkish harems is altogether a different affair,
and however revolting to our notions and habits, has nothing
in common with the condition historically known to us as
slavery. The essential fact in this condition, as will be seen,
was the forfeited life; all other facts hinged on that, and the idea
of property or chattelism was incidental—a mere result. When
the man's life was forfeited, when he was deemed to be dead
in law, when his captor could do as he pleased with him,
crucify, torture, or destroy him altogether, then it necessarily
followed that he was a chattel, or a thing that he would be
apt to make as profitable as possible, and this self-interest was
the sole protection of the miserable creature. It therefore
was, doubtless, a great interest—some of the Roman nobles
owning many thousands of them, though, except in respect to
the servile wars, almost constantly raging within some portion
of the empire, the government seems to have had nothing to
do with slaves or slavery. It was wont, however, to resort to
terrible punishments to keep them in subjection, and it was
not uncommon to line the highways leading into the city for
forty miles with crosses, on which these wretched beings were
suspended, and left in sight and hearing of each other, until
death relieved them from their sufferings.

Such was Roman slavery, as it has been described by his-

torians of the time—a condition not at all involving what we
call freedom or rights of any kind, but simply that of a forfeited existence, and which, if given back by the owner, the
man was restored to life, to a legal existence, to his normal
condition, and, without the slightest interference of the government, was at once absorbed in the general citizenship. Of
course there is no resemblance or even approximation to the
social order of the South ; indeed, as observed, it is difficult to
conceive of conditions more utterly opposed or unlike each
other. As has been shown elsewhere, the labor, the service,
the industrial forces of the negro were essential to the cultivation of the soil and the growth of the indigenous products that
belong to the great intertropical regions of the American continent. Ships, therefore, were fitted out for this purpose to
bring negroes to the New World, not to make slaves of them,
or to transform them into things, but to make their labor
available for the common good of mankind. Much wrong,
cruelty, and inhumanity, it is quite likely, have been practiced,
but the motive and the object were right, of course, for these
had their origin in human necessities and human welfare. The
abuses we have nothing more to do with ; the object and the
essential fact—the service—remains, and will remain forever,
if the great tropical centre of the continent remains civilized,
instead of being transformed into a bàrren waste. The service
of the negro, his industrial $_cap_{acity}$, his labor, is a thing that
may be estimated as easily and accurately as any other species
of property, and therefore is property, and to the precise extent necessary to enforce this labor or this service the owner
of it has absolute control over the person of the negro. There
is not, nor should there be, any difference between this property and other property, and to this extent it may be called
chattelism, for, as observed, it may be as easily and precisely
fixed or defined as any other property. The master takes care

of him in childhood and in sickness, clothes, feeds, and provides for his old age, or for the loss of health, etc., and estimating or comparing these things with his services, he is able to fix a positive value to the labor of the negro, and this, like any other property, he may dispose of to any one else, if he chooses to do so. This property he must have absolute control over, and therefore, to the precise extent needed to make it available, he has absolute control over the person of the negro. The ignorant abolition writer says, "the slave is put upon the auction-block, examined and handled precisely as the horse, or other animal, and knocked off to the highest bidder; he follows his master home, to be dealt with just as any other animal."

It is true, there is a seeming resemblance, but if we follow them home and observe what follows, then it will be seen that there is no resemblance at all. The master takes care of his horse, for such is his interest; he may even have a liking, a kind of affection for him; but if sick or worn out, or if he falls and breaks a leg, he blows his brains out, and after taking off his skin, leaves the carcass to be devoured by the dogs or vultures. In the case of the negro he also takes care of him and treats him well, for it is his highest interest to do so, and often feels an affection, and a very strong one, for him. If ill, he sends for a surgeon and treats him as men usually treat their children. He is a part of the household, belongs to the family, and is usually strongly attached to the master and the master's children. His own wants are all attended to. He has his cabin, his patch of garden, his poultry, etc., very often his bale of cotton. He is permitted to choose his own wife, to enjoy all the domestic happiness that his nature is capable of, and if he fulfils his duty industriously, promptly, and honestly, then the master may be said to have no more control over him; but should he reach old age, break his leg, or in any way become disabled and useless, if the master should blow his brains out he would be hanged as a murderer. There is surely no resemblance in these things, none whatever; indeed it may be said that the one essential fact accomplished, the "service" duly rendered, the master's absolute control ceases. He must still care for and protect the negro and provide for him in sickness and old age, but his absolute rule is always within well-defined limits, and beyond them the master may not go. He may enforce service, and if the negro disobeys, punish him, or if he resists the reasonable will of the master, compel obedience—absolute, unquestioning obedience. But the laws of every Southern State protect the "slave" from the caprices and cruelties of the master just as in the Northern States they protect the child from a sometimes passionate and brutal father.

In the previous chapter it has been shown that the negro is in his normal condition only when in social subordination to the white man—for that is the natural relation of the races whenever or wherever they are in juxtaposition; but the precise form of this subordination may be modified, perhaps, by time and circumstances. Subordination and protection exist together—indeed, are inseparable. The strong should protect the weak: the superior white man, who demands the obedience of the inferior negro, should also protect this feebler being; and such is the social condition at the South. Owning the the service of the negro, it is the highest interest of the master to take the utmost care of him, while the latter has an equal interest—relatively considered—in being honest, industrious, and faithful to the master. Indeed, it is impossible to perceive any antagonism of interests in this condition, and compared with any other, it may be said, without chance of successful contradiction, that it is the most harmonious in its essential principles known to our times. It originated in an absolute want—the service of the negro—that industrial capac-

ity which he alone can furnish, and this service is the essential
feature of the domestic institutions of the South. It was and
is made a property that may be sold or exchanged as promptly
as any other property, and the person of the negro is subject
to the absolute control of the master to an extent necessary to
enforce this power, but no further. There is still a large margin for self-control, for all the self-government that nature demands, for the gratification of all his wants and the full development of all his faculties. This is demonstrated beyond
doubt, for he rapidly multiplies, while if he were denied the
rights that nature accords him, his instincts repressed, his
wants forbidden gratification, like the Roman slave, or like the
so-called free negro of the North, he would become languid
and diseased, and tend rapidly to extinction. But while the
existing condition is thus healthy, natural, and just, as before
remarked, it is quite likely that, in the future time, it may be
widely changed in its details. This relation—the subordination with the inseparable protection—can never be changed
without destruction to both, or without social suicide; but
the social condition may some day be modified sufficiently,
perhaps, to do away with any defects, if such exist at
present.

In another place the subject of climate and industrial adaptation is fully considered, and it will suffice to remark in this
place that the tropics are the natural centre of existence of the
negro, and some day not very remote our negro population,
with a few exceptions, perhaps, will be found within the intertropical region. And when that day comes, it is quite likely
that some modification will be worked out which, while the
essential principles of the existing condition are preserved,
chattelism, or that seeming personal property in the negro now
so extensively associated in the popular mind at the North as
wrong, may disappear altogether. We are only just emerging,

as it were, into a boundless field for progress, for inquiry, for experiment, for social development, for working out the great problem of humanity. All Europe is in utter ignorance and blindness; and if the whole political and social order is not in conflict with the natural order, the latter, is, at all events, repressed, and forbidden a development. We, ourselves, have reached a comparatively far advanced position—the grand position and declaration of the men of 1776, that all men (of course of our own race) are created equal, and designed by the Almighty for the same liberty, etc.; and we have based our political order on this fundamental and everlasting truth; but while in theory we have thus recognized the relations that nature has decreed between individuals, in practice we have made but little advance over the people of Europe.

Our cities and towns are filled to overflowing with poverty, ignorance, vice, and misery, and though much of this is the direct result of the wrongs and oppressions of the Old World, and all of it legitimate consequences of the European practice which yet prevails among us, especially in the States most connected by commerce, literature, and opinion with the Old World, our social progress is small, indeed, compared with our political enlightenment. But the masses are, however slow the progress, becoming more and more intelligent, and consequently more virtuous and happy, for, however frequent the exceptions among individuals, morality among the masses always keeps pace with their intelligence. And though the social condition at the South is less, infinitely less defective than at the North, and social progress in the future has a comparatively circumscribed field of action, there are many things, doubtless, which, in the future time, will be widely altered from the present. God has organized and fixed the nature and relations of His creatures, so that there is no conflict of duties, and that which best secures the happiness of ourselves, also accomplishes the happiness of others, whether they be our equals or our inferiors, men of our own race or negroes. Thus, when the dominant race—the citizenship of the South—comprehend most clearly and truly what their own welfare demands, then, too, and of necessity, will the best interests of the negro be secured. The perverse fanatics at the North, who, unmindful of, and indeed dead to the woes of their suffering brethren, imagine the most terrible miseries among negroes at the South, can not continue much longer in their unnatural delusions, and when the pressure of their attempted interference is withdrawn, earnest and conscientious citizens will doubtless inquire into those possible social defects that may exist among them, and strive to apply the appropriate corrections. What these defects may consist in, the writer does not assume to decide or to understand, but after a long-continued and patient investigation of the social condition of the South, he thinks he can not be mistaken when he declares that they are wholly or mainly confined to the citizenship, and he is wholly and absolutely incapable of comprehending any wrong whatever in the fundamental social relations of the races or so-called slavery of the South.

CHAPTER XVII.

THE *fact* that the negro is a negro, carries with it the inference or the necessity that his education—the cultivation of his
faculties, or the development of his intelligence—must be in
harmony with itself, and therefore must be an entirely different thing from the education of the Caucasian. The term
education, in regard to our own race, has widely different sig-
nifications. It may be the mere development of the mind, or
it may mean, with the cultivation of the intellect, the formation of the character, as Pope says:

> " 'Tis education forms the common mind;
> Just as the twig is bent, the tree 's inclined."

But without restricting the term to the former limit—the
development of the intelligence—it will be found that the education of the negro at the South is in entire harmony with his
wants, the character of his mind, the necessities of his mental
organism; and that they are the best educated negro population ever known in human experience.

Common sense and experience teach us to educate all creatures committed to our charge in accordance with their wants.
No one would presume to teach a horse as he would a dog, or
any other animal. We have our schools for girls as well as for
boys, and the education varies continually as the child changes
into youth, adolescence, and finally into manhood. The nature
and condition of the pupil are the great central facts—whether

a horse or a dog, a boy or a girl, a youth or a man, a negro or a Caucasian; the education must, if natural and proper, always hinge on this central fact. The negro brain and mental character, as has been shown, differs from our own both in degree and in quality, in the extent of its powers, and the form or modes of mental action. As still more strikingly manifest among animals, the negro child has more intelligence than the white of the same age. This is in harmony with the great fundamental law which renders the most perfectly organized beings most dependent on reason—in the parents, if not that of the offspring. The calf or pig of a month has more intelligence than the child of that age; the negro child has more than that of the Caucasian, but the character of this intelligence, of course, varies in each and every case. In the lower animals it is instinct; in the ease of the negro child it is more than instinct, but it is also radically different from that nascent rationality peculiar to the white child. Nevertheless, it is intelligence, and, as observed, more active in the negro child than in that of the white of the same age—an intelligence which enables it to preserve life where the former would, perhaps, perish, and thus to preserve the race amid the exigencies of savagism and the absence of care and forethought in the parents. It is this smartness of the negro child that has often deceived and deluded those perverse and deluded people of our own race, who get up negro schools. They see, or rather think they see, in this smartness the proof of their theories in regard to negroes, and parade their pets to admiring visitors with the utmost confidence in the justice and humanity of their exertions in behalf of an "oppressed and down-trodden race." But a few years more of these negro pupils would be sufficient (if any thing could be) to open the eyes of these perverted people, who, shutting their eyes and closing their ears to the ignorance and miseries of their own race, waste their money and time on a different one; indeed worse than waste, for they inflict much evil on the mistaken objects of their labors, evils though perhaps not traceable, that must necessarily attend every one of these negro pupils thus forced into a development opposed to the laws of their organism, and in contradiction to the negro nature.

The cultivation and development of the mental faculties, the mode or modes of education, are instinctive with our race, though constantly improved and perfected by reason resting on experience. The Greeks, Egyptians, and other ancient nations practiced substantially the system now common to modern times—that is, they taught their children by abstract lessons as well as oral instruction. They studied arithmetic, or the science of numbers, grammar, history, etc., under the direction of parents or guardians, as well as listened to lectures on rhetoric and philosophy in the " groves of the academy." History and biography were the legends and traditions of gods and goddesses, it is true, but modern history is mainly that of kings and queens, and as the former were once human, the only substantial difference consists in the greater accuracy of the latter.

The Mongol mind has its specific tendencies in this respect; that is, children are taught, not by abstract lessons, but by material emblems which represent *their* ideas. They have no history, in our sense of the term. It is utterly impossible that the Mongol mind can trace back events beyond a certain number of generations, and the crude and contradictory mass of nonsense which passes for Chinese history or the "Annals of China," is the work of Caucasian Tartars or those of predominating Caucasian innervation.

The negro has never taken one step towards mental development, as we understand it. He has never invented an alphabet—that primal starting-point in mental cultivation—he has

10

never comprehended even the simplest numerals—in short, has had no instruction and can give no instruction except that which is verbal and imitated, which the child copies from the parents, which is limited to the existing generation, and therefore the present generation are in the same condition that their progenitors occupied thousands of years ago. But the Almighty has adapted him to a very different condition from this fixed and non-progressive savagism. All the subordinate races have a certain capacity for imitating the higher habitudes of the Caucasian, unless it be the Mongol, which, perhaps, does not possess this faculty. The English have been masters in Hindostan for more than a century—their power rests on the same tenure of force on which it was founded—they have made no impression whatever on the habitudes of the Hindostanee—their language, their schools, their religion, their mental habits, are untouched, and it may be doubted if God ever designed that they should be in juxtaposition or made subject to a superior race.

In regard to the negro, there can be no doubt, not merely because, by himself, he is a non-producing and non-advancing savage, but because his entire structure, mental and physical, is adapted to juxtaposition. All the other races have a certain specific character to overcome first, or to be understood and properly harmonized, but the negro is a blank, a wilderness, a barren waste, waiting for the husbandman or the Caucasian teacher to develop his real worth, and gifted with his wonderful imitative powers, he not only never resists, but reaching forth his hands for guidance and protection, at once accepts his teacher, and submits himself to his control. Of the four millions now in our midst, a considerable proportion are the children of native Africans, indeed, there are not a few natives still among us, and yet everything connected with Africa— their traditions, language, religion, even their names have wholly disappeared. The Normans conquered the Saxons eight centuries ago, but the Saxon names, and even their language, are now as entirely Saxon as if a Norman had never landed on the shores of England. This blank, this feeble mental capacity and readiness of the negro nature to imitate the habits, bodily or mental, of the superior race, adapts the negro to his subordinate social position, and the purposes to which Providence has assigned him. The child-like intellect does not resist the strong and enduring mental energies of the Caucasian—its first impressions pass away in a few years, while its imitative capacities sit so gracefully on the negro nature that multitudes of ignorant people confound the real with the borrowed, and actually suppose that the " smart" negroes to be met with occasionally at the North are examples of native capacity. Of course, the borrowed intelligence is equally short-lived, and were our negroes carried back to Africa, they would lose what they had acquired here with the same rapidity that they have parted with their original Africanism, and names among them now celebrated would be as utterly lost a hundred years hence as their African names have disappeared here. These things being so, it obviously follows that negro " education" must be oral and verbal, or, in other words, that the negro should be placed in the best position possible for the development of his imitative powers—to call into action that peculiar capacity for copying the habits, mental and moral, of the superior Caucasian. It may be said that all mental instruction is through the imitative capacity, or that our own children are thus educated, but the negro mind, in essential respects, is always that of a child. The intelligence, as observed, is more rapidly developed in the negro child—those faculties more immediately connected with sensation, perception, and perhaps memory, are more energetic, but when they reach twelve and fifteen they diverge, the reflective faculties in the white are now called into action, the real Caucasian character now opens, the mental forces are fairly evolved, while the negro remains stationary—a perpetual child. The negro of forty or fifty has more experience or knowledge, perhaps, as the white man of that age has a more extended knowledge than the man of twenty-five, but the intellectual calibre—the actual mental capacity in the former case is no greater than it was at fifteen, when its utmost limits were reached—its entire power in full development.

The universal experience which, in this as many other in-stances, usually rests upon truth, leads the people of the South to designate the negro of any age as a " boy"—an expression perfectly correct, in an intellectual sense, as the negro reaches his mental maturity at twelve or fifteen, and viewed from our stand-point, is, therefore, always a boy. Indeed, this psycho-logical fact, together with his imitative instinct, constitutes the specific character of the race, and present the landmarks neces-sary for our guidance when dealing with the mental and moral wants of the negro. Intellectually considered, he is always a boy—a perpetual child—needing the care and guidance of his master, and his instinctive tendencies to imitate him, therefore, demand that, as in the case of children, the master should present him a proper example. His mental wants, it is be-lieved, are provided for, and his capabilities in these respects fully developed at the South. They are in pretty extensive intercourse with the white people; even on the large planta-tions they have the master's family or that of the overseer to copy after and to guide them, and though it may be that something more is needed, that a better mental training is pos-sible in the future, it is, at all events, certain that this verbal instruction is better adapted to their wants than the schools and colleges of a different and vastly superior race. If any one should propose to teach children of five the branches proper to those of ten and twelve years of age, or the latter those that occupy young men in the universities, it would be seen at a glance that this teaching was unnatural and improper. And our every-day experience will show that it is injurious, not alone to the mental, but to the bodily health of the pupil. The same or similar results must attend the school education of negroes. It is, perhaps, difficult to trace the consequences of negro education at the North. There are but few negroes, and the mulattoes and mongrels who pass for such must pay a penalty for this education according, doubtless, to their proportion of negro blood.

The mongrels, and possibly some negroes at the North, often seem as well educated as white men, but it must be at the expense of the body, shortening the existence, just as we sometimes witness in the case of children when the pride, vanity, or ignorance of parents have stimulated their minds, and dwarfed or destroyed their bodies. An " educated" negro, like a "free negro," is a social monstrosity, even more unnatural and repulsive than the latter.

It is creditable to the people of the South that no such outrage on nature and common sense is found in all her borders. God has made the negro an inferior being, not in most cases, but all cases, for there are no accidents or exceptions in His works. There never could be such a thing as a negro equaling the standard Caucasian in natural ability. The same Almighty Creator has also made all white men equal—for idiots, insane people, etc., are not exceptions, they are results of human vices, crimes, or ignorance, immediate or remote. What a false and vicious state of society, therefore, when human institutions violate this eternal order, and by withholding education from their own brethren, educate the inferior negro, and in a sense make him superior to white men, by setting aside the law of God!

Some of the States have passed laws against teaching negroes to read; a more extended and enlightened knowledge of the negro will, doubtless, some day govern this matter through public opinion, and without governmental interference. The negro learns from his master all he needs to know, all that he can know, in a proper sense, all that is essential to the perform- ance of his duties, or necessary to his happiness and the fulfil- ment of the purposes to which nature has adapted him; and though there might, perhaps, be no good reason given why he should be prohibited from learning to read, it is sufficient to say that it is absurd, as well as a waste of time that should be carefully employed. His mental powers are unable to grapple with science or philosophy, or abstractions of any kind, and it would be folly to suppose that he would be or could be inter- ested in history or biography, in which his race, his instincts, his wants have no share, record, or connection whatever.

All this applies, of course, to the South—to negroes in their normal condition and natural relation to the superior race. It may be well enough at the North, as long as they have mongrels and free negroes, to provide schools for them, as they have no other guide or protector but the State itself, but though they thus acquire a certain kind of mental activity, as observed, it is at the expense of the vital forces, and another of those incidental causes that tend to the final extinction of this abnormal element. It is, however, a disgrace, and, to a certain extent, a crime in any State to educate negroes or mongrels, so long as they have one single uneducated white man within their limits. The proof of this is seen every day in the *fact*, that however educated, or whatever the seeming mental superiority of the " colored" man, the uneducated white man tolerates no equality. Thus nature vindicates her rights, and whatever the ignorance, delusion, or crimes of society, the eternal order fixed by the hand of God is inevi- table and everlastin .

CHAPTER XVIII.

THE instinct of paternity—the love and care of offspring—is common to all creatures, animal and human, and is indeed necessary to the preservation of their existence. The animal frequently exhibits it more decidedly than the human creature, and however unseemly it may be, we, even our own supremely endowed race, may take a lesson from it. The animal instinct, however, is limited to the mere preservation of the life of its offspring, and the latter, when a certain development is reached, no longer needs it, for its own instinct then guides it to preserve itself.

The love, and care, and guidance of the Caucasian mother for her child is both a profound instinct and a lofty sentiment, and indeed calls into action the highest capabilities of her nature, her profoundest intelligence as well as the most exalted and self-sacrificing affection. It begins with the birth and ends only with the death, for though it is constantly modified by time and changes in the development of her offspring, it accompanies the latter through life, and disappears only at the portals of the grave.

God has endowed the parents with the highest intelligence, and laid on them the command or the duty of caring for their offspring—not the mere bodily preservation, as in the case of the animal, but the education, the guidance and development of the faculties, the moral capabilities as well as the intellectual powers of their children. He, therefore, has endowed them with affections of corresponding breadth and strength, and adapted them to these duties, and, moreover, rewards them with corresponding enjoyment or happiness in the affections and love of their offspring. These duties are too often imperfectly performed, indeed often misunderstood. They are sometimes delegated to others, sometimes carelessly fulfilled, and often disregarded altogether. They should never be delegated to others unless the loss of health or some imperative cause exists. The mother should always nurse her own child—if able to do so—and the parents should always educate their own children. In the main, this is done in our American society, for though children go to the public schools, the impress of the character is generally made at home. The child arriving at adult age, and no longer needing the care and guidance of the parents, marries and leaves home, but the affection of the parents, especially that of the mother, accompanies it through life, and not unfrequently, after a separation of forty years, it is found to be as strong and fresh as in the days of childhood. The large brain of the Caucasian mother, or her large intellectual nature, as has been said, is associated with corresponding capabilities of affection. The interests of life, the social welfare, the progress of civilization—in short, absolute social necessities, demand this, for were it otherwise, were the affections limited to the infancy of the offspring, society, as it now exists, or indeed anything at all resembling it, would obviously be impossible.

The interest of parents in their children, years after they have left home—their grandchildren, etc., though separated thousands of miles—their letters to them, their visits to the old homestead, and the ten thousand other nameless things that bind together those of the same blood, constitute a large portion of our social existence, and is indeed an essential part of our civilization. And *all* of this is dependent on the affec-

tions and in harmony with the elevated intellectualism of the
race, the breadth and strength of the former corresponding,
of course, with the mental endowments and specific capabilities of the Caucasian.

The negro, of course, is endowed with affections, approximating in some respects, indeed in many respects, to those of our
own race, but there are some things, some qualities in his
emotional nature utterly different, and then again some things
specific with us totally absent in the negro. The mother has
a similar love for her offspring at an early period in its existence, possibly stronger, or rather more imperatively instinctive, than that of the white woman. Instances are not unfre-
quent among the lower classes in England, and other European
countries, where mothers destroy their offspring, and painful as it is to acknowledge it, the same thing sometimes
happens at the North; but though an instance of the kind is
possible, there have been so few among negroes at the South
as to warrant us in saying that not one person in a thousand
has ever heard of such a thing. It is true, the negro is in a
normal condition, and the European peasant is, to a certain
extent, in an abnormal one, and vice and crime, and consequent
misery, are always in exact proportion to the extent of the
latter in all races. Nevertheless, it is quite certain that, both
living under equally favorable circumstances, the negress is less
likely to destroy the life of her offspring than is the white
woman. Her maternal instincts are more imperative, more
closely approximate to the animal, while that sense of degradation which the higher nature and more elevated sensibilities
of the white woman prompts to the hiding of her shame by
the destruction of her offspring, is entirely absent in the negress.
She may possibly destroy her child in a paroxysm of rage, but
here nature has guarded her too strongly by the imperative maternal instinct, while those ten thousand chances in our higher
10*

habitudes and social complications which may involve the most exquisite suffering of the unhappy mother, and impel her, by one terrible and supreme crime, to destroy her own offspring, can never happen or influence the negro mother.

A few years since a " slave" woman escaping from Kentucky to Ohio was recognized and taken back to her home, but on the way down the river cut the throat of her child, whom she had carried off in her flight. The Abolitionists, of course, admired and praised this bloody deed, and declared that, rather than her child should live a slave, she, with Roman sternness and French exaltation, herself destroyed its life. If they had said that the mother had killed her child because it was not permitted to have a white skin, or straight hair, or to have any other *specialty* of white people, it would have been quite as rational and as near the truth as to say that she killed it because it was not to grow up with the freedom of the white man. The woman was doubtless a mulatto or mongrel, who in revenge possibly for the supposed wrong, inflicted this punishment on those whom she had been taught to believe had wronged her. But while this unnatural crime was quite possible, as indeed any unnatural vice or crime is always possible to the mixed element, it is scarcely possible to the negress, whose imperative maternal instinct, as has been observed, shields her from such atrocity. The negro mother has always control and direction of her offspring at the South so long as that is needed by the latter. The master, of course, is the supreme ruler—the guide, director, the common father, the very providence of these simple and subordinate people, but while his is the directing power that sees to all their wants, and protects them in all their rights, the relations of mother and child are rarely interfered with, for both the interests of the master and the happiness of the mother demand that she should have the care and enjoy the affection of her own offspring. This, however, is confined to a limited sphere when contrasted with the instinctive habitudes and enlarged intellec- tualism of our own race. The negro child, in some respects, at the same age, is more intelligent than the white child. This same fact is manifested by our domestic animals. The dog or calf of six months is vastly less dependent on the mother than the human creature. The negro child, with its vastly greater approximation to the animal, is also less dependent at a cer- tain age than the white child. As frequently stated in this work, the negro has absolutely nothing in common with ani- mals that our own race has not.

There is an impassable chasm, wide as it is deep and ever- lasting, between the human and animal creation. But while the negro has nothing whatever in common with animals that we ourselves have not, in all those things or qualities in a sense common to both men and animals, the negro has a vastly larger approximation to the latter. As the intelligence or the capac- ity of providing for itself, therefore, is more rapidly developed in the animal, so, too, in the case of the negro child, at a cer- tain age it is less dependent on the care and affection of the mother than is that of white people. Those ignorant and per- verse persons who stifle the impulses and sympathies with which God has endowed them for their kind, and engage in teach- ing, as they suppose, negro children, have been so impressed by this fact, that in their utter ignorance of the negro nature, they have inferred that the latter was really the superior race; they have often found a negro boy or girl of ten years, for example, whose perceptions, memory, etc., seemed to them, and, doubtless, sometimes were, more clear, prompt, and de- cided, than those of white children of the same age, and there- fore they were quite convinced of the superiority of the negro and of the sublimity and immensity of their own labors in thus helping on the intellectual development of a wronged and down-trodden but really superior race.

But if they could have followed out the future of these children for a few years, and were persons of sufficient underderstanding to analyze facts at all, they would have made a still more startling discovery than that of the fancied superiority of the negro. The negro mind reaches its maturity, its complete development, at from twelve to fifteen years, and though there may be vastly more knowledge or experience, the negro of fifty has no more actual mental capacity than he had at fifteen. The faculties directly dependent on the senses are actively and rapidly developed in the negro child, but the reflective faculties, the faculties in regard to which the senses are mere avenues through which external influences are conveyed to the brain, are absent, of course, in the negro, for there is an absence of brain itself, and therefore it is just as absurd to imagine him possessing them as to suppose the sense of sight in any creature without eyes or without an organism for that faculty. The white boy, on the contrary, only begins at this age to manifest the reflective faculties, which, constantly expanding, doubtless reach their maturity from twenty to twenty-five. Of course the mind may continue to expand in a sense for many years, for a life-time, but the actual mental capabilities, like those of the body, doubtless reach their normal standard from twenty to twenty-five. Thus, a white boy and negro of ten, with the faculties directly dependent on the senses possibly most active in the latter, begin a year or two later to diverge from each other. The negro at fifteen, with scarcely perceptible reflective faculties, remains stationary, while the Caucasian, with constantly increasing powers, with imagination, comparison, and reflection, superadded to the mere perceptive faculties, requires several years more for the development of his complete intellectual nature. It is not merely that the negro mind becomes stationary at twelve to fifteen, for to *them* it is complete development, but if we can suppose a white boy of twelve to fourteen remaining thus—mentally considered—through life, then we can form a pretty accurate conception of the mental differences between white men and negroes, for the latter are intellectually boys for ever. This is a common and familiar expression at the South, which originates in the nature and necessities of things, and the term boy expresses the intellectual existence of the negro as truthfully as the term *man* expresses the physical condition of the white man.

The affections harmonize, of course, with the mental nature, and the love of the negro mother corresponds with the wants of the offspring. She has a boundless affection for her infant; it grows feebler as the capacities of the child are developed; at twelve to fifteen she is relatively indifferent to it; at forty she scarcely recognizes it; and all of these phases in the maternal instinct or domestic affections of the race are in accord with its specific nature and the purposes assigned it by the Almighty Creator. Without the enlarged brain and reasoning power of the white mother, nature has made amends to the negress, and provided for the wants of her offspring by giving her a more imperative maternal instinct, that shall insure its safety and welfare. When the negro reaches maturity, at twelve to fifteen, nature has accomplished her purposes. The offspring no longer needs her care, and the mother becomes indifferent to it, and it cares little for the mother. A few years later, and she forgets it altogether, for her affections corresponding with her intellectual nature, there is no basis, or material, or space for such things. Of course, living in juxtaposition with the superior race, and the imitative faculty of the negro constantly brought into action, there is a seeming resemblance to white people in these respects. But one only needs to remember the

mental qualities of the negro—the small and widely different
brain, and consequently feeble, and, as compared with us, limited sphere of intellectualism, to see the absurdity of endowing the negro with domestic affections corresponding with
ours. At twelve to fifteen, as has been said, the purposes of
nature are accomplished. The offspring no longer needs the
care of the mother—the affections with which nature endowed
her are no longer needed. Why should they exist, then?
Isolated in Africa, they perhaps rarely feel any interest in their
offspring after the latter reach maturity, and, separated a few
years, would not know them, would have no recollection of
them, for there is no civilization, no social development, nothing
whatever of that which we call society, and in which with us
the domestic affections—the family relationship—the love of
mother, wife, sisters, brothers, and offspring constitute so large
and essential a part. The limited intelligence of the negro, the
small brain and feeble (scarcely perceptible) reasoning faculties, it will be evident to the reader, must be accompanied by
corresponding domestic affections and an emotional nature that
accords with this limited intellectualism. And this is manifested in the habits, wants, and condition of the negro at the
South, in his feeble and capricious love for his wife and indifference to his offspring, redeemed only in the potent and instinctive affection of the mother in its earlier years for her
child. The strongest affection the negro nature is capable of
feeling is love of his master, his guide, protector, friend, and
indeed Providence, who takes care of him in sickness and
shelters and provides for him in old age and helplessness. God
has adapted all His creatures for the wisest and most beneficent purposes, has endowed the negro with affections harmonizing with his wants, has given the negro mother imperative
maternal instincts that shall secure the safety and welfare of
her offspring, but little more, for little more is needed; for

society or civilization neither does nor can belong to negro existence, while affection for his master, love and devotion to him who protects and provides for him through life, is both a necessity and an enjoyment, and therefore God has made it the strongest and most enduring feeling of the negro nature. Of the four or five millions in our midst, great numbers are the children or grand-children of African parents, a few even are of African birth, but probably not one has any distinct memory, recollection, or tradition of their forefathers*—not one that cherishes any past family sentiment or affection of any kind whatever, indeed not one that even preserves an African name! We trace back not alone the general but the family histories, the loves and affections, the hopes and fears, and sacrifices and sufferings of our pilgrim forefathers of two or three centuries ago, because all this accords with the large brain and expanded intellectualism, and the corresponding strength and breadth of the affections, which may be said to be the motive forces which impel the whole social phenomena in question. But the negro neither has nor can have any thing in common with this. He has no capacities of the kind, no civilization or social development, and therefore no wants of the kind, no affections even resembling our own, though at the same time God has endowed him with all that is necessary to his happiness and to the mutual welfare of both races when in juxtaposition.

The affection of the mother for her child, and the husband for the wife, though widely different from that which we witness in our own race, is abundantly sufficient for the purposes that nature has in view, and with the accomplishment of these

---

* These facts, and some others mentioned in this chapter, were referred to in a previous one, but they need to be repeated in this connection to fix them fully on the mind of the reader, as well as to explain the subject here under discussion.

purposes they subside. The affection for the master, which is necessary to their welfare through life, remains—the sole enduring affection of the negro nature, as it is obviously the sole permanent want of the negro existence. The laws and legislation of the Southern States generally accord with these facts of the negro nature, for though those who have made these laws were unable to explain them even to themselves, their every-day experience and practical knowledge of the negro enable them to legislate for the wants and welfare of these people as well and justly as for themselves. Probably all, or nearly all of the States forbid the separation of the mother and child, so long as the maternal instinct remains, or her care of her offspring is needed by the latter ; and even if there be no law of this kind on the statute-book of some States, it is in the hearts and instincts of the dominant race, and is equally potent in the form of public sentiment to prevent such an outrage on nature as the forced separation of mother and child.

There are, doubtless, instances where wrong is done at the South, as well as elsewhere, to the subordinate negro as well as to our own kind, but with the same political and social system as that of the North, and with vastly more political intelligence and faithfulness to the principles of that system, it is only reasonable to conclude that, in regard to the negro element, the same enlightened spirit of justice and fair dealing generally pervades Southern society. And when it is remembered that the social adaptation is in harmony with the natural relations of the races, and not only that there is no social conflict, but, on the contrary, that it is the utmost interest of the master to treat his negroes kindly, then whatever the temporary exceptions, the general result must be in favor of the happiness and welfare of these people.

CHAPTER XIX.

MARRIAGE.

NOTHING, perhaps, is so repugnant to the northern mind as the notion that marriage does not exist among the "slaves" of the South, and the Abolition lecturers have given this subject the most prominent place in their terrible bill of indictment against their southern brethren. The spectacle, or the seeming spectacle, of four millions of human beings living without marriage, without family, without children, with nothing but offspring, shut out, like the brutes that perish, from all the household charities, and doomed to live in universal concubinage, as it has been termed, was, to the northern and European mind, such a stupendous outrage on "humanity," that we need not wonder at their fierce indignation, or at the wild and unsparing denunciation heaped upon the authors of such boundless and unparalleled iniquity. Especially were northern women shocked and indignant, and above all others, the women of New England were excited at times to a "Divine fury" when contemplating this mighty "wickedness." Our fair countrywomen are believed to be equally virtuous and lovely, but the *domestic* education of those of New England, in some respects, is more admirable than that of others or any other country. They are taught to labor, to be their own housekeepers, to regard life, and the duties of life, as a solemn mission to be faithfully and conscientiously fulfilled, and though it imparts a certain materialism bordering on hardness, perhaps, to the New England woman, it is associated with such simple and trans-

parent love of truth, and such an earnest and abiding sense of
duty, that the harsher features of the character are lost in
these gentler and more exalted qualities. Hence they are
taught to regard a violation of the family relation as the one
most heinous and unpardonable sin. To women thus educated,
with the utmost abhorrence of any violation of marital obligations, the seeming universal disregard of this relation, and
the duties embraced in it, among the "slaves" of the South,
was probably the most transcendent wrong that the mind
could conceive of, and the "anti-slavery" delusion of the
North has doubtless been increased to a considerable extent
by this strictness or severity of female education. And if the
facts were what they suppose, then indeed would their indignation and abhorrence be just enough, but strange that they
should never have doubted or mistrusted these facts. Many
of the most intelligent have known their sisters of the South,
known them to be as virtuous, refined and womanly as themselves, and yet living every day of their lives in the shadow of
this mighty wrong, and in the midst of this supposititious iniquity. Could that be possible? Could woman retain her
purity, her womanly delicacy, or expand into the full stature
of a true womanhood with such surroundings, in an atmosphere thus corrupt and corrupting, in a social condition where
four millions of people were living without marriage, in open
and utter disregard of the fundamental principle of morality
as well as of social order? No, indeed, it could not be possible, and, as remarked, it is strange that the women of the
North have not had misgivings of this kind, or have not mistrusted the assumed *facts* of "negro slavery" in this respect.
But before the actual facts involved are presented to the reader, it is necessary to clearly understand what marriage itself
is. It may be defined as the pledge of two persons of different sex to live together for life—pledged to each other and to

society, for the presence of witnesses to a marriage contract
or a marriage ceremony has simply this meaning, and none
other. With us marriage is a mere civil or legal contract. It
is the same in France, and, to a certain extent, in England, but
in other countries it is combined with religious considerations,
and the Catholic church makes it a sacrament. This. is marriage, as ordinarily understood, as the necessities of the social
order compel us to accept and regard it. Nevertheless, every
one's instincts will assure him that marriage consists in reality
of vastly more than this description of it. A man and woman
may pledge themselves to each other and to society—all the
legal and customary forms may be complete, and yet we know,
or may know that there is no true marriage, for these parties
may be entirely indifferent, or even objects of actual dislike to
each other. The obligations or duty to society may be fulfilled, the interests of families provided for, the legal rights of
the parties themselves properly protected, even the welfare of
offspring appropriately guarded, nevertheless, if the parties are
not united by affection, by those mysterious affinities with
which God Himself has endowed them, and for this precise
purpose, then there is no true marriage, and, abstractly considered, they are as entirely separate as if they stood on different sides of the Atlantic instead of at the altar where the ceremony is being performed. It is clear, therefore, that marriage,
truly considered, involves vastly more than the mere external
ceremony or legal formularies, which the universal interest
demands, however, as an essential accompaniment. "Increase
and multiply" is an ordinance of nature as well as the command of holy writ. All the innumerable tribes of inferior
beings obey this command with a regularity, order and completeness that admit of no exception or interruption. They
are all governed by instinct, by a wise necessity which impels
them to fulfill this Divine decree and in modes adapted to their

specific nature. Birds choose their mates, are faithful to them, share together, in some instances, the care and nurture of the common offspring, and all other animals of the higher order exhibit a tendency to form these temporary unions. But in addition to the natural instinct impelling us, in common with all other creatures, to fulfill the universal command to "multiply and replenish the earth," the Almighty Creator has given us reason and endowed us with capacities of affection which are designed to guide us in these respects. A youth and maiden are thrown into each other's society, an acquaintance, an intimacy, a mutual affection and reciprocal love follow. They feel themselves united, not merely harmonized, but morally consolidated, as it were, into a single being, and they mutually pledge each other to be thus as long as they both shall live. They are united, not by their pledges to each other, their mutual declarations of affection, but by those beautiful and mysterious affinities that God has planted in the soul itself, and the pledges and promises are the mere outward expression of their actual existence.

It is thus sometimes said that marriages are made in Heaven, for there is an eternal fitness, a complete unity or oneness in these impalpable agencies which, whatever may be the seeming incongruities of character in some instances, thus link together for ever these human souls as well as persons. Alas! that it should so often be mistaken—that pride and vanity, or a groveling and sinful lust, should be imposed on the simple and loving heart of woman as the counterpart of her own glowing and beautiful affection; and the man guilty of this frightful sin, this "gallantry," as the corrupt and rotten society of Europe designates the desecration of a woman's soul, commits a crime infinitely more atrocious than murder or the mere destruction of the body of his victim. Unfortunately, too, accident, imperfect education, circumstances, a thousand things may and do lead both parties to mistake each other or themselves, and to rush into marriage only to discover a few months later, that they were deluded and deceived, and instead of that perfect unity of feeling, of affection, of soul, which they had believed in, there were contradictions and repugnances that no gentleness of temper or strength of reason or length of time could ever change, and therefore in sullen despair they settle down into hopeless apathy, or still worse, shock and scandalize society by a reckless violation of its laws as well as of the personal vows so sacredly pledged at the altar. But when the instincts of natural affection have been guided by reason and a true perception of the wants and nature of each other, and that perfect unity of feeling and of purpose exists which flows from this reciprocal adaptation of the parties, then there is marriage in its true sense, for then two relatively imperfect beings are united into one complete whole. And if we could suppose this husband and wife living for themselves alone, and isolated from all association with others, then nothing more would be needed. They were united by affection, by adaptation, by true perceptions of each other's wants, by those mysterious affinities which we call love, in short, by an organic and eternal fitness, and their mutual pledges would be abundantly sufficient for themselves. But we are not permitted to suppose such a thing as isolation or separation from others, or from society. Our existence is necessarily complex, and our duties relative as well as personal, and therefore, marriage must be witnessed, and pledges given to society as well as made to each other, for the due fulfilment of the duties involved. A modern doctrine, if it may be called thus, has been set up that people who have mistaken their "affinities," and only discovered their true ones after marriage, have a right to correct their mistakes and form a new marital union which they may suppose essential to their happiness. But they would disregard utterly their relations to others, their duties to society, their reciprocal obligations to their fellows, and trample on the fundamental principle of social order, indeed, society would itself be rendered utterly impossible could such individual caprice and selfishness prevail to any considerable extent. All their so-called arguments against the "institution" of marriage are, therefore, simply absurd, for while their conception of an essential portion of it may be correct enough as far as it goes, the assumption that the parties are alone responsible to each other, and are not called on to give pledges to society in the form of a civil contract or legal and indissoluble marriage, is founded on a total misconception or total disregard of their relations to others and of the duties necessarily involved. But enough on this point. Marriage is a natural relation that springs spontaneously from the necessities of human existence, and though a civil contract, it has a deeper and holier significance than the mere external ceremony or pledge which is thus given to the world as well as to each other.

Marriage, is of course, a natural relation among negroes as well as ourselves, and were it true that these four millions of people were living without it, then the denunciations heaped upon the people of the South would doubtless be merited. But a moment's reflection should be sufficient to convince any one, at all events any American, that with a different nature, with different faculties, different wants, and different duties of these people, there must follow a different form or modification of this relation. The negro is substantially a child or undeveloped and undevelopable man, with affections, moral wants and faculties approximating, of course, to our own, but yet so different that his happiness as well as that of the white man demands a corresponding development. The affection of the sexes strongly resembles that of our school-children. It is

sudden, capricious, superficial, and temporary, and sometimes
violent, but rarely permanent, or would be rarely permanent
were it not for the example of the whites, whose habitudes in
these respects the imitative instincts of the negro impel him
to copy after. In their native Africa, and without the influence and example of the superior race, polygamy is universal,
the affection of the husband being a mere caprice in most
cases, they sell their wives and children without compunction,
but the mother, with that universal maternal instinct common
to all human creatures, and to animals of the higher classes,
clings tenaciously to her offspring, while perfectly willing to
change husbands or owners, as they really are in fact. Many
of the "rich men" of Africa are only so in the number of their
wives and children, and they trade and traffic in this property
as coolly and regularly as if they were legitimate subjects of
commerce. Nevertheless, the natural law and the natural ten-
deney of this people is to a single union, and probably a large
majority of the native Africans have only one wife. There is
no natural tendency to polygamy in any race, for the numbers
of the sexes being equal, the natural impulse is to a single
union. But their feeble and capricious affections lead to polygamy, and their incapacity to purchase or support wives is the
only limit to the negro practice in these respects. Under the
teachings and restraints of the superior race at the South, the
negroes, male and female, are vastly elevated in this regard, as
well as others above their African habitudes. They form sexual unions or marry essentially like the whites. The parties
become intimate, an affection springs up, they ask and receive
the consent of their masters, and they are married by a white
clergyman or by a minister of their own people. Thus far,
marriage among "slaves" is, on the surface at least, an exact
copy of the marriage of whites. They ask the consent of their
masters, as white persons ask the consent of their parents **or**

guardians, and they are married with the same ceremonies either by a minister of their own, or, as very often occurs, by a white clergyman. But here they diverge. The negro does not and can not constitute a part or portion of that mighty fabric we term society. He has no social interests, no property to guard or to devise, for though he receives and enjoys a larger portion of the proceeds of his labor than any mere laborer in Europe, every thing legally belongs to the master. There are no family interests for which to provide, no reputation or character to protect, no social duties to perform, or rights to defend in his case; in short, he has no connection whatever with that vast and complicated machinery which we call society. Marriage, therefore, from our stand-point—that legal formula and social pledge so vital to the very existence of social order—is obviously absurd and impossible in the case of negroes. The natural affinity, the union of affection, the perfect adaptation so essential to a true marriage in our race, is substantially imitated and substantially similar in the case of negroes at the South, but to seek to force the negro beyond this—to force upon him the social responsibilities that attach to white people; or, in other words, to make marriage a legal contract in the case of negroes, would be as absurd as to force him to vote at an election, or to perform any other high social duties, and which are evidently impossible. In regard to his own wants, the well-being of his offspring, every thing connected with the best welfare and highest happiness that his race is capable of, he now enjoys, and any attempt to force him to marry as white people marry—that is, to make marriage a civil or legal contract—is not merely impossible, but it would be a crime and a monstrous outrage upon the nature God has given him. The Almighty has endowed the negro with wonderful imitative powers: of course, it is impossible for him to

imitate all our higher ·qualities—he can only approximate to
them—but when the master has presented him with a proper
example, in this respect as well as in other respects, as parents
and guardians are expected to do in the case of children, they
have fulfilled their duties to these "slaves," and generally the
negro is restrained and governed by these examples. But the
feeble and capricious affections of the negro give their masters
much annoyance, and perhaps the greatest trouble they experience with these people is their faithlessness to their marital
obligations. The ignorant "anti-slavery" lecturer at the North
has distressing tales to tell of cruel masters who separate wives
and husbands, and break up families; but while such things
have doubtless happened, it is quite certain that masters have
interfered a hundred times to keep them together to one
instance to the contrary, or to sell them apart. Such things
happen occasionally, when estates are to be settled and property divided; but the instincts of the whites and the happiness of the whites are more disturbed by them than the negroes
themselves. The limited intellectual power—the feeble moral
nature, and superficial and capricious affections of the negro
lead him to regard these separations of wives and husbands—
of parents and children, with indifference, or rather we should
say he has none of our perceptions or our instincts in respect
to these family relations, and therefore when they do happen
he is relatively or comparatively unconscious of suffering. In
his native Africa he sells his wife and children without hesitation, and all the suffering he now feels is borrowed or imitated from the whites—a feeling scarcely perceptible in his native
state, but in his better and higher life at the South, it is doubtless exalted into something like a sentiment of family. Nevertheless, he readily adapts himself to whatever changes the
chances of life may bring him, and where the white husband,
and certainly the white wife, might despair and die, the negro
11

and the negress, with new partners and another marriage, are
quite as happy as if they had never been separated from their
former ones.

But these things are exceptional, and husbands and wives
are doubtless far less frequently forced apart by these accidents
of society than are the wives and husbands of the "lower
orders" in England by the pressure of want and that necessity
of self-preservation which so often rends them asunder. The
real trouble, however, as has been said, is in the negro himself
—his feeble and capricious affections—substantially similar to
those of white childhood, and which it requires the constant su-
pervision and influence of the master to restrain so as to keep
them faithful to each other. The limited mental endowment
and the feeble moral perceptions of the negro render him incapable, in these respects, of little beyond the fulfilment of the
universal command to "increase and multiply." White husbands and wives, when one dies in early life, often remain
unmarried, faithful to a memory forever; and still more frequently, perhaps, the affections that bound them together in
their youth remain bright and untarnished in age and to the
borders of the grave. Such a thing never happened with a
negro. Not one of the countless millions that have lived upon
the earth was ever kept from marrying a second time by a
sentiment or a memory. With their limited moral endowment
such a thing is an absolute moral impossibility. They live
with each other to extreme old age, because they imitate the
superior race, and because it has become a habit, perhaps, but
the grand purposes of nature accomplished, there is little or
nothing more, or of those blessed memories of joy and suffering—of early hope and chastened sorrows, which so bind and
blend together the white husband and wife, and often render
them quite as necessary to each other's happiness as in the
flush and vigor of youth. Affection for his master is, in fact,

the strongest, and it may be said to be the only enduring affection of the negro nature, for it remains an ever-present feeling
long after the feeble and capricious "family sentiment," or
love of wife and offspring, is entirely obliterated from his
memory. Marriage of "Southern slaves" thus briefly presented, will be seen to be as real, decent, orderly, and natural,
as the nature of the negro admits of, or relatively speaking, as
the Almighty Creator himself has designed or decreed. *He*
has endowed the negro with different and vastly subordinate
moral wants and affections, but at the same time given him an
imitative capacity that enables him to copy the higher nature
and more exalted habitudes of the superior race. They therefore marry as white people marry, with the same forms and the
same ceremonies, and such a thing as polygamy, or what the
"Abolitionist" calls concubinage, is utterly unknown among
these people. They are no portion or part of society, have no
place in the social compact, they are unable to fulfil its duties,
and therefore have none of its rights, hence legal marriage is
obviously absurd and impossible. To the ignorant Abolition
writer it may seem quite plain that marriage should be a civil
contract with negroes as well as white people, for his theory
that the negro is a *black* Caucasian, neutralizes all difficulties in
this as in other things. But even they must see that to force
them on the same social level in this vital respect must necessarily involve social equality in all other respects—a result, unless their theory be sound, obviously unnatural, monstrous, and
wicked. The negro, isolated in his native Africa, is at this
moment exactly what he was four thousand years ago, selling
his wives and offspring with as utter disregard of marital relations, and unconsciousness of a family sentiment, as in the
time of the Pharaohs; and when we contrast these things—
the universal polygamy, the trade in wives, the caprice and
savagism of the lawless husband or master with the decent and

Christian marriage of " Southern slaves," imitated from the superior race, and generally restrained by its example, may we not say with entire reverence and truth, that marriage, as it now actually exists among these people at the South, being all that their natures are capable of, and all that their wants and their highest happiness demand, is also, and of necessity, all that God Himself has decreed or designed in respect to this race ?

There is no other comparison to make, or contrast to present, but that of African savagism; for that modern product of a world-wide delusion, " freedom," or free negroism, as shown elsewhere, is a social abnormalism, a diseased condition, that necessarily ends in extinction ; and unless it can be proven that disease is preferable to health, and death itself a greater good than life, no argument or proof drawn from it is legitimate or allowable.

CHAPTER XX.

THE surface of the earth is naturally divided into zones or centres of existence. These great centres of creation have each their *Fauna* and *Flora*, their animal and vegetable life peculiar to themselves alone. Geographical writers use these terms, and speak of the temperate, frigid, and torrid zones, etc., as mere designations of certain portions of the earth where the climate is widely varied; but this is very subordinate to the real differences that separate the great centres of organic life. All creatures, indeed all organic and living things, have their centres of existence, their local habitations, their places in the mighty programme of creation. They are all adapted to these great centres of life—their organic structure, their faculties, and the purposes they were designed to fulfil, all harmonizing with their localities, the positions the Almighty has assigned to them. There are approximating forms of life, certain genera among animals and plants, that may be said to belong to the same family or group, but which are found in different zones or centres of existence, but there is no such thing as the same *species* being found in more than one centre of creation. All the animals and plants of Europe are, therefore, different from those of America, as all the creatures that belong to the northern region of this continent are specifically different from those of the tropics.

Each and every *specific* creation is different from every other specific existence, and differs just as widely in the circumstances that surround it, and to which it is adapted, as it does in its own organic structure. If an animal, for example, it has a special structure with special instincts, qualities, etc., and the external circumstances, the climate, the vegetation, all things are in perfect harmony. This law may be said to be universal, for the few seeming exceptions scarcely deserve notice. There are a few plants and cereals suited to all climates. The potato, of American origin, is cultivated with equal success in Europe, while most of our ordinary vegetables are of European origin. Wheat grows with equal luxuriance in the Valley of the Nile, the table lands of Mexico, and the great Northwest. But while all of these things, and many more, are thus capable of successful cultivation in different localities from those in which they were originally created, the external conditions must be preserved—the same or similar soil, and, to a certain extent, the same climate or the same heat and moisture are essential in their cultivation. This is also generally true of animals. Our domestic animals are all suited to different climates. The horse, dog, ox, sheep, etc., are of European origin—some of them Asiatic—and they live and multiply with equal certainty under the fervid suns of the tropics, or amid the icy blasts of the extreme North. They are striking exceptions, however, to the general law which adapts all creatures to their own centres of existence, and, it would seem, were designed by the Almighty and beneficent Creator for the especial purpose of benefiting man. They have accompanied him in all his wanderings, especially the dog and horse, shared his fortunes, aided in fighting his battles, and however subordinate, played an important *rôle* in the civilization of mankind. They are closely associated in this capacity for resisting external circumstances with man himself, that is, the Caucasian, or master man, who, as regards mere climate, is capable of living and of enjoying the healthy development of all his faculties in all climates alike, unless, perhaps, the polar regions, or extreme North. As a general law, all creatures, as they ascend in the scale of being, become less and less subject to external influences ; but some of our domestic animals are certainly exceptions, for the dog and horse, at all events, are capable of living where the negro, and possibly the Mongol, would surely become extinct. The same general laws of climate affect the human races, not exactly similarly, of course, but approximatively as they do animals, and with a certain modification, as they do plants—that is, they have all centres of existence to which they are *specifically* adapted, with the sole exception of the Caucasian, as some of our domestic animals, and indeed some vegetable existences are exceptions. The white man, as has been said, can exist everywhere, where life of any kind is possible, except the extreme North, and even here, as shown by Kane and other explorers in those bleak and barren regions, by proper precautions, or by complying with certain conditions, life is possible for certain periods. He is, doubtless, designed for the temperate latitudes, industrially considered, but, as regards climate, he is at home everywhere. Writers, ignorant of the laws of climate, and indeed ignorant of the specific character of races, have supposed that they become weak, effete, and imbecile in tropical latitudes, and this notion is, perhaps, very generally entertained by otherwise intelligent people. The population found in these regions are negro, Indian, or Malay, intermixed often with white blood, and these inferior people are supposed to be a result of climate, and to exhibit the natural consequences of a warm and enervating atmosphere ! The white man under the equator, living, or rather attempting to live, the life of the negro—to labor under the rays of a vertical sun— would rapidly decline and die, for his organic structure could not resist the external influences that tend to destroy him. The *malaria* springing from the decomposition of the rank vegetation, which ascends in the early portion and descends to the earth in the later portion of the day, would soon poison all the springs of life, and fever would close the scene. Any attempt at labor in midday would be still more rapidly fatal, for the caloric generated by the exertion, without an excretory system to relieve it, would end in fatal congestions of the vital organs, especially the brain. We constantly witness an approximation to this in our Western States and Territories, where nearly a generation voluntarily sacrifice themselves in the effort of preparing comfortable homes for their offspring. But after a certain progress is made, the causes of disease subside, and the temperate climate enables them to labor at all times.

But while the white man is forever forbidden by the laws of his physical nature to labor, or by his own hands to grow the natural products of the tropics, he can live there, and enjoy all his faculties of mind and body with the same certainty and success that belong to the temperate latitudes. It may be that the temptations to indulgence, to voluptuousness, or to the gratification of the animal appetites, are greater in these warm and glowing climes, but surely no more so than in our own summers, compared with the winter or other less attractive seasons. On the contrary, the necessities of cleanliness and the less potent demand for stimulants, with the cooling and delicious fruits of the tropics, tend to delicacy of tastes and appetites. At all events, it is certain that the grossest, most brutal, and most immoral populations of Europe are found in the far north, while those of southern Europe are the most temperate and the most delicate in their habitudes of any people in the world. But climate has little, if any, influence in these respects. The white man under the same circumstances is the same being, and his grossness and immorality, or his delicacy, temperance, and morality, are things of chance, according as he has been educated, and circumstances, public and private, have formed his character. As a master, as the guide and protector of the subordinate negro, he may live wherever the latter can, otherwise the negro would have been created in vain—a blank in the economy of the universe, a contradiction in the designs of Providence, and a blotch on the fair form of creation. Generally speaking, climate or other external circumstances have influence over the life, either human or animal, according as they are low in the scale of being, and therefore while the Caucasian man can live and enjoy the full development of all his powers in the tropics, the negro and other inferior races are absolutely limited to their own centres of existence. The Mongols have been confined to those portions of Asia where they now exist, ever since known to history, for though in the mighty invasions of Genghis Khan, Tamerlane, and others, when millions of them spread like a flood over other regions, and even as far as Chalons, in France, they almost as rapidly receded, and are now just where history first found them.

The modern slave-trade, carried on so extensively by the English of our day, where these people, under various pretexts, are placed aboard ships and sent to Jamaica, and other West Indian Islands, to supply the place of the abandoned negro, must be a far greater wrong than the importation of negroes from Africa, for it is a violation of the laws of climate that must rapidly destroy them, while in the case of the negro he is still within that centre of existence, where God himself placed him. The Malay, too, is in his own centre of life, and like all the inferior races, never migrates from it. The Esquimaux, buried in the bleak and desolate North, never ventures beyond it, and should he be carried into the tropics by the white man, would doubtless soon succumb under its burning suns. We know but little of the Indian or aboriginal in these respects. They now constitute the industrial forces of Mex-

11*

ico, and, except Brazil, of all South America. There are some ten millions of them, and as we know that the negro never can labor on the table-lands, or live at all in an atmosphere several thousand feet above the level of the sea, it may become a question of immense importance to the civilization of this continent to determine the natural position and our true relations to this race. The negro, more distinctly, perhaps, than any other race, is limited to his centres of life. If Dr. Kane had taken any with him in his Northwest explorations, it is hardly possible that they could have lived through it, if of pure negro type. His organic structure, while as perfectly adapted to a tropical climate as the eye is to sight or any other organism to a given purpose or function, utterly forbids him to live beyond a certain latitude. An individual may do so, of course, or a generation or more may linger out a miserable existence, but his structure forbids that he should multiply himself or become a permanent resident in the extreme north. There are great numbers in Canada, the result of that wide-spread ignorance of his true nature that has worked out such tremendous evils to these poor people as well as to the deluded and mistaken whites. Their situation in Canada is the most miserable, perhaps, that human beings can possibly endure. It would be miserable enough if they had masters, guides, protectors, and providers for their wants, but, without these, with none of the external circumstances with which God surrounded them when He first called them into being, and then left to compete with white men for the means of subsistence, it is repeated that their condition must be the most deplorable to which unhappy human creatures could be subjected. The constant accession to their numbers through the Underground Railroad renders any thing like an estimate of the fatality among them quite out of the question, but when, in addition to their abnormal social condition, there is the pressure of an unnatural climate or of external influences utterly opposite to those that God originally provided for them, and directly in conflict with their organic structure, then it is obvious, of course, that they must perish rapidly.

All those physicians in the North who have had any experience of the diseases of these people, know the tendencies to consumption or disease of the respiratory organs so common, almost universal among them, but few if any have known that this was a necessary result of the peculiar structure of the negro. His entire surface is studded with innumerable sebaceous glands, which are the safety-valves that nature has provided for relieving his system from the action of vertical suns, but these rendered torpid, indeed incapable of performing their functions in the icy atmosphere of the North, congestion and disease of the lungs necessarily follows. Almost every one has seen negroes in Northern cities, who have lost their legs by frost at sea—a thing rarely witnessed among whites, and yet where a single negro has been thus exposed, doubtless a thousand of the former have. Climate, therefore, has a fixed and absolute control over the existence of the negro. God has adapted him, both in his physical and mental structure, to the tropics, and though he can live in the temperate latitudes, his welfare, his happiness, and the development of his faculties are secured just as he conforms to the designs of the Almighty, as written in his organism, and lives within the centre of existence where he was created. And those ignorant and terribly mistaken people who have seduced and led him into the bleak and forbidden North, have unconsciously committed a crime that would appall them if they could truly comprehend it.

Such are, briefly, the more prominent laws of climate, and their influence on men and animals; but as climate itself, in the ordinary meaning of the word, has regard only to degrees of latitude, or to modifications of heat and cold, they are of secondary importance, or, at most, are only a portion of those general laws of adaptation which govern animal existence, and harmonize it with the locality in which it was originally created. Beyond the few exceptions referred to, all organic existence is adapted to its own centre of life, and incapable of living in any other. This is illustrated every day, and familiar to the least observing among us. Cereals and vegetables of every kind demand, if not always a special climate, certainly a special soil. Corn, wheat, etc., require a soil suited to them— there must be a special adaptation of external circumstances, for there is an eternal relation between the organism and the circumstances that surround it. The most ignorant among our agriculturists know from their own experience that certain things can only grow on certain soils, and this fixed and indestructible law, thus manifested in the simpler forms of being, pervades the whole organic world. And, as remarked, it is in exceptional instances, or the instances where climate does not govern, that these adaptations to particular soils are essential. In general, it can not be transplanted or removed from its own centre of existence. The products of the tropics —the sugar cane, coffee, indigo, cotton, etc., the numerous fruits, etc., can not be changed, or, at all events, can not be grown successfully outside of their original centre of creation.

As we ascend in the scale, the laws of adaptation, are, of course, multiplied, or become more elaborate, and in the case of human beings, they are widely diversified with numerous secondary relations; but the great universal and all-dominating law that unites men to their centres of existence, is as indestructible and everlasting as it is in the simplest form of vegetable exis- tence. God has created both them and the external circum- stances, has given them a specific structure and corresponding faculties, and He has made the earth, the soils, the form of its products, its climate, etc., in perfect accord with the former, and as time and chance, or human forces, can never change or modify the works of the Almighty, this law of adaptation is everlasting.

The white man—as a laborer—is adapted to the temperate latitudes, not because mere climate, or heat and cold, demand it, but because such is his natural adaptation. All the external circumstances accord with his nature—his physical structure and his intellectual endowments. The soil, its natural products—the time and mode of their growth, their ripening or maturity, in short, their cultivation is in perfect harmony with his faculties. The farmer of Ohio or Illinois, for example, ploughs and prepares his fields through the early summer, for sowing them with wheat in the early autumn. The process is elaborate. The land must be manured, ploughed carefully at different times, harrowed over at intervals, and gradually made ready for the reception of the seed. Then he carefully selects that which his experience assures him is best. After it is sown he again harrows over his fields, watches them carefully for several months, and then, the crop having ripened, another process begins.

This is equally elaborate and demands the fullest exercise of his mental faculties as well as the labor of his body. He must watch and judge of the weather, when he shall gather in his crops, how dispose of them, etc.; then comes the threshing, the separation of the grain, etc., the disposal of the straw, the feeding of his stock, all again needing the fullest exercise of all his highest faculties. Then, again, begins another process—if not personal or where he himself is the leading party, where men like himself or with the same faculties as himself are associated with him and engaged in completing the process which he began. That which he planted and gathered is now still more elaborately manipulated. The wheat is changed

into flour by a lengthened and elaborate process, and then passing through another elaboration, it becomes bread—the sustenance of the race, the natural food of the millions, the legitimate result of a healthy exercise of his specific faculties and
of the industrial adaptation of the race. Beginning with the
selection of the land, its preparation, the selection, etc., of the
seed, the planting, the care and estimate of the weather, the
ripening, the gathering, the separation of the grain, the transformation into flour, the still greater change into bread, in the
entire process, from the occupation of the land to the moment
when placed on the table of his household, the *tout ensemble*
needs and calls into action the highest faculties of reasoning
and comparison, and however uneducated or ignorant the individual may seem, when compared with the man of books,
the process, or rather processes, would be impossible, of course,
to any race except our own, or to beings with capacities inferior to those of the white man.

It is the same with all the other products common or indigenous to temperate latitudes. They all demand the highest
capacities for their cultivation. The nature of the soils, the
fitness of particular products to particular soils, the periods of
growth, of ripening, the influences of the atmosphere, the
action of heat and cold, the change of seasons, etc., are all in
harmony with the elevated faculties, while the result, their
cultivation and uses, are all essential to the welfare and happiness of the white man. The industrial adaptation is complete,
the varying soils, often widely different on the same farm, the
numerous regulations, the multiplied relations and connections
involved, the changing seasons and complicated circumstances
render the temperate latitudes as absolutely the centre of life to
the white man, industrially considered, as the tropics are to the
negro, or as any of the simpler forms of being are to the localities in which we find them. The industrial and specific adap-

tation of the negro to his own centre of life is, however, more
palpable and demonstrable, for his limited intelligence and
more direct relations to external circumstances enable us to
grasp the facts involved more readily. The soil of the tropics
has little variation, and rarely needs any manure or preparation like those of temperate latitudes. And the indigenous
products, those that need care and labor for their cultivation,
however luxuriant their growth, are few in number. There
are almost innumerable species of fruits that grow spontaneously, and indeed a great number of plants that are nutritious,
which need no care or labor, and which the negro, in his isolated or barbarous state, lives on to a great extent. But the
great natural products of the tropics, those that are essential
to human welfare, which are at this instant the most important elements of modern commerce, and are vitally affecting
the civilization of our times, are few in number, and need only
the lowest grade of intelligence for their cultivation. Cotton,
for example, needs but little beyond planting and picking, and
sugar, so far as the labor is concerned, is even more simple.
It is true, in the complete elaboration and final perfection of
these products, the manufacture, etc., the highest order of intelligence is called into action, but this has no necessary connection with the negro. Cotton is shipped to the North or
Europe, and passes altogether into other hands, and though the
negro labor was vital in the preliminary stages, it has no more
connection with the ultimate disposition of this material than
the labor of mules that were employed to prepare the earth
for its original cultivation. Coffee, tobacco, indigo, etc., are
all equally simple, all in accord with the simple soils, the uniform atmosphere, the primitive laws of development, as they
may be termed, and in perfect harmony with the grade of intelligence, the specific nature and industrial adaptation of the
negro.

His physical organism is adapted to the cultivation of these products as perfectly as is his grade of intelligence. His head is protected from the rays of a vertical sun by a dense mat of woolly hair, wholly impervious to its fiercest heats, while his entire surface, studded with innumerable sebaceous glands, forming a complete excretory system, relieves him from all those climatic influences so fatal, under the same circumstances, to the sensitive and highly organized white man. Instead of seeking to shelter himself from the burning sun of the tropics, he courts it, enjoys it, delights in its fiercest heats, and malaria —that deadly poison to the white man, which, in the form of yellow fever, has swept from existence vast multitudes of our race, is as harmless to the negro organism as the balmy breezes of May or June to the organization of the white man. Of course mulattoes and mongrels may have something that approximates to the yellow fever of the white man, but to the negro it is simply an organic impossibility. His faculties, his simple grade of intelligence, his physical organism, his specific, climatic, and industrial adaptations are therefore in perfect harmony with the primitive soils, the simple products, and uniform atmosphere of the tropics, and in complete relation and perfect union with the circumstances that surround him in the centre of existence where the Almighty has placed him.

The late Daniel Webster once declared that God had limited " slavery" to certain climates, and that he, at least, would not " reënact the will of God," and this declaration, though as a form of speech absurd enough, was certainly in close neighborhood, to a great and vital truth. If he had said that the Almighty had adapted the negro to certain climates, he would have expressed just what we are now ·considering; but the relation of the negro to the white man, the thing he called slavery, is, of course, as proper and as natural in New York or Ohio as in Mississippi. The vulgar notion, therefore, that "slave labor," the industrial capacities of the negro, is unprofitable in temperate latitudes is only partially true. The "slave" relation, the normal condition, as contrasted with the so-called free negro, presents just the difference between a useful negro and a worthless negro, or a negro who adds to the productive forces of a State, and one who lives on the State—a healthy and a diseased social element, and therefore wherever found, if, indeed, in the extreme North, it is simply absurd to speak of the former as unprofitable when contrasted with the latter. But when the negro is contrasted with the white man in Ohio or New York, then the whole subject is changed. His industrial capacities are incompetent to grow the indigenous products of the temperate latitudes.

The reasoning, the reflection, the elevated faculties called into action, that are absolutely essential to the cultivation of their products, the varying and complicated soils, their elaborate preparation, the care and judgment needed in gathering them, etc., the still more elaborate processes before they are rendered fit for human sustenance, all this needs the high intelligence, and therefore the large brain, of the white man, and to the isolated negro is impossible, of course.

It is true, the master may guide them, and the owner of a hundred negroes in Ohio may carry on these processes and cultivate the soils of the Western and Middle States sometimes, perhaps, when all labor is scarce, with tolerable success. But their inferiority, their lower grade of intelligence, the time and trouble expended in this guidance, must be so palpable to every one who reflects a moment, that the case only needs to be stated to convince them of the relative worthlessness of this labor. And leaving out of view the force of climate, the changing seasons, the sudden frosts which sometimes disable and very generally affect the negro injuriously, and in the end destroy him—leaving all this out of consideration, and contemplating his mere industrial adaptations, it is obvious that the negro can never be, as he never has been, able to cultivate the soils or grow the products of the temperate latitudes. But while the great dividing lines are distinct enough, while the white man and negro, in their industrial adaptations, can never be in conflict when each is within that centre of existence to which the Almighty Creator has adapted and designed him, there is a large extent of territory where they may both labor to advantage, and where time and circumstances may often determine their presence and their fitness for such labor. The white man is forever forbidden by the laws of his organization to labor under a tropical sun, or to grow by his own physical efforts the products indigenous to the tropics. The negro, by the laws of both his physical structure and mental nature, is forever incapable of cultivating the soil or of growing the products indigenous or common to the temperate latitudes.

These great elementary and indestructible truths, which, fixed forever by the hand of God, admit of no exception, change, or modification whatever, which time, and circumstances, and human power can not influence, any more than the laws of gravitation, or animal growth, or the term of animal existence, or any other law of the Creator of the universe, will not be mistaken; but when we come to consider the approximating latitudes, then there is a wide field opened up, to our view, to chance, to time, to a multitude of considerations.

In general terms, it may be said, that wherever the white man can labor with effect, that is, can preserve his health and the full exercise of his faculties, there his labor must be more valuable than is that of the negro. People who are ignorant of the laws of climate and industrial adaptations, and still worse, ignorant of the nature of the negro and his relations to the white man, when traveling on the Ohio River, observe that the populations on the Ohio side are more energetic, industrious, and prosperous than they are on the Kentucky side of the river, and they infer that it is because Kentucky has "slavery." The author is not prepared to admit their assumption, for though there may be greater wealth and apparently greater prosperity in Ohio, the true and only test of well-being in a State is the equality of condition and of the happiness of its people, and we have no means of determining this truth by applying this test in the present instance. England is vastly more wealthy than any other State in Christendom—its annual production is vastly greater, but this wealth is monopolized by a fraction of the population. While the great body of the people are steeped in poverty to the lips, and while the few are every day growing wealthier, the many are, with equal rapidity and certainty, becoming more abject in their poverty, and, consequently more ignorant, vicious, and miserable. If, therefore, it were true that Ohio did increase in wealth more rapidly than Kentucky, it would by no means follow that the people of Ohio were in a better condition than those of Kentucky. But it is reasonable to suppose that the production is greater than that of Kentucky, for while the climate and industrial adaptation are suited to the white man, there are none but white men in Ohio, while nearly half of the laboring population of Kentucky are negroes. The same absurd assumption and inference have been made in respect to Virginia and other so-called Slave States, when contrasted with New York and other so-called Free States. It has been said, " Virginia falls behind New York in general prosperity." " It is because she has half a million of slaves, and if she will abolish this slavery, then she will soon equal, perhaps surpass, New York, for Virginia has certain natural advantages which New York has not." Or, in other words, it is said that Vir-

ginia is less prosperous than New York, because her half a
million of negroes are in a normal condition, and if she will
thrust them from this condition and turn them loose, as New
York has done, then Virginia will soon be equally prosperous
as the latter! Possibly one out of twenty of the negroes in
New York, Ohio, or any other so-called Free State, is engaged
in productive labor, while the nineteen others live—temporarily—ou the labor of the producing classes of those States.
The argument of these political economists, therefore, is simply this: Virginia with half a million of industrious and productive negroes, is less prosperous than New York, but if she
will transform them into half a million of idle, non-productive,
and good-for-nothing negroes, then she will rapidly recover
from her present depressed condition. But enough—these
people who set up an abstraction entirely nonsensical, must
reach conclusions equally preposterous. They are not only
ignorant of what they argue about so pompously, but they
imagine conditions that not only do not but can not exist,
either here or elsewhere, in our own times or any other, in the
existing, or any other world.

Virginia, Kentucky, all of the transition States, all the States
with considerable negro populations that are in the temperate
latitudes, are, of course, less productive than those bordering
on them with entire white populations, for the negro is greatly
inferior in his industrial capabilities, as in all other respects,
where white men can labor. Thus far there can be no doubt,
for there is no room for doubt, but it by no means follows
that the people of Ohio or Pennsylvania are in a better condition than those of Kentucky and Virginia. The people of Virginia, if not homogenenous in race, are so in interest, and that
one great fact underlying the social condition, is itself, or in
the results that flow from it, of vast benefit. The interests of
the State, of all its people, the "slaveholder," "non-slave-

holder," and the negro or so-called slave, are homogeneous, universal, and indivisible, and therefore without social conflict, or
causes for social conflict, the tendencies of the social order are
harmonious and beneficent. The only seeming conflict or the
sole thing that superficial thinkers might mistake for such, is
the fact that the negro is not adapted to the locality, and they
might suppose that therefore the owner of his services, or of
this so-called slave property, might, to a certain extent, monopolize the soil that of right belonged to the white laborer.
But a moment's reflection will be sufficient to convince any
rational mind of the unsoundness of this supposition.

A Virginia planter may, perhaps, inherit a thousand acres of
land and a hundred negroes. His poor white neighbor is without land perhaps, and thinks it hard that these negroes, whom
his instinct as well as reason assures him are not as well
adapted to the locality as himself, should occupy it, while
he has none. But the planter himself is worse off still. The
land is worn out—the negro capacity can not resuscitate it—
they barely earn sufficient for the common support—the
planter finds it hard to live at all, and only does so, perhaps,
by parting with some of his people, and therefore whatever
the evil of this negro element in localities which the changes
of time and circumstances have brought about, it is an evil
that presses upon the owner of this species of property with
vastly greater force than it does on the non-slaveholder. Of
course the remedy is obvious—"Slavery Extension"—free and
full expansion—the acquisition of new territories suited to the
industrial capacities of the negro. For example, if we suppose the late General Walker had been successful, and opened
Central America to American settlement, energy, civilization,
and prosperity—the Virginia or Maryland planter, who now
finds it difficult to "make both ends meet," would gather up
his household and migrate to these inviting and fertile regions.

His negroes producing double or treble, or even more, in their new homes, he could afford to send his children to the North or Europe to be educated, and himself spend his summers at the Springs or abroad, and live as luxuriously as he pleased, while his negroes or so-called slaves, in their centre of existence, where God ordained that they should live, laving themselves in the genial heats of the tropics, with all their best and highest capacities called into action, and the best qualities of their nature healthily and naturally developed, would be even more benefited, perhaps, than the master himself. The vacancy would be filled by the increasing white population, by the constant inflowing of the mighty masses pouring in upon us from the Old World, by the poor German or other European peasant, who only needs liberty and the means for developing the high nature with which God endowed him, to exhibit himself as the equal of the kings and aristocrats who have crushed him into an artificial inferiority actually resembling the natural inferiority of the negro, and these impoverished soils being resuscitated by his industry, his intelligence, in short, his industrial adaptations, the now wasted and wasting lands of the transition States would become, and doubtless will become some day, the very garden of the republic. Nor would this be the whole of the beneficial process in question. The world needs, and especially our own farmers and working classes need, the products of the tropics. Sugar, and coffee, and tropical fruits should be had at half their present prices, while the increased production, the extension of commerce and general progress would have a vast influence over the civilization of our times by this simple application of industrial forces in conformity with the fundamental laws of climatic and industrial adaptation. A large majority of our negro population are at this moment outside of their own centre of existence, and a time will come when the border or transition States will probably have few of these people. As observed, it is absurd, a contradiction, an abuse of language, to speak of "slavery," or the social subordination of the negro, as an evil, or as being, under any possible circumstances, unprofitable, for that involves the anomaly of supposing the idle and good-for-nothing negro a benefit to the State; but the negro is profitable to his master, beneficial to the State, and happy himself in such proportion as he approximates to the tropics, and is placed in juxtaposition with the external circumstances to which God has adapted him. They or their progenitors were mainly landed at northern ports. They were, in the then scarcity of labor, possibly needed even in the Central States. As an advanced guard in the rising civilization of the New World, they were once, perhaps, essential to the Provinces of Virginia, Maryland, etc., for the rich soil, the rank vegetation, the extensive marshes and wild river bottoms generated an extent and degree of malaria that was often fatal to the white man, and rendered the labor and aid of these people of vital importance in the early settlement of the country. But as the country became cultivated and white laborers became plenty, it was seen that the labor of the negro was less valuable; so that Mr. Jefferson, and many of his cotemporaries, actually fancied it an evil, and desired to be relieved from it. And indeed, what was worse still— they confounded the existence of the negro with the relation, the so-called slavery, of the negro; and it was only when Louisiana was occupied, and new and appropriate regions were opened to the negro, and in harmony with his industrial capacities, that this erroneous notion of Mr. Jefferson and others disappeared from the southern mind. Virginia has still a large negro population, but while they are mainly employed in cultivating tobacco, suited to the simple capacity and subordinate nature of the negro, the demand for cotton, rice, sugar, etc., in the great tropical regions of the republic, is rapidly attracting them southward, and in conformity with their own happiness as well as the welfare of the white citizenship, this process is destined to go on until they are all within their own centre of existence. Whether or not Virginia, or any other transition State, would be better without them at this time, it is of course impossible to say, or to conjecture even. The simple fact, however, of their presence there would seem to indicate that it was desirable to have them among them yet, or at all events in considerable numbers, but the industrial attraction is constantly carrying them further south—to Texas, Florida, and other Gulf States, where their labor is more valuable.

These general laws of climatic and industrial adaptation, which thus underlie the social fabric when made up of mixed populations, are also illustrated by the national history, and demonstrated in every step of the national progress. When negroes were first introduced into the British North American Colonies, there was, of course, and for many years after, a great demand for labor. Here was a mighty continent, a new world, open to the enterprise and energy of the most energetic and most enterprising branch of the great master race of mankind. All that was wanted was labor—labor, too, that was of the lowest kind in some respects, and laborers whose imperfect innervation and low grade of sensibility could resist the malarious influences always more or less potent in new countries and virgin soils, even in temperate latitudes, were often desirable. The Bristol and the Liverpool " slave merchants," therefore—the progenitors of the saints and philanthropists of Exeter Hall—supplied these wants, ordinarily with negroes, but occasionally with some of their own poorer and more helpless brethren, whom they did not hesitate to kidnap and send out to labor on the American plantations. Negroes, therefore, were forced from the sea-board to the in-

terior, even as far as Canada, while the Central Colonies had
even very considerable numbers of these people. With the
downfall of the British dominion, however, the Bristol merchants were forced to engage in other enterprises, and as the
genius and daring of Clive and his companions had just then
opened a new and boundless empire in India, English capital,
enterprise, and polity took another direction, and though the
African trade was continued for some years afterward by our
own people, there were, comparatively, but few negroes imported after the overthrow of the British rule. After the removal of a foreign and artificial rule, and the establishment of
a political system in harmony with the instincts and wants of
our people, the social and industrial laws were permitted a
natural development, and from this period a widely different
movement began. Negro labor was less profitable in the
Eastern than in the Central States, and of course less profitable
in the latter than in Virginia, the Carolinas, etc., and therefore
the industrial attraction carried them from the interior to the
sea-board, and from the North to the South. The acquisition
of Louisiana, of Florida, etc., the opening of new regions and
the formation of new States adapted to the climatic wants and
industrial capabilities of the negro, drained them off still
more rapidly. Mr. Jefferson and others, as has been observed,
confounding the relation of the races, or so-called slavery, with
the non-adaptability of the negro labor in temperate latitudes,
desired to exclude, not negroes, but the social relation which
they supposed an evil, from the northwest territory, and the
old confederation, it will be remembered, passed an ordinance
to that effect. This "ordinance," which ignorance and folly
have so long worshipped as a "bulwark of freedom," with
as abject a spirit and total absence of reason as the Hindoo
worships his Juggernaut, of course never had, nor could have,
the slightest influence over the subject.

12

If there had been no extension of our southern borders, no Louisiana, Florida, Alabama, or other States adapted to the wants and industrial capabilities of the negro, the whole Northwest, at this moment, would be what these blind and mistaken people term "slave territory." The cheap lands and fresh soils of the West, would attract the holders of this species of property even more strongly than any others, and the only difference, so far as the negro is concerned, would be, or could be, that their numbers would be less than at present. As he approximates to his centre of existence, or as the negro is in harmony with the external conditions to which the Almighty has adapted him, his well-being is secured, his vitality is greater, and he multiplies himself more rapidly ; therefore as regards the negro element, it would have been less in the Northwest than it is now in the Southwest, but the relation, of course, would be as at present, for however willing Vermont, or some other State without negroes might be to pervert these relations, and in theory place themselves on a level with a subordinate race, those who are in juxtaposition with negroes have never done so, or thus voluntarily attempted social suicide.

Mr. Jefferson, by the acquisition of Louisiana and the extension of our Southern limits, therefore, "saved" the Northwest from a negro population and so-called slavery, just as the acquisition of Texas by President Tyler and the eminent and far-seeing Calhoun and others, at a later day, opened other and still wider regions adapted to the wants and specific nature of our negro population, and which are now, by the natural and indestructible laws of climate and industrial adaptation, gradually withdrawing this population from the border or transition States. Indeed, one only needs to examine the several census returns of the federal government, from 1790 to 1860, to understand both the history of the country, in these respects, and the operation of the laws of climate and industrial adaptation. They will then see that the negro element constantly tends southward—a black column ever on the march for its own centre of existence—an advance guard of American civilization, that moves on without cessation, and that must continue to advance until it is in perfect accord with those external conditions to which it is naturally adapted. Nor is the interest of the master—the increased value of the negro labor—the sole motive power, though certainly the leading cause of this progress southward. The increased and increasing white population, with the vast European emigration, is pressing on its rear, while the demands of modern society for the products of its labor, and many other influences, are every day increasing in force, and impelling the negro tropicward with greater rapidity at present, perhaps, than ever before.

Persons wholly ignorant of these causes, or of the laws underlying this progress of the negro southward, have blindly labored against it, and in regard to the annexation of Texas, which opened such a wide and beneficent field for negro industry, and therefore for the true welfare of these people, they doubtless really believed they were doing them a kindness when thus foolishly striving to reverse the ordinances of the Eternal, and to prevent the expansion of this negro population. And this expansion, or this industrial attraction constantly going on from Virginia and other border States to Texas and the Gulf States, doubtless does appear unjust, and, perhaps, inhuman to those ignorant of the negro nature, as well as of those laws of industrial adaptation which always have and always must govern the subject. The sale of negroes in Richmond and Norfolk, to be sent South, seems to them, perhaps, a great hardship, but while it is believed that the larger portion are accompanied by their masters, who naturally seek new homes in Texas, etc., there is no other possible mode or means through which they could reach a more genial clime, and therefore, even if it were indeed a harsh procedure to sell them in Richmond, it would still be vastly more inhuman to keep them from approximating to their specific centre of existence. As it is, it is true beneficence and kindness to facilitate their progress southward; but if they really were black-*white* men, as the ignorant anti-slaveryite fancies they are, and without any specific affinity or adaptation for a tropical climate, even in that case their public sale at Richmond or Norfolk, to supply the labor market of Texas, would not involve a thousandth part of the misery and physical suffering endured by a very considerable portion of those British subjects who annually arrive at New York. Indeed, it is safe to say that the thousand or so diseased, half-starved, and miserable British *subjects*, which the Mayor of New York had penned up and out of sight of the Prince of Wales at Castle Garden, in order not to offend the olfactories or revolt the senses of that young person, embodied more physical suffering, more wrong and outrage on humanity, than *could* be inflicted on negroes through all eternity, so far as this process of extension southward may be concerned. The master, or the man who purchases the service of the negro, has, of course, the utmost interest in taking care of him and providing for all his wants, while the negro himself, on the way to the climate and the external conditions for which the Almighty has adapted him, *must* be in the pathway of progress, and advancing generally toward that goal of happiness and well-being which the common Creator has designed for all His creatures.

No law or legislation would seem to be needed—nothing but the removal of all obstructions from the path of progress, and the free and full development of the laws of industrial attraction. The demands for tropical products, and the greater value of the negro labor—the necessities of modern civilization and the interests of the master—have carried the negro from the Central, as they are now carrying him from the border States, toward the great tropical centre of the continent. And by a beneficent and inevitable necessity which God himself has fixed forever in the economy of the universe, the welfare of the negro is secured in exact proportion as these laws of industrial attraction and adaptation are permitted free action and full development.

In conclusion, therefore, it would seem that a simple removal of all obstructions to these fixed and fundamental laws would be all that was needed to secure the best welfare of all —white men and negroes—of the North equally with the South, for while the industrial attraction would remove the negro element just as fast as the interests of the border States may demand, the West can always secure themselves from a considerable negro population, by aiding in the removal of obstructions from our southern borders, as Jefferson saved them sixty years ago.

CHAPTER XXI.

NORTH AND SOUTH.—ORIGIN OF THE AMERICAN IDEA OF
GOVERNMENT.

ALTHOUGH the progenitors of our so-called slaves were
mainly imported at Northern ports, and all of the Northern
and Middle States have had, at times, considerable negro populations, the process of transition southward has been so rapid
that the Northern communities, or the people of the Northern
States, have been but little impressed by them or influenced
in their ideas and mental habits by the presence of this widely
different and subordinate element of our general population.
But when they became a fixed population, when Virginia,
especially, had acquired what, by comparison, may be called a
large negro element, then the actual presence of these negroes
called into existence new ideas, and gave development to new
modes of thought or mental habitudes. All our ideas and
mental habits are, in a sense, accidental, the result of circumstances, just as language, which is the outward expression of
our ideas, becomes changed by time and circumstances. The
English of the tenth century were widely different, of course,
in their ideas and mental habits from the English of the four-
teenth century, under the rule of the Normans ; and this difference was widely varied from anything that mere time or ordinary circumstances could have produced.

And the different mental habits of the people of America
generally, when contrasted with those of Europe, show sufficiently that all our ideas are accidental, the result of local circumstances, though, of course, all are in subordination to

those fixed and fundamental laws of mind that are specific with the race. The presence, therefore, of the negro—of a widely different and subordinate element of the population of Virginia, and other States, when it became stationary and had to be provided for by the local legislatures, its specific wants as well as those of the citizenship looked after, and its social adaptations rendered harmonious with the welfare of the former—naturally developed new ideas of government and new modes of thought in the dominant and governing-race. Except, possibly, some of the Spanish colonies south of us, there was no portion of the New World where so many of those who could claim connection with European aristocracy originally settled as in the province of Virginia.

In the earlier days of Massachusetts a great number of the most respectable of the middle classes of English society, and some few instances of the old hereditary nobility, found new homes in the colony, but in the latter case they had abandoned the old Norman traditions, and to enjoy their religion and "freedom of conscience," identified themselves with Puritanism. In the Dutch province of New York, there was, perhaps, a somewhat larger infusion of the aristocratic element, but as Holland itself was essentially republican, and the Dutch really the originators of modern liberty in Europe, and, moreover, had a very limited landed aristocracy compared with England, France, etc., but few persons identified by tradition and association with the hereditary aristocracy of the Old World found their way into the Dutch settlements of the New.

But Virginia was originally settled—to a very large extent —by the offspring of the old Norman chivalry, by the cavaliers—the descendants of the proudest, most warlike, most chivalrous, heroic, and enterprising, and, at the same time, most tyrannical and oppressive aristocracy the world has ever seen. Those who belong to the race—the same species--of course will, under the same circumstances, manifest the same qualities, and therefore, if at any time the child of the princely Plantagenet or lordly Warwick had been exchanged in its cradle with the "base" progeny of some Saxon churl, who fed and kenneled with their hounds, the latter would have grown up with all the pride and chivalry, and princely bravery common to the former. Nevertheless, a class, an aristocracy, a privileged order, forms sentiments, ideas, etc., and transmits its traditions, rules, etc., to its descendants, that may, for centuries perhaps, preserve their integrity. Even in our social every-day life, and changing society, we often see families transmitting their family usages, habitudes, modes of thought as well as action, for several generations, and with only slight departures from the family model left by some original or venerated ancestor. Aristocracies, however, usually destroy themselves by the very means they resort to to preserve their ascendency over the great body of the people. In order to preserve the respect, the awe, the continued belief of the vulgar mass in their seeming superiority, they must avoid the populace and intermarry with their order, and the more completely this is done, the more they become a close corporation as it were, and violate the laws of consanguinity, the more rapidly they are deteriorated and fall below the general average of the people. The Northmen, the robust and enterprising fishermen of the Baltic, the fillibusters and pirates of the Northern Seas, invaded France and conquered Normandy, and Rolla and his roving horde of followers threatened to overrun Paris, and indeed the whole kingdom. They finally settled down in Normandy, from which, at a later date, they emerged into Italy, conquered Naples, the island of Sicily, and for a long time threatened an invasion of the Oriental World, which could hardly have resisted such an indomitable race of men. A Duke — a bastard Duke of Normandy, at that time

laid claim to the crown of England, and with forty thousand
followers landed in that country, and in a single battle so completely demolished the "Anglo-Saxons" and Anglo-Saxonism,
so much boasted of in these days, that the former have remained slaves ever since, and the latter was so utterly annihilated that it disappeared for ever on that fatal day at Hastings.
Then, for the first time, the Normans assumed the distinct
form of an aristocracy or privileged order.

Though they had long since cast off the rude habits and
uncouth manners of adventurers and conquerors, and when
they invaded England were, perhaps, as intelligent and refined
as any similar number of European people, and a great deal
more so than those they conquered in England, they had never
assumed the form, enacted laws, or established rules and regulations as an aristocracy or governing class. From this time
forth, however, the Norman aristocracy ruled England with an
iron hand, and though the wars of the Roses, and the still
more fatal conflict with the Puritans or middle class, exterminated or drove out the remains of the Norman blood, and
there is little, if any, in England at this time, the country is
still governed by the traditions, the habits, in short, the system established by the old Norman aristocracy. Most of the
great families became extinct, while the younger sons and
others of broken fortunes emigrated to Virginia, and with the
establishment of the commonwealth, very many of the Norman ancestry abandoned England. So many and so strong
were the remnants of the old Norman families in Virginia, that
they refused to recognize the commonwealth, and actually set
at defiance the formidable power and iron will of Cromwell.

But these remains of the old Norman aristocracy—that aristocracy which for several centuries governed England—that
have left their impress, their habits, their laws of primogeniture, their feudalistic customs, so deeply engraven on the
12*

English mind, that the aristocracy of the day, though entirely modern, and with scarcely any family connection with it, are able to govern the masses, through these habitudes, as absolutely as the Normans once did by the sword and the strong hand of arbitrary power, these descendants of the old Norman race in Virginia have changed completely about, and though their ancestors were the main supporters of kingly despotism, they are the originators and champions of democracy in America.

In all the changes and mutations of human society, there is scarcely any parallel to this change of ideas in Virginia, or to this extraordinary transformation which has changed the descendants of the old Norman aristocracy into the firmest and most reliable defenders of democracy. Of course, the early colonists of Virginia were of all classes and conditions of English society; not a few of them, perhaps, were kidnapped young peasants, without friends or relatives to protect them or to punish the base wretches who carried them over the sea and sold them here, as elsewhere, in the American colonies. But it is undoubtedly true that a larger, vastly larger body of "gentlemen" emigrated to Virginia than to any other colony, and as these were all cadets, or younger branches of the great houses in England, nearly all of which were Norman in descent, and nearly all of which in the direct line afterward perished in the wars of the commonwealth, it would seem equally certain that if there be any Norman blood anywhere, it must now be found, or mainly found, in Virginia.

The cause of this transformation, this radical and extraordinary change of opinion, which has made the descendants of the proudest and most despotic aristocracy ever known the authors and main supporters of democracy, must be a potent one, and as far removed from the ordinary causes which, in the progress of time, modify men's opinions and habits, as the results themselves are extraordinary and without parallel. As has been remarked, all our ideas and mental habits are the result of circumstances, the external influences that surround us, the changed conditions of our existence, which give origin to new thoughts and new modes of mental action. And when we take these things into view and contemplate the changed conditions, the new and altogether different circumstances that surrounded these Virginia descendants of the cavaliers and gentlemen of England, then the causes are obvious—the new ideas that sprung up in men's minds, legitimate and consistent with the extraordinary and indeed unparalleled circumstances under which they lived. They were in juxtaposition with negroes, with an inferior race, with widely different and subordinate social elements, and new thoughts, new ideas, as well as altogether different habits, naturally and necessarily followed. They saw these negroes were different beings from themselves, not in color alone, or in other physical characteristics, but in their mental qualities, their affections, their wants, in short, in their *nature* and the necessities of their social life, their welfare and happiness, and indeed the welfare of this subordinate element, demanded corresponding action, with, of course, corresponding ideas and modes of thought. They saw that this negro was not artificially or accidentally, but naturally different from themselves, that God himself had made him different and given him different faculties and different wants, and therefore designed him for different purposes, and that it was an imperative and unavoidable duty as well as necessity to adapt their social habits and legal and political institutions to this state or condition of fixed and unalterable *fact*. But this was not all, nor the limit to the new ideas that thus originated in the changed conditions under which they were living. Their traditions, the mental habits of their old cavalier ancestry, the ideas they carried from the mother country, taught them to regard the person of a king as something quite sacred, and to whom an absolute and unquestioning obedience was always due, while the class of gentlemen, the nobility, or aristocracy, that more immediately surrounded royalty was deemed to be altogether superior and different from the vulgar multitudes that made up the people. The celebrated formula of Archbishop Laud, that "passive obedience and non-resistance" was the absolute and universal duty of the people to the will of the king, expressed with brevity and accuracy the prevalent sentiment of the cavaliers, and they demanded from their special retainers the same unquestioning submission which they themselves accorded to royalty. The ignorance of the great mass of the people on one hand, and the actual power and tyranny of the nobles on the other, sunk so deep into the common mind of England and other European people during the middle ages, that though many generations have passed since, the sentiment of superiority in one class and of inferiority in the other, remains yet, and in England at this day is nearly as potent as ever.

But the descendants of the cavaliers in Virginia were placed face to face with *facts* that utterly exploded these factitious sentiments that had their origin in a certain condition of society, and not in nature or in the natural relations of men. They were in juxtaposition with negroes, with different and subordinate beings, human, it is true, like themselves, but different human beings, just as pigeons, while birds equally with robins, are different *birds*, or as hounds, though *dogs*, were different dogs from spaniels or bull-dogs. This was a great, starting, fixed *fact*, that no amount or extent of sentiment, theory, or mental habit could explain away or modify, or avoid in any respect. They saw this fact daily staring them in the face; they were compelled to recognize it, to legislate for it, or for these people, to adapt their social customs to it, in short, to conform to it, and therefore were forced to cast aside their preconceived notions, the traditions and mental habits of their ancestors, all their ideas of loyalty to a creature like themselves and of their own class-superiority which they had brought from the Old World. What was their fancied superiority over their own humbler brethren, when contrasted with this *natural* inferiority of the negro ? What was the accident of education, of wealth, of refinement of manners, or any other factitious, temporary, or accidental thing worth, which separated them from their less fortunate neighbors, when compared with the handiwork of-nature, with the fixed and impassable barriers that separated them both from negroes ? What, in short, were the petty distinctions of human pride, vanity, and accident, in comparison with the ordinances of the Eternal ?

Such were the facts that confronted them, such the external circumstances that developed new ideas and new modes of thought in the colonists of Virginia, such the potent *causes* that changed the descendants of English cavaliers into the earliest, most consistent, and most reliable champions of democracy in America. The same causes, to a certain extent, influenced the inhabitants of other colonies, and it will be found that in precise proportion to the amount and the fixedness of this negro element in any locality, there were clear, corresponding views of liberty and equality among white men. Indeed, this is as true now as ever before, and almost invariably there are sound and rational views of liberty and of democratic institutions in precise proportion to the presence, or imperfect and unsound notions in proportion to the absence, of this negro element. Those States like Mississippi, Texas, Arkansas, and Alabama, that have relatively the largest negro population, are the most decidedly and consistently democratic, while Massachusetts, Vermont, etc., with the fewest negroes among them, are the most unsound in these respects, and however intelligent in regard to other things, are certainly behind most of the great American communities in political knowledge.

South Carolina, and perhaps some others, may seem exceptions to this very general truth, but if so in reality, it is owing to peculiar causes, such as the education of many of its people abroad, in Europe, and at the North, etc., but even as regards that State, so exceptional in many respects, land is more equally divided than in any other State, and where such a fact obtains, the general tendency to equality in citizenship must be strikingly manifested.

The great revolutionary movement of 1776 gave full expression to the new modes of thought, the grand ideas, the glorious truths thus developed in the mind of Virginia, and relatively in the other colonies, where this *cause*, this negro element had anything like a stationary existence. It was no accident or chance that made Mr. Jefferson the author of the great idea, or rather the exponent of the idea embodied in the Declaration of Independence, the grand and immortal truth, that all white men are created equal, and therefore entitled to equal rights, or, as he expressed it, to "life, liberty, and happiness." True, some other Virginian might have done this, and possibly some mind in the Middle Provinces, New Jersey, or New York, might have formed a tolerably clear conception of this great fixed and unchangeable truth that underlies the whole superstructure of our political society; but no man in the Northern Provinces could have risen to this mental elevation at that period in our history; indeed comparatively few are even now capable of it. Massachusetts and the neighboring colonies grasped the idea of independence with great clearness, and urged it with an earnestness, bravery, and indomitable perseverance certainly unsurpassed, if equalled elsewhere, but it was independence of a foreign dominion, and not independence of foreign ideas or of a hostile system. They were without negroes, without any natural substratum in the social elements, without any test or standard to determine men's natural relations to each other, and clinging to the mental habits of their British ancestors, they were therefore incapable of forming those grand and truthful conceptions of equality which Mr. Jefferson, and Virginians generally, under the influences that have been stated, so clearly apprehended. The accidental and artificial distinctions of society—family influence, wealth, education, etc., were as in England, though, of course, not to the same extent—the standards, the tests, the land-marks of the political as well as the social order, and the phrase often used by New England writers of our own day, that "representation was inseparable from taxation," fully expressed the mental habits and imperfect political conceptions of the Northern mind. In England, except the titled aristocracy, the House of Lords or Peerage, which pretends to rest on blood or birth (?), wealth alone gives rights. The *man* is nowhere, no part or portion, or element even of the political system. In every county where he happens to have property, he has a vote, but if without property, he has no voice whatever, and, as observed, is not even an element of representation, as are the negroes of the South. Taxation and representation, therefore, are inseparable, so far as forms are concerned, in the British system, though, as a fact, it is the working classes, who are not represented at all, that must pay all the taxes in the end. The mental habits of the North, in 1776, were fashioned on this model; they saw only those accidental things that separate classes in England, as, wealth, education, etc., and though they had an earnest desire for liberty, this liberty was a vague, undefined, shadowy sentiment, rather than any precise idea resting on fact as in Virginia. The immediate want and common impulse of independence, however, impelled all parties to act harmoniously

for its accomplishment, and though the grand truths presented
by Jefferson in the Declaration of Independence were far above
the then intellectual standard of the North, it did not conflict
with the mental habits of the Northern people sufficiently to
interfere with the common object. But when that object was
accomplished—when the foreign dominion was overthrown
and the common independence secured, and a new political
system was to be created, then a conflict of ideas was developed that was found to be so grave, that many good and patriotic men for some time feared it could not be compromised.
The leading men of the North—the representative men—the
men who desired independence from foreign domination, but
with, at best, vague notions of liberty, or of a new political
system—Hamilton, Adams, Morris, etc.—now came into serious
conflict with the democratic ideas of Virginia. They desired a
monarchy without a king, or a republic without the rule of
the masses. The general notion was, the British model without its defects, or the British system without its corruptions,
and so entirely were some wedded to this, that they declared
it, with all its corruptions, the best government in the world.

The leaders very generally assumed, as they often expressed
it, that society was *naturally* divided into the few and the
many—the educated minority, and the laboring majority—and
as such was the actual social condition of the population as
well as the mental habits of the leaders, it is not at all surprising that they sought to found a government on such a basis.
The agricultural population of the Northern and Middle States
were then very ignorant indeed, when compared with the
present. Feudalism had not been long overthrown in England
or Europe, and the serf transformed into the peasant, and
though the American farmer of 1776 was a great advance over
the latter, he still largely partook of that general apathy, sto-
lidity, and ignorance which in all times, until now, in our own

favored land, have distinguished the tillers of the soil. The large population at the North otherwise employed, the mechanics, artisans, shop-keepers, laborers, etc., were generally, as in the mother country, without representation in the provincial legislatures, and as the interests of the educated classes, the capitalists, merchants, lawyers, divines, etc., were supposed to be, and were in fact, in conflict with those of the former, they always desired strong governments to hold them in order. Indeed, the idea of mob ascendency, of anarchy, the wild rule of the rabble, was the constant terror of the Northern leaders, and in all the arguments of Hamilton, the Adamses, etc., this was put prominently forward. Their rhetorical formula was always the same—" the rule of the uneducated mass will degenerate into license and anarchy, from which the country can only be saved by the strong hand of some military chief, who, first a dictator, will finally don the purple, and the *rôle* so often played in the Old World will be repeated in the New." This notion and this reasoning was legitimate—the consistent result of the social condition as well as the offspring of the inherited traditions of the Northern mind. The capitalists, all those who inherited wealth, the " well-born" and educated class, in short, the few who had the power in their hands, naturally sought, to preserve it and to build up a strong government; which, while it specially benefited themselves, should always be able to " preserve order"—that is, while founded on existing social distinctions, was sufficiently strong to repress the efforts of the multitude to change the social condition. They had no negroes, no natural substratum in the social elements or natural distinctions of society. They had nothing before their eyes but the results of chance, of the accidents of life—nothing but wealth and education—nothing, in short, but the *débris* of the old societies—those class distinctions which in the Old World constitute the basis of the political and social order, and their mental habits, their opinions, their notions of government and its uses, were, of course, in accord with these things, and their minds were incapable of rising above the existing condition, of overleaping the barriers and escaping from the external circumstances that surrounded them. There were, doubtless, individual exceptions—some men who were deeply imbued with the grand idea promulgated by Jefferson in the Declaration of Independence. There were many in the Middle States who had an imperfect but advancing conception of this glorious truth, and there was still a larger number, perhaps, who were groping in darkness with a vague but earnest desire to embrace it. But the dominant thought, the prevalent opinion, the general mental habit, was reflected by the representative men, the great Northern leaders, Hamilton, Adams, Otis, and their companions, who desired to found a government on the British model, which, though it should be a great improvement over the former, was to be based on the same foundation—for, to *their* minds, their mental habits, there was no other, or, at all events, no other *safe* basis for government. They were honest and patriotic men—men of gifted minds and large attainments—men sorely tried and tested by the hardships and sufferings of a seven years' war, through which they walked with their lives in their hands, and the scaffold always frowning on them in the distance, and the purity of intentions, the unselfish and patriotic desires of such men, should never be questioned. They could not rise above the circumstances that surrounded them; they could not comprehend the grand idea of Mr. Jefferson; they saw before them only class distinctions, the rich and the poor, the educated few and the toiling many, and they desired to build the government on the *status quo*, and therefore demanded a strong government, that should always be able to restrain the multitude and keep them in subjection to their "rulers."

On the contrary, as has been stated, Virginia had cast off the mental habits of the Old World, the offspring had long since outgrown the traditions of their ancestors ; the descendants of English cavaliers had changed entirely about in their opinions, and the children of those who held to the doctrine of " passive obedience" and " non-resistance" declared that " resistance to tyrants was obedience to God." The cause or the causes of this wonderful transformation of opinion, this radical change in mental habitudes, which has made the descendants of the supporters of royalty the originators and special champions of democracy in America, have been already considered.

The presence of the negro, the existence in their midst of a different race, was and is, and always must be, a test that shows us the insignificance and indeed nothingness of those artificial distinctions which elsewhere govern the world, and constitute the basis of the political as well as the social order.

The importance of education, of cultivation, the refinement of mind and manners, the possession of wealth, of family influence and social distinction, may all be duly appreciated, as all have their value or social consideration, but where there is a *natural* substratum of society, where a different and subordinate race are in juxtaposition, where negroes exist in any considerable number and in natural relation to the whites, then it naturally follows that the great natural distinctions fixed forever by the hand of the Almighty become the dividing lines and the fixed landmarks of the social order.

This radical change in the mental habits of all brought face to face with the negro ; this instinctive consciousness of their own natural equality that accompanied their perception of the negro's inferiority ; in short, this development of the democratic idea to which Mr. Jefferson gave such grand expression in the Declaration of Independence, was and is accompanied by corresponding uniformity or harmony of interests. Agriculture, labor, production, was and is the one great dominating interest of Virginia and of all other communities made up of these diverse social elements. It is impossible to divide the interests of "master" and "slave"—of the white man and negro—when placed in natural relation to each other. It is the utmost interest of the master to treat his "slave" kindly, to care for him in sickness, to feed him well, and not to overwork or abuse him, and it is the utmost interest of the latter to be faithful to the former. It is a sort of partnership, a species of socialism, when the brain of one being and the hands of fifty other beings labor for the common good, for the general welfare; and though possible exceptions are found where a brutal master beats and abuses his people, or a worthless "slave" runs off and hides in the swamp, both alike injure themselves, the master gets less work from his "slave," and the "slave" brings upon himself a corresponding evil. The so-called "non-slaveholder," if an agriculturist, has the same interest; he is also a producer, and can not separate his interests from the "slaveholder," which, perhaps, he was himself yesterday, and may be again to-morrow. If he be a mechanic, a lawyer, physician, or merchant, then, though not identified as a producer with the "slaveholder" or "non-slaveholder," and in a sense may be said to have different interests, these interests do not and can not conflict with the former, unless, as in the Northern States, government is called on to "protect labor." But as government is confined to its legitimate sphere in Virginia and most other Southern States, and protects all, without favors to any, there is then no conflict of interests, even when some are engaged in widely different pursuits from the one great common interest of production. There is, therefore, universal harmony in Southern society; the interests of master and "slave" are entirely indivisible, while those of the " non-slaveholder," if engaged in production, are similar, and as to all others, when they do not involve the government, though the pursuits or interests be widely different, there can be no social conflict.

The ideas of Jefferson, Madison, and their cotemporaries were naturally formed by these circumstances, and after the revolutionary contest was over and a common government was to be created, they naturally proposed a system in harmony with the condition they represented. The North, as has been said, with no social substratum or natural distinctions, desired a government based on artificial distinctions, those separating classes, the same substantially as in England, though, of course, dispensing with a titled class, a king, and laws of primogeniture. It is true all the States had a few negroes, and they were all in their normal condition of so-called slavery, but their numbers were so inconsiderable that they did not influence society or modify the mental habits of the Northern people. All over, and especially in the New England States, the same ideas were reflected by the representative men ; they wanted a government based on the *status quo*, on wealth, that should keep power in the hands of the few who then exercised it, and with sufficient force to hold the multitude in subjection. They proposed an executive for life, who should also appoint the governors of the States, that senators should serve ten years, and various other projects of similar character—all ending in or embodying the same common idea, that is, a government for the few at the expense of the many.

The Southern men, on the contrary, proposed a government embodying *their* idea—the idea of democracy, and that should reflect the advanced opinion and living spirit of their own society, rather than a thing based on the model of Britishis...., and involving substantially the principles of the old European order. While they duly appreciated education, cultivation,

and other accidental social distinctions, those whose ideas were
advanced by juxtaposition with negroes, or with this natural
line of demarcation, would not listen to the creation of a central government that tended in any respect to place power in
the hands of a class, or that enabled the few, however indirectly it might be, to govern the many. The contest, both in
the convention and before the people, assumed the form of a
contest for a strong or a weak government—a government
that should be supreme, like the British Parliament, or a gov-
ernment.of delegated powers, which, while carefully defined,
should be extremely limited in its functions or scope of action.
But back of all this were the fundamental ideas—the British
and the American—the spirit of the old societies and the spirit
of the new order—of British oligarchy and of American
democracy.

Massachusetts and Virginia were respectively the head-quar-
ters and embodiments of this conflict, this struggling of ideas,
these tendencies to return to the past or to advance into the
future, and it is as remarkable, perhaps, to find the former
arrayed on the side of power and privilege, as that the descendants of the cavaliers should now be the champions of democracy, and the advocates of the broadest liberty. But, as has
been observed, our ideas are the results of accident, our opinions originate in the circumstances that surround us, and
therefore while the mental habits of the North were only
slightly modified from those of the mother country, those of
the South, under wholly different conditions—conditions, in
fact, utterly unknown to the English mind—were radically
different.

The Northern masses, as has been remarked, were then
ignorant and helpless, and the agricultural class, though advanced considerably beyond the same class in England, as the
tillers of the soil had then barely escaped from the old feudal

slavery or serfdom, were utterly powerless and without defenders in the great civil contest that succeeded the revolution. As against the advocates of strong government—those who represented the governing class—they could make no resistance whatever, except a physical and revolutionary one. The right of suffrage was very limited, and, indeed, as in England at this time, property and not population was the basis of representation, and therefore the vast majority had no voice nor representation whatever. Under such circumstances, it is obvious and beyond question that if a similar state of things had existed at the South, a government would have been formed on the British model—a republic, doubtless, but a bastard one—with powers so extensive and absolute that, as we now witness in Europe, nothing but revolution and physical force could ever enable the masses to overthrow it or to regain their natural liberty.

But the planters of the South, unlike the farmers of the North, were an educated class, and fully competent to compete with the great leaders of the Northern oligarchy. Their ideas were widely advanced beyond those of the Northern farmer, but their *interests* were identical—those of agriculture, of production, of labor, of democracy, of manhood against privilege, and therefore they naturally fought the battle against strong government and class distinctions. The government actually adopted was, with the exception of a life tenure in its judicial department, substantially that which was originally advised by the leading minds of the South, and which, instead of being supreme and absolute over the States, as desired by the Northern leaders, was, with certain well-defined exceptions, as utterly powerless and indeed disconnected with the States as the government of England, or any other foreign power. And perhaps no higher or more patriotic example can be found in all history than that of the graceful assent and acceptance of the Northern leaders, when they consented to adopt

the present system. As has been said, it was no selfish or
base spirit that prompted their desire for a strong government.
They saw that the great body of the people were ignorant;
all history and all experience warranted them, as they believed,
in retaining power in the hands of the few who then possessed
it—in a word, they could not rise above the circumstances that
surrounded them, or act otherwise than in conformity with
their mental habits. But when fairly beaten in the convention
and the great forum of popular discussion—for when the ideas
of Jefferson and other Southern leaders were brought before
the Northern masses, thousands of earnest and enthusiastic
apostles of these new and glorious truths sprung up in every
direction—then Hamilton and his associates generously assented
to the adoption of the present system, and became its warmest
advocates. They in no respect changed their views of government, but they became convinced that these views were then
impracticable, and however unquestioned their ascendency at
the North, that the Southern States would never consent to
any union on such basis, and as a federal union on almost any
terms was essential to the maritime States, they had the mag-
nanimity to accede to the Southern or democratic view embodied in the present government, and to become, as has been
said, the warmest advocates for its adoption before the people.
But if this patriotic and high-minded course of Hamilton and
the great leaders of Northern opinion, which thus, it may be
said, secured to the country and to the world the noblest government ever known in human annals, is worthy of the esteem
and admiration of posterity, what a stupendous and boundless
benefit Jefferson, Madison, George Mason, and their associates, who not alone assented to, but who originated this government, have conferred upon posterity, and indeed the race
itself!

    For the first time in human history the grand idea of equal-

ity, of an equal freedom or of equal rights, was declared to be
the sole foundation of government, and made the vital principle
of the political order, the starting-point of a new and more
glorious civilization than was ever before dreamed of in the annals of mankind. Christ had promulgated the Divine command,
" do unto others as you would have them do unto you," or
recognize in all other men the same rights that you claim for
yourselves; but however faithful some may have been to this
command in a religious sense, all the " Christian" governments
that have ever existed, or that exist now, are in utter conflict
with it, and therefore the government created in 1776, which
embodied this glorious truth and clothed it with the flesh and
blood and body and bones of material power, is unquestionably the most important worldly event that has ever happened in human affairs. The revolt against England, its
success, the subsequent independence, the creation of a new
government, the beginning of an independent national existence, might all occur without any radical change of principles
or any revolution of ideas, as indeed it is certain would have
been the case if the views of Hamilton and other Northern
leaders had been embodied in the new government. But the
grand idea of Jefferson in the Declaration of Independence,
and afterwards embodied in the federal government, was the
starting-point of a revolution the greatest, most beneficent,
most radical, and most important, that has ever happened in
the history of the race—a revolution, moreover, that has gone
on ever since, and must continue until all the governments of
the Old World are overthrown, and society reorganized on the
basis of the great, indestructible, and immortal truth that
underlies our own—that fixed, natural, and unchangeable equality which God has stamped forever on the organism of the
race. If, therefore, we compare the services of Jefferson,
Madison, and their associates with those of other men in other

13

times or other lands, it will be seen that they rise to a dignity
and importance immeasurably greater than even the most elevated and most glorious among the benefactors of mankind.
How paltry, in comparison, the Barons of Runymede, who
overthrew a tyrant king that had oppressed their order! How
mean and selfish Brutus and his fellow-conspirators, when slay-
ing the man they envied as well as feared! How insignificant
even Hampden and the great leaders of revolution in England,
who fought to defend themselves from the increasing oppression of a ruling class, when compared with Jefferson and his
associates, who proclaimed an idea and organized a basis for
the freedom of the race—for the equal rights of all whom God
had made equal!

But great, and, when compared with what others may have
done, immense as may be the benefits conferred by Jefferson
and his associates on mankind, they only did their duty, and
honestly represented the ideas and desires of their constituencies. Or, in other words, they merely expressed the opinions
and reflected the mental habits that had their origin in the
social condition, and followed as a necessary consequence of
juxtaposition with negroes. If there had been no negroes in
Virginia—no widely different race with its different capacities
and different wants to provide for, in short, if there had been
no natural distinctions, then those accidental and artificial
things—wealth, education, family pride, etc.—which separate
classes would have remained as elsewhere, the basis of political as well as social order. The descendants of English cavaliers, with their traditions and mental habits, would, perhaps,
be somewhat liberalized, for their condition was widely
changed from that of their ancestors, but without negroes,
without the presence of natural distinctions, without those
lines of demarcation fixed forever by the hand of God for
society to repose upon, they would have remained the most

aristocratic community in America. Neither Thomas Jefferson, nor any of the great controlling minds of the day, would
have been heard of; or, at all events, would not have figured
in that grand *rôle* where history has always placed them—the
authors of a new idea and the founders of a new political system.

· They *might* have had, as Sir Thomas Moore and Algernon
Sidney, and, indeed, men of all ages have had, feeble glimmerings of the great truth promulgated in 1776. All who belong
to the race or species are created equal; and this great, fixed,
and eternal fact, embedded in the physical and mental organism of the race, has always been dimly perceived, but without
juxtaposition with a different race, without the actual presence of the negro, without the constant daily perception of
those natural distinctions that separate races, in contrast with
the artificial distinctions of classes of their own race, neither
Jefferson nor any one else could have risen to the level of the
grand truth embodied in the Declaration of Independence.
They *might* have been distinguished actors in the great drama
of independence, but that, as an historical event, would not
have differed from a score of similar events where one people
or portion of a people have separated and set up an independent government. The overthrow of the Moorish dominion in
Spain—of the rule of the Spaniards in Holland—and the recent
independence of Belgium, are parallel events, and many others
might be named where foreign dominion has been overthrown
and new governments set up without resulting in any change
or progress of ideas, or without working out any fundamental
revolution in human affairs. And if Jefferson, Madison, and
their associates had had the same mental habits as Hamilton,
Adams, and others of the North, it is obvious that independence would not have been accompanied by a revolution in
ideas. As has been said, a more liberal system than that of

the mother country would have been established, but a new system, a radical and fundamental change in the political order —a new starting-point in the progress of the race—a government founded on the universal equality of the citizenship as actually established, it is obvious would have been impossible. And as the public men of a country can never rise above the level of the average opinion or the ordinary mental habits of the people, it is equally obvious that Jefferson and his associates would never have done so, and therefore; if there had not been a condition of things that gave origin to new ideas and new habits of thought in the people of Virginia and elsewhere where these widely different social elements were in juxtaposition, then it is equally obvious that the world would never have heard of them in 1776, and whatever time and circumstances might have brought about in the future, no *revolution* at that time would have been possible.

In conclusion, therefore, that is repeated in direct terms which has been rather inferred than directly stated. The presence of the *negro on this continent, our juxtaposition with a widely different and inferior race, and the existence of natural distinctions or natural lines of demarcation in human society, originating of necessity new ideas and modes of thought, has been the happiest conjunction that has ever occurred in human affairs, and has led directly to the establishment of a new system and a new civilization based on foundations of everlasting truth—the legal and political equality of the race, or of all those whom the Almighty Creator has Himself made equal.*

CHAPTER XXII.

In the foregoing chapter it has been shown how "slavery," or the presence of the negro element in our midst, has given origin to the American idea of democracy—to more expanded and truthful conceptions of our true relations to each other—to mental habits which led Mr. Jefferson to promulgate the grand idea of equality in 1776—to make that great movement a revolution of ideas as well as a war of independence—to render the latter a mere preliminary for ushering in a new political system based on the equal rights of citizenship and the starting-point of a new civilization widely and radically different in its fundamental idea from anything ever before known in the political experience of mankind. It has been shown that Hamilton and Jefferson, the respective leaders and exponents of the opposing ideas and tendencies of the time, merely reflected the mental habits that belonged to the different social conditions then existing, or of the different constituencies which they represented, and after the great contest for independence which they passed through harmoniously was closed and a new system of government was to be created, that the ideas of Jefferson generally prevailed and the present government embodying these ideas was established.

It has been shown, moreover, that both of these great men and those who acted with them were equally honest and equally patriotic; that neither, nor any of them could rise above the level of opinion in their respective sections, for then they would no longer have been representative men or able to influence the people; that the opinions of Hamilton reflected the mental habits of the North which clung to the forms and spirit of the British system founded on artificial distinctions, while Jefferson, reflecting with equal fidelity the mental habits that originate in a different social condition—where a subordinate race is in juxtaposition—advocated a democratic system resting on the fixed and indestructible laws of nature. And in view of all these historical facts and inductive facts the conclusion was deemed irresistible that the presence of the negro element in our midst, the existence of a natural substratum in the social elements which thus secured the liberty of our own-race—the legal and political equality of white men—was the happiest event or conjunction of circumstances that has ever happened in the history of mankind. But while the great northern leaders thus consented to the establishment of a democratic system they were driven on by their own tendencies as well as the mental habits of their people to neutralize its forces and to pervert its spirit. At that period suffrage was extremely limited, while the agricultural class in the Northern States—compared with the present—may be said to have been extremely ignorant.

The northern or federal party were thus enabled to get possession of the new government and to give it such direction as their opinions and interests doubtless seemed to demand. The President himself—the illustrious Washington— was without decided political convictions. His instincts and his family traditions, it is believed, inclined him in the direction of the northern party, while the local tendencies of opinion—the general mental habits of the Virginians to regard the distinctions of race as the legitimate basis of political order— generally restrained him, and in the mighty conflict of opinion kept him in a neutral position. He formed his cabinet out of wholly incongrous materials, made Jefferson Secretary of State, and Hamilton Secretary of the Treasury, and selecting other exponents of the conflicting opinions, sought to neutralize the contending forces by an equal selection of subordinates from the hostile camps.

The public credit, the restoration of commercial confidence was the first and most pressing want of the country as well as of the new government, and in this Hamilton found a pretext for adopting,the British system of finance which he foresaw would enable his party to recover to a great extent the ground lost in the creation of the government, and in practice, whatever might be the theory entertained, restore it or closely approximate it to his darling model—that favorite British system which he and his associates believed to be an embodiment of political wisdom. The idea of the British aristocracy that government is an instrument designed for their benefit was deeply implanted in the northern mind, and is so still.

In England it is a practice which the idea has simply originated in. Official employments, pensions and special legislation or monopolies in England, embrace all or nearly all the ruling class, and therefore, the idea that government is established for their benefit necessarily follows. This idea of government is generally embraced by the northern mind even in our own times, and the habit of looking to this vast and beneficent power as the source of pecuniary benefits to the people, if not to a class, is almost universal among the northern people.

Hamilton, brought up under the British system, was deeply imbued with it, and, placed in power, it was natural enough that he and his associates should construe the Constitution in a way to give it effect. The state debts that were contracted for carrying on the war were assumed by the new government and formed a basis for a national bank which was soon established, and the rapid restoration of public credit that followed the restoration of public order and a settled society in a young and vigorous country was claimed by the federal writers as a proof of the wisdom of their policy and the extraordinary ability of their leader.

Mr. Jefferson opposed this policy from the beginning in all its aspects—the adoption of the British system of finance, the assumption of state debts, the creation of a national bank, in short, the entire programme of federal policy. He held with the state-rights democracy of our day, that the central government was a factitious and limited government, whose powers were derived, not from the collective people but from the people of the several or *United States*, that the Constitution should be literally construed, and the practice under it strictly confined to the plainly enumerated objects, and, therefore, that the creation of a national bank, assumption of state-debts, etc., were unconstitutional in principle and dangerous in practice.

Hamilton and his party, on the contrary, held that the financial policy they adopted was not only the wisest that was possible under the circumstances, but that the consequences likely to follow—the consolidation of power and prestige of the central government—would be of the greatest possible value to the people. Indeed, the old contest between Massachusetts and Virginia—the conflict of ideas—the warfare of widely different mental habits which preceded and ushered in the government were renewed and accompanied by a bitterness of spirit quite unknown in the former case. Hamilton, impelled by the opinions of the North, assumed in practice, if not in theory always, that the central government sprung from the collective or the American people instead of the people of the States, and was almost unlimited in its powers, and he doubtless believed that the more extended its powers, the safer and more stable would become the country and the more prosperous the people. He had failed to obtain such a government as he especially desired—a government after the English model—republican in form but aristocratic in fact, a government based on those artificial distinctions which the mental habits of the North were accustomed to regard as the only safe foundation, and now in power, with the prestige of the great name of Washington to support his policy, he doubt-less believed himself a patriot, and as performing vital service to his country and to posterity, when he thus construed the Constitution and consolidated the powers of the federal system.

Indeed, the fear of the people—of a reckless and dis-orderly multitude—was the abiding sentiment of the great northern leaders, and the consolidation, power, and grandeur of a central government that should restrain them was the object of all their efforts. Thus, the very objects the federal-ists aimed at—doubtless from patriotic motives, for there being no laws of primogeniture there was no permanent class to be ben-efited by their policy—were the very things that Mr. Jefferson and his friends contemplated as the greatest danger to the country. Hamilton desired to construe the Constitution in a way to build up an enormous central power that should hold in check the tendencies to disruption and disorder, while Jef-ferson believed that the greater the assumption and the con-solidation of power in the federal system the greater the dan-ger to the freedom of the States and to the people.

Or, in other words, the federalists believed that the more the central power was enlarged the greater the scope and strength of the federal government—the more certain were the States to be kept from disunion and the restless multitudes from anarchy, while Jefferson and his party believed that this assumption of power in the central government would result in the overthrow of the government itself if there was no other way of obtaining redress and of preserving on the part

of the States and the people of the States the liberties which
they fought for in 1776. Such was the great civil contest that
sprung up under the administration of Washington, but which
was constantly restrained by the presence of that great man,
who, without any very decided leanings as regarded the parties
to it, was, moreover, eminently practical and earnestly disposed
to favor conciliation and peace rather than commit himself to
the abstract opinions of either side. It was only, therefore,
during the succeeding administration of Adams that this fundamental conflict of ideas—this conflict which involved the
very foundations of government itself, and which, back of the
immediate actors that figured in the scene, originated in the
different mental habits that spring of necessity from different
social conditions, reached its culmination and prepared the way
for that final solution which the great civil revolution of 1800
afterwards accomplished.

The federalists, or, more properly, the centralists, had construed the Constitution in a way to make the government in
practice substantially what they believed it should have been
in theory. They had adopted the British system of finance,
had created a national debt and a national bank, which, as in
England, was to be the agency for the deposit and disburse-
ment of the public revenue, and, from the necessities of the
case, a vast and overshadowing monopoly which was to hold the
credit of the States, and of every individual in the States, at its
mercy. In fact, the States were rapidly sinking into mere dependencies and subject provinces of the vast and overshadowing
power of the central government, which, not content with its
usurpations over the States—tending, in practice, to almost
obliterate the lines of State sovereignty—even sought to
strike down the liberty of the individual citizen, and in its
alien and sedition laws to exercise absolute powers. These
laws authorized the president to imprison and punish citizens

and others as his fears or caprices might dictate, with few, if any, greater safeguards for the citizen than in absolute governments of the Old World.

The federal party embodied the British idea of government, and their notions of liberty differed little, if any, from those of the mother country. *Liberty* in England consists in the equal protection of person and property in an ordinary sense, but, as liberty, in fact, consists in an equal citizenship or an equal voice in the creation of laws that all are called on to obey, of course those who have no vote or voice in these laws are, to that extent, slaves. It was the policy of the federalists to limit this great natural right of suffrage, and in all the States where they were in the ascendency they sought to do so, as indeed was legitimate and consistent with their fundamental idea of government. Equally consistent and legitimate was their habit of expecting pecuniary benefits from government, for this, as has been said, was the practice in England, and the idea or theory that sprung from it was deeply engraved on the northern mind. While the federalists, therefore, sought to consolidate power in the hands of the federal government and to weaken the States, all the selfish and mercenary interests of the day were naturally attracted to a party whose public policy thus favored and invited their coöperation.

The conflict of labor and capital—the frightful antagonism between those whose labor produces all wealth and those who own the wealth produced by past generations of laborers—is at the bottom of all the revolutions and civil commotions of modern times, for it involves the whole subject of government, as well as all those mighty social evils which so disfigure and deform European society. In England this conflict has, in one sense, reached its utmost limit—while in another respect it may be said to be least active or less palpable than anywhere else.

The few who own the wealth produced by past generations
are the wealthiest in the world, while the many who produce
all the wealth of the present are undoubtedly the poorest!

*Those who produce every thing enjoy nothing, while those
who produce nothing enjoy every thing!* A political econo-
mist of great eminence has made an estimate of the present
wealth of England, and declared that, if equally divided, every
man, woman, and child in England would have ten thousand
pounds, or fifty thousand dollars, and yet supposes that there
are ten millions of people who never own a dollar beyond their
daily support! The land is owned by some thirty-five thousand proprietors, many of whom have large parks containing
many thousand acres, filled with game and left untilled, while
millions of men and women of their own race—their own kind
—are without a single foot of that which God designed for the
common sustenance and comfort of all! Education, moral
development, and happiness must go hand in hand with these
things, of course; indeed, it is a truth that should always be
recognized when estimating the well-being of masses of men,
that their moral and physical well-being are necessarily inseparable.

No one, however ignorant or prejudiced in favor of British-
ism, or "British liberty," can suppose for a moment that such
stupendous results as these, or that such a social condition as
that of England, could ever be brought about by natural causes.
They are all of the same race, with the same natural capacities
as well as wants, and if there be any difference, or any natural
inferiority, it is within the governing class, whose intermarriage
among the landed aristocracy has deteriorated their blood, and
reduced them below the normal standard.

It is the government, therefore—the contrivance or political
machine which has worked out these tremendous results—that
has dug this mighty chasm between beings whom the Almighty

has created alike, and therefore forbidden any governmental distinction.

The notion that government should benefit their condition, therefore—should make them richer and happier—originates in the fact itself in England, and those who, like the federalists, formed all their ideas of government after the British model, sought naturally enough to wield it for these supposed beneficent purposes. There was the same social conflict, in a degree, at the North as in England. It was the interest of the capitalist or employer to get all the labor possible with as little expense as might be, while the laborer would naturally seek to get as high wages as possible, and in return give as little labor as possible.

The capitalists, the men of wealth, the professional classes, merchants, indeed all classes of Northern society, except the agricultural class, were attracted to the federal party, and, in addition, speculators and projectors of every kind were naturally drawn in the same direction. These classes, embracing all the wealth, and cultivation, and social influence of the day, rallied in support of the federal party, which, with the government in its hands, with the prestige of power, and nearly all of the intellectual men of the time on its side, was irresistible, so far as the North was concerned. The producing classes, the farmers and laborers—those only that were naturally opposed to its policy, or whose real interests were in conflict with its policy—were then comparatively helpless. The right of suffrage was exceedingly limited, and though the agricultural class largely outnumbered the others, they were ignorant, without guides, and indeed quite helpless in the grasp of the federal leaders. The federal party, as has been stated, had, by so construing the constitution, usurped power that rendered the government substantially such as they originally desired to establish, and the masses, without intelligent leaders, were

powerless to resist. And any one intelligently contemplating
the condition of things in the Northern States during the
administration of the elder Adams, must be irresistibly forced
to the conclusion that the masses—the laboring and producing
classes—were wholly unable to relieve themselves from the
oppressions of this party, short of a physical revolution and an
appeal to arms. They were largely in the majority, but the
right of suffrage being mainly confined to property-holders, laborers, mechanics, artisans, etc., were, as in England, disfran-
chised; while the agricultural classes, though greatly advanced,
no doubt, beyond the same classes in the Old World, were
yet extremely illiterate and ignorant, and therefore powerless.
The policy of the federalists was absolutely the same as in England—that is, the government was a machine or instrument
through which the few who produce nothing were to enjoy
every thing, and the many, who produce every thing, were to
enjoy nothing. In a new country, with cheap lands and virgin
soils, it might be many centuries before the awful results now
manifested in England could be worked out, but the process
was the same—the same causes were in operation, and the
same results would surely follow—differing only in degree.

Nor, had the Union been confined to the Northern States,
was there any reasonable prospect before the masses of overthrowing the oppression foisted on them, by a resort to revolution and physical force. They were the immense majority,
it is true, but without leaders, without education or intelligence, or prestige of any kind, their doom was sealed, their
subjection certain, their slavery inevitable. It would have
been the old story over again—the revolt of the people against
their oppressors in 1776 to be again subjected to other oppressions in 1796—a change from one master to another; though,
doubtless, as all the efforts of the race have been in the direction of progress, a certain advance towards a better condi-

tion. But, fortunately for mankind and the cause of free institutions, a widely different state of things existed in Virginia and other States in the South.

As fully considered in another place, the negro element was here stationary, and in numbers so considerable that rules and regulations were necessary in regard to it. It had to be provided for; its capacities, its wants, its necessities, in short, harmonized with the wants and well-being of the dominant race. The colonial legislatures, as the State legislatures of the present day, were constantly called on to enact laws and establish regulations for this subordinate social element, as well as for themselves, and therefore habits of thought grew up that gave them widely different notions of government from those of the people in the North.

There was no social conflict; all had the same interests, and if one man inherited wealth, and another had nothing but his labor to depend on, they never came in conflict, for the former never sought the aid of the government to benefit himself at the expense of his less fortunate neighbor. In the North, if a citizen inherited ten thousand dollars, he invested it in some special corporation—a bank, a manufacturing company, or something else—that had its origin in special legislation, and perhaps doubly increased his income, which, of course, was drawn from the laborer, the producer, the class that creates all wealth.

In Virginia, on the contrary, if a citizen inherited ten thousand dollars, he invested it in lands, in the industrial capacities of negroes, in short, in labor; and though he may never have labored an hour with his own hands himself, he became of necessity a producer, with the same common, universal, and indivisible interests of all other producers and laborers, and therefore never sought the aid of government. Indeed, the government could not nor can not at this time legislate for the benefit—special benefit—of the planter of the South, or the farmer or producer at the North; and from the day it.was created to this moment, there has never been an act of Congress or of the federal government that specifically benefited the South. Congress *might*, it is true, "protect" cotton or wheat, or other of the great staples which the producers of both sections furnish, but it would be a "protection" quite as useless to the parties interested as it would be harmless in its results to other classes and interests among us.

The clear mind of Jefferson grasped these bonds of industrial interest between the southern planter and northern farmer—the slaveholder of the South and the laborer of the North—at a very early period, and declared them "natural allies" in the great conflict then pending. The planter or "slaveholder" of the South asked nothing from government but its protection. He had grown up under a condition of things where there was no social conflict of any kind. There were no opposing interests—no class distinctions—nothing to appeal to his selfishness or to blind his judgment. Society was *naturally* divided, not into the rich and poor as elsewhere, but into whites and negroes, and, as the latter was owned-by the former there was no contradiction, no motive or possible inducement to employ the government as an instrument for the special benefit of any body. The old European notion of government, therefore, that clung and still clings to the northern mind, that government should regulate the religion, the commerce, the industry, etc., of the country, was exploded, and the modern and true American idea that it should simply protect all alike and give favor to none became the general idea of the populations of the South; and, indeed, of the great agricultural populations of the Central States so far as it then could find expression. And, when this was the general notion of Virginia and other States at the South as regards their own legitimate government, of course they would not permit the federal and factitious government resting on delegated and strictly defined limitations of power, to be perverted in its spirit and transformed by its practice into a machine, as in England, to benefit others at their expense. The Southern States, therefore, especially Virginia and Kentucky, met in their legislatures, consulted with other States, and, in the celebrated Kentucky and Virginia resolutions of 1798, made a declaration of principles, and pledged themselves to a policy that will always serve as the true landmarks of our State and federative systems so long as the republic, or, indeed, American freedom itself lasts to bless the world and illuminate mankind.

These resolutions offered a common platform for the agricultural States—for the producing classes of all sections—for the masses, the millions, in short, for all men who believed in the American idea of government and demanded equal rights for all and favors for none.

Thus the Middle States, the great agricultural populations of the North, who, unaided and alone were powerless in the grasp of the federal party, led as that party was by the intellect, and sustained by the wealth and social prestige of the North, found themselves naturally allied with the agricultural populations of the South who were led by men quite the equals in general attainments, and vastly the superiors in political knowledge, of the great northern leaders. These men—Jefferson, Madison, George Clinton, and their associates—had already conquered in the great intellectual contest that had preceded the creation of the government, and though in the great battle now pending, the centralists occupied vantage ground, for their banks, state debts, and consolidated federal powers, attracted to their standards all the selfish interests and mercenary influences in the country, the former again carried the day, and in the great civil revolution of 1800 restored the government, as Mr. Jefferson expressed it, to "the republican tack." This restoration of the federal government to its original purposes was surely second only to the revolution of 1776 in importance, and without it it is obvious that the fruits of the former must measurably have been lost. As has been seen, the northern masses were at that time wholly unable to contend with the opposing minority which embraced within its ranks the wealth, talent, education, and social influence of the day. And though largely in the majority as regards numbers, it was powerless even as regards physical force, for it was without leaders to direct its energies or to cope successfully with that brilliant array of able and accomplished civilians and soldiers that gathered about the administration and directed the councils of the federal party. If the rule of the federalists in the course of time became personally oppressive—if that personal "freedom" which in England permits the *subject* to enjoy locomotion as he pleases and protects his person from violence were stricken down, then it may be supposed that the northern masses would have resisted, and, perhaps, in the progress of the future have overthrown such government.

But the government actually established by the federalists— by the false construction of the Constitution, and the usurpations in practice which would have kept the producing classes —the toiling millions—in the same or similar subjection to a ruling oligarchy, as is now witnessed in England, and which, in the course of time, would render them equally abject, poverty-stricken, ignorant, and miserable, would seem to be, in view of all the circumstances then existing, beyond their power to change or reform by a civil revolution like that which did occur in 1800, or to overthrow by the strong hand of physical force. The great civil revolution, therefore, when able and accomplished statesmen of the South, the equals in talent, and vastly superior to any class in Christendom in political knowledge, led the northern producing classes through the great conflict then pending, and overthrowing the centralists restored the government to its original purity and simplicity, must be deemed, as has been said, only second in importance to the great event of 1776.

And the social condition in the South, the so-called slavery, which invariably renders the southern planter the natural ally of the northern farmer, must be considered, as it obviously is in fact, the sole, or at all events the leading cause for the successful working of democratic institutions, as it was originally the sole and unquestionable *cause* that originated the great American idea of government embodied in the Declaration of Independence. Nor are the consequences of that condition of so-called slavery—the existence of a subordinate social element at the South which has thus, with more or less directness, worked out the equality, freedom, and happiness of the laboring classes of the North—limited to our own land or to our own people. As has been observed, the conflict of capital and labor is the great question of the day—the question that is at the bottom of all the European revolutions of modern times, and its solution must, of necessity, involve the destruction of every government now in existence except our own. *Capital* in the old world has the education and intelligence as well as the government on its side against the people, and the simple fact that, in half of the American States, capital and labor are united, inseparable, and indissoluble, is of transcendent importance to the future liberation of the laboring millions of Europe.

Here—for the first time in the experience of the race—wealth, cultivation, and intellectual power are arrayed on the side of production and in defence of the rights of labor, not by a warfare on northern capital, as it is sometimes charged, but by

demanding that government shall not legislate for the latter at
the expense of the former. Nor is the subordinate element—
the inferior race in our midst, which, in the providence of God
has thus been made the mediate or immediate cause of such
vast and boundless benefit to the freedom, progress, and well-
being of the superior race—without participation in these benefits. God has designed all His creatures for happiness, and this
happiness is always secured when they are in their true position, and in natural relations to each other; and when the condition of the negro is compared with his African state—the
existing population with their African progenitors—then it is
seen that the progress and happiness of the inferor has
marched *pari passu* with those of the superior race.

CHAPTER XXIII.

THE FUTURE OF THE NEGRO.

THERE are something like twelve millions of negroes in America, on the mainland and the adjacent islands—as large a proportion, perhaps, in view of their industrial adaptation, as there are of the Caucasian or dominant race; and, therefore, whatever may be the contingencies or the wants of the future, there would seem to be no necessity now for any further importation of these people. Of the twelve millions, there are between four and five millions in their normal condition at the South. There are, perhaps, half a million of so-called free negroes, about equally divided between North and South. There are about four millions in Brazil, Cuba, and Porto Rico of so-called slaves, but really in a widely different condition from that common to the South. Finally, there are between three and four millions of so-called free negroes in the tropics, in Jamaica, Hayti, and the other islands, with some thousands, however, scattered about the coast towns, and in the *terra caliente* of the mainland. The free negro, in the American Union, as has been stated, is destined to extinction. It is only a question of time, when this doom will be accomplished. The census returns, and the universal experience, recognize this deplorable truth; but beyond them, and independent of any demonstration whatever, their extinction is a necessity—is as legitimate and unavoidable as any other *effect* or effects linked by inevitable necessity with their predetermining cause or causes. They are not merely turned loose—abandoned to their fate without masters or protectors to look after them, but they are assumed to be Caucasians, *black*-white men, creatures like ourselves, with the same capacities, and the same wants, and though no one assumes to do so individually, *society* forces them to live up to the theory in question, and, as this is impossible, as no human force or forces can set aside the ordinances of the Eternal, it destroys them. If, for example, laws were passed to change the color, the hair, the form of the limbs, or any *physical* quality of the negro, and the whole power of the State was brought to bear upon him to compel him to be like the white man in these respects, it is obvious that nothing could be accomplished save the destruction of the unhappy creature. The capacities, the wants, the moral and intellectual nature of the negro, differ from our own to the precise extent that his physical nature or bodily structure differs from ours, and, therefore, Northern society, or rather that monstrous and malignant philanthropy which in its ignorance and blind impiety deems itself kind and beneficent, necessarily destroys the object of its solicitude when it strives to give him the rights of the white man, or to force him to change his moral and intellectual nature into that of the white man.

If all the children of the age of ten, in a given community, were turned from their homes into the street and left without their natural protectors to care and provide for their wants, they would perish in time, of course, if we could suppose them to remain at this age or condition. But if, in addition to this abandonment of these helpless ones, a theory were set up that they *had* all the capabilities of the adult, and should, therefore, enjoy the rights and perform the duties of men and women, they would, of necessity, perish still more rapidly. If a dog, or horse, or other domestic animal were turned loose or lost its owner, it would sooner or later perish, but if some deluded "philanthropist" should set up the assumption that his bull-

dog, for instance, was entitled to the rights and should enjoy
the life of the hound, and therefore attempt to force it to exhibit the same qualities, the scent, sight, or swiftness that God
has given the latter, he would, of course, destroy the poor
thing with far greater rapidity than if he had simply turned it
loose to shift for itself. Similar results do attend and must
attend that malignant philanthropy and blind impiety which
would impose the rights or force the duties of the white man
on the differently organized and differently endowed negro.
In Virginia and Maryland he is simply turned loose without
any guide or protector or white man's rights whatever, not
even the right of free locomotion common to British subjects,
and, therefore, lives longer, for there is no especial violence
attempted—no direct effort made to force him to live out the
life or to manifest the nature of widely different beings. But
in Canada and Massachusetts, where white manhood is held
so cheaply that the negro is supposed to be entitled to the
same rights, and direct efforts are made to compel him to fulfill the same duties, where the little Prince of Wales in his
recent visit declared that *he* would not recognize those distinctions of race that originate in the mind of the Eternal
and are fashioned by the hand of Omnipotence, which no
amount or extent of human force, folly, impiety, or crime can
obliterate even to the millionth part of a primordial atom, and
which millions of years after those paltry distinctions of human
invention which transform this common-place lad into an
imaginary superiority over his fellows shall have disappeared,
then he rapidly and miserably perishes.

The tendency to extinction, therefore, is always accelerated
or diminished in exact proportion as "impartial freedom" is
thrust upon him—as he is permitted "to enjoy equal rights"
with the white man, or as ignorance and folly, in their blind
and cruel kindness and exterminating goodness, strive to force

him to manifest the nature and live the life of a different being. This assertion, doubtless, startles the reader, as it once certainly would have startled the writer himself. We are all so accustomed to mental habits directly-in conflict with this assertion, that it is somewhat difficult to lift our minds out of them and to take true cognizance of the facts, and inductive facts, that daily confront us.

The negro *is* a different being from the white man, and therefore, of necessity, was designed by the Almighty Creator to live a different life, and to disregard this—to shut our eyes and blindly beat our brains against the decree—the eternal purpose of God himself, and force this negro to live *our life*, necessarily destroys him, for surely human forces can not dominate or set aside those of Omnipotence. Nor is the negro the sole sufferer from this blind impiety, this audacious attempt to disregard the distinctions and to depart from the purposes of the Almighty Creator. The large "free" negro populations of Maryland and Virginia are the great drawbacks on their prosperity, and if the hundred thousand or so of these people were supplanted by the same number of white laborers, or, indeed, the same number of "slave" negroes, a wide and beneficent change would rapidly follow. Furthermore, they are vicious as well as idle and non-productive, and every one of them a disturbing force—a dangerous element—which, in conjunction with those hideous wretches maddened with a monstrous theory like those miscreants at Harper's Ferry, are always liable to be made instruments of fearful mischief. The consequences of the fifty thousand "free" negroes in juxtaposition with the three millions of white people in New York are barely perceptible, but as scarcely one in fifty of these people are engaged in productive labor, they are a considerable burden upon the laboring and producing ctizens. True, they do not see it or feel it—and multitudes of honest and laborious citi-

zens in the rural districts are profoundly interested in the
"cause of freedom," while thus contributing a certain portion
of each day's labor for the support of some fifty thousand non-
productive negroes. Again, in the cities and larger towns,
the vices and immoralities of the whites have an extended association with this free negro element.

The negro in his normal condition has attractive qualities.
He is not degraded, for none of God's creatures are naturally
degraded, and his fidelity and affection for his master and his
master's family, sometimes reach a dignity that would reflect
honor on the white man. Nor is there any prejudice or
hatred between the races when they are in true relation to
each other. One may travel for months, perhaps years, in the
South, and never witness a collision or the slightest disturb-
ance between them; but, on the contrary, they will often see
a kindly feeling displayed even when the negro is not owned
by those who exhibit it. The negro is in a social position and
relation that accords with his nature, his wants, the purposes
that God has adapted him to, in short, lives out his own life,
and therefore, all that is good, that is healthy in his moral
nature as in his physical nature, is duly manifested. But at
the North, where he is thrust from his natural sphere and
forced to live out the life of a different being, he exhibits the
same moral defects that he does in his physical nature. He
is a social monstrosity—and though his subordinate nature
renders him less likely to commit great crimes than the superior white man, the tendencies to petty immoralities are almost
universal. Some, indeed, bred up in well-regulated families,
and others who are nearly white, escape the general demoralization of this people, but the instances are probably few—the
moral defects march hand in hand with the physical, and, as
they tend continually to disease and death, so, too, do they
tend to universal immorality. And as it would be strange,
14

indeed, if Providence visited the sins of the dominant race on these poor creatures alone, they are extensively associated, as has been observed, with the vices of the whites. With feeble perceptions of moral obligations, with strong tendencies to animal indulgences of every kind, and an utter repugnance to productive labor, they congregate in the cities; and the social exclusion to which they are exposed, as well as the absence of moral sentiment among them, renders them, to a wide extent, the instruments of the vices and corruptions of the whites.

Thus, it is not alone the negro's non-productiveness—the burden, the absolute tax imposed on the laboring classes—but the demoralization of this abnormal element, of this social monstrosity, that is inflicted on society as the legitimate and unavoidable punishment for having placed the negro in an abnormal condition. God created him a negro—a different and inferior being, and, therefore, designed him for a different and inferior social position. Society, or the State, has ignored the work of the Almighty, and declared that he should occupy the same position and live out the life of the white man; and the result is, the laboring and producing classes are burdened with his support, and society, to a certain extent, poisoned by his presence. To the negro it is death—necessarily death, as it always must be to all creatures, human or animal, forbidden to live the life God has blessed them with, or to live in accord with the conditions He has imposed on them. The ultimate doom of the poor creatures, therefore, is only a question of time. The great " anti-slavery" imposture of our times, which has rested on popular ignorance of a few fundamental truths in ethnology and political economy, has at last culminated, and few, if any more of these people will ever be turned loose, or manumitted as it has been called. Whether they will be restored to society and to usefulness at the North may be doubted, but necessity as well as humanity will doubtless prompt such a policy at the South;

but, in any event, it is absolutely certain that, as a class, they will become extinct, and a hundred years hence it is reasonable to suppose that no such social monstrosity as a "free negro" will be found in America.

But another and far more embarrassing question is presented by free negroism outside of the American Union, and that now confronts us in Cuba, Jamaica, Hayti, Mexico, and on the whole line of our Southern border. This is the danger, the sole danger of the so-called slavery question, and it involves possibilities that are fearful to think of, though scarcely dangerous at all if our own people were truly enlightened on the general subject.

In a previous chapter it has been shown how climatic and industrial laws govern our mixed populations, and, without the slightest interference of government, the negro element goes just where its own welfare as well as that of the white citizenship and the general interests of civilization demand its presence. This law of industrial adaptation has carried it from northern ports into the Central States, from the latter to the Border States, and is now, with even increased activity, carrying it from Virginia, etc., into the Gulf States, and thus permitted to go on, with all obstacles removed from the path of its progress, a time will come when the negro population of the New World will be within the centre of existence where it was created, and where the Almighty Creator has provided for its well-being. A sectional party in the North, taking advantage of popular ignorance, and actually enacting a law prohibiting it to exist anywhere where white labor is best adapted, could not by that sole act do any practical injury to the social order of the South. Such an act would indeed be a violation of the spirit of the federal compact, and, as an adjunct of the hostile policy of the foreign enemies of republican institutions, its moral bearings would be full of mischief; but, disconnected or disunited with the British free negro policy, it would be harmless, for, as Mr. Webster once declared, it would only be a " reënactment of the will of God." But, as already observed, the danger of this whole question lies beyond the boundaries of the American Union, and if it be true that we have a considerable number in our midst disaffected to democratic institutions— then every man opposed to the existing condition, or so-called slavery, is, however ignorant of it, to a certain extent an instrument of the enemies of these institutions; and the policy of any such party, as well as the action of any among us, whether in concert with, or independently of any such party, for the same common object or end, becomes treason, and treason the most wicked and revolting that the mind can conceive of, for it involves the natural supremacy of the white man over the negro, as well as the permanence, peace, and prosperity of our republican system.   The Spanish, still less the Portuguese conquerors of America, have never exhibited that healthy natural instinct which preserves the integrity of races, so universally as the Anglo-Americans have done.   They have intermixed and amalgamated with the Indians or Aboriginals with little hesitation ; and though they have always manifested a certain repugnance to an equality with the still more subordinate negro, they have largely intermixed, and therefore, extensively deteriorated and ruined themselves.

In Brazil there are nearly four millions of negroes that are called slaves, but held more by the bonds of pecuniary interest than they are by nature, as with us.   There is a large mulatto and mongrel population, often highly educated, possessing vast wealth, with, of course, all the advantages that these things give when society does not rest on natural distinctions.   A mulatto or mongrel in Virginia or Mississippi may be left to take care of himself, or be a so-called freeman, but he can never be a citizen—can never in any thing whatever be legally endowed with the social attributes, any more than he can with the natural attributes, of the white man. But in Brazil, and, indeed, in Cuba, the mulatto, mongrel, or negro may by law become a citizen, may own slaves, may, in short, be artificially invested with all the "rights" by the government that nature— that God himself has withheld or forbidden. The white man in Cuba is a slave to a foreign dominion, and this same foreign power, while it withholds from him his natural rights, forces the negro by the same arbitrary power into legal equality with him. The arbitrary force is less in Brazil, but the low grade of manhood in the white element, its extensive affiliation and consequent deterioration with the subject race, has rendered them incapable of either comprehending liberty or of enjoying free institutions. The negro that was a slave once becomes a citizen, with all the legal rights of the white man, and, if he inherits wealth, educates his children, etc., then these artificial and accidental things, instead of the distinctions of nature, become the line of demarcation in society. If a planter has a family of children by his negro slaves, and educates them and leaves them his wealth, then they become influential citizens, makers of the government, etc., and leaders of fashion, perhaps, in Rio Janeiro and other cities. The white man is so degraded, the instinct of race so perverted, the sense of superiority so obtuse—in short, the nature of the Caucasian so completely corrupted by extensive affiliations with the subject race, that natural distinctions are no longer a line of demarcation, and wealth, accident, etc., as in Europe, and as the Federalists once desired, are the basis of the political and social order. It is somewhat different in Cuba, for here the American instinct of race and the high appreciation of manhood common to all societies based on the order of nature have a certain influence. But even in Cuba, in our own neighborhood, within a few hours' sail of our coast, society rests upon an artificial basis, and what is called slavery rather involves pecuniary considerations than a question of races.

The social condition, therefore, or so-called slavery may be overthrown any day in Brazil or Cuba, for, resting on a basis of property instead of the distinctions of nature common with us, there is no permanent security for the social safety, and in view of the policy of England on this subject and its influence in Brazil, we should not be surprised at any moment to hear that a revolution had broken out, and that slavery was overthrown in every portion of the Brazilian empire. This result which may happen at any moment, and which circumstances alone may protract for an indefinite period, would seem to be ultimately inevitable—for the white element is every day becoming more deteriorated and feeble; and, without the mental and moral power, without the healthy instinct of the race to buoy it up amid such corrupt and corrupting tendencies, without that high sense of manhood which makes the American "slaveholder" the perfect type and complete embodiment of the strength and power of the great master race of mankind, without, in short, the natural superiority of the white man to restrain this negro and mongrel population, it is certain sooner or later to escape from all legal restraint, and any hour the whole social fabric may collapse into utter and hopeless ruin. It will be well for Americans who desire to preserve American institutions and American civilization to heed this and ponder well on the uncertain and rotten foundations of social order in Brazil and Cuba, and which, already fatally undermined, may at any moment, as has been said, collapse into a huge mass of free negroism, and thus become a portion of that diseased, monstrous, and nameless condition which ignorance, and folly, and imposture, and hatred to American democracy have combined to pervert language as well as stultify reason and call freedom.

Elsewhere it has been shown that the negro isolated in Africa is in a natural condition, for he multiplies himself, but that he is in his normal, healthy, educated or civilized condition at the South, for he then multiplies with vastly greater rapidity than in a state of isolation, and consequently, *must* be more in harmony with those fixed and eternal decrees that God has ordained for the government of all His creatures. It has also been shown that the negro abandoned and left to himself in Virginia, etc., dies out, but, of course, less rapidly than at the North where the notion prevails that he is the same being as themselves, and therefore, in their efforts to make him manifest the same qualities, or, in other words, to force on him the same " rights," he rapidly tends to extinction. But there is still another phase of free negroism vastly more extended and more dangerous to republican institutions and the future civilization of America.

The negro is a creature of the tropics, and his labor is essential to the cultivation of tropical and tropicoid products, which, in turn, are essential to the happiness and well-being of all mankind. But, as has been shown, his *mental* organism renders him incapable—as absolutely and inevitably as the *physical* organism of the white man renders *him* incapable of tropical production. In the brief space allowed in this work to the consideration of this vital and most momentous truth, the author could only present a few leading facts in its support, but these *facts* are so overwhelming that no rational or honest mind in Christendom will venture to dispute the truth in question. Furthermore it may be stated without chance or possibility of historical contradiction, that in the entire experience of mankind no single instance has ever been known when the isolated negro or the labor of the white man has cultivated the soil or grown the products of the tropics. The mind of the white man and the body of the negro—the intellect of the most elevated and the industrial capacities of the most subordinate of all the known human races, therefore, constitute the elements and motive forces of tropical . civilization. Every mind capable of reasoning at all will know that civilization is impossible without production, and production in the great tropical centre of our continent being forever absolutely and necessarily impossible without negro labor guided, controlled, and managed by the higher intelligence of the white man—it is therefore absolutely certain that the social relation which English writers have taught the world to regard as a condition of slavery, is simply that social adaptation of the industrial forces of the subordinate race, essential, not alone to their own welfare but to the welfare of all mankind, and without which there can no more exist what we call civilization in a large portion of America than there can be life without food or light without the sun. This is obvious, and indeed unavoidable to those who are in actual juxtaposition with negroes. But in Europe where there are white men only, and where negroes, Indians, Malays, etc., are in the popular imagination beings like themselves except in the complexion, and only need to be civilized, as they suppose, to be like others, it was an easy matter to excite a public feeling hostile to the prosperity of the people of the tropics. The theory, or rather dogma of a single race, that all mankind was a unit, and negroes, Indians, etc., had a common origin and common nature, and therefore common rights, had been set up by English writers during the conflict with the American colonies; and Dr. Johnson, with his usual coarseness of expression, had declared that " the Virginia slaveholders were the loudest yelpers for liberty" — thus, in utter unconsciousness, paying them a compliment when he believed he was inflicting a sarcasm of peculiar virulence.

The doctrine of the Declaration of Independence had reacted

in Europe, and the French Revolution, which followed so
closely on the American, threatened to overthrow the whole
social fabric in the Old World and to reconstruct its governments on the basis of the great American idea promulgated
by Jefferson. To counteract these tendencies, the English
statesmen of the day sought to distract the attention of the
people from their own wrongs to the fancied wrongs of the
negro—and Wilberforce, Dr. Johnson, and other tory leaders
and writers, originated that world-wide delusion and imposture
which, in the name of freedom, has probably done more damage to freedom than all other influences combined, within the
last seventy years. The assumption of a single race—that the
negro was a *black*-white man, and therefore entitled to all the
rights of white men, naturally attracted the attention and
aroused the sympathies of the English masses, and when the
supposed wrongs of the negro in America were contrasted with
their own, the latter, doubtless, seemed utterly insignificant in
comparison.

The English government, therefore, entered on an "anti-
slavery" policy, which, beginning with the abrogation of the
"slave trade" has continued ever since, and though it has impoverished, and, in fact, destroyed some of the finest provinces
of the British empire, it is as avowed, defined, and energetic at this moment, perhaps even more so than at any other
period since it was commenced. Mr. Calhoun and others have
supposed that the so-called emancipation of negroes in the
British West India Islands originated in a spirit of commercial
rivalry, and in order to monopolize tropical production in their
East Indian possessions that they were willing to sacrifice
utterly their West Indian colonies. There can be no doubt
that British statesmen universally believed that the example
they were about to give us in this respect would be followed
by universal "emancipation" in the United States, as, indeed,

14*

it has been followed by all the European governments owning American possessions. But while this was expected by every body in England, and thus far may be said to have been the prime motive of their action, it is not reasonable to assume that British statesmen were prompted by a spirit of commercial rivalry or believed for a moment that they were concocting a grand scheme for securing a monopoly of tropical pro-· ducts. The policy begun by Pitt forty years previous, naturally and necessarily culminated in the "emancipation" of 1832, though the desire to neutralize the popular excitement then prevailing in respect to parliamentary reform, doubtless hastened the action of the government. English statesmen may be unable, and probably are unable to explain the motives for their "anti-slavery" policy, but they never mistake or fail to recognize its vital importance to the preservation of their system. Democracy and aristocracy are necessarily antagonistic in all their tendencies, and the progress, strength, and extension of the former necessarily involve the downfall and destruction of the latter. And, as it is the South—the "slaveholders," the States, and the people whose social life rests upon natural distinctions that have always struck the deadliest blows at the British system, and, as declared by the old tory, Dr. Johnson, eighty years ago, have been the warmest supporters of liberty, British statesmen, in their turn, desired to break down a condition thus dangerous and thus in conflict with their own.

Indeed, they can not avoid making war upon the social order of the South. It is a necessity that exists in the nature of things, and springs spontaneously from the circumstances that constitute the opposing conditions, and therefore, from 1776 to 1860 this warfare, openly or secretly, on the battle-field, or the still more dangerous arena of public opinion, has been uninterrupted. Their system is based on artificial distinctions—on things of human invention; ours on natural distinctions—those fixed forever by the hand of the Almighty; and so long as England is an American power her policy must be in conflict with our own. If it could ever be successful—if the twelve millions of negroes on this continent could ever be forced from their normal condition of subordination into a legal equality with the whites—then it is obvious democratic institutions would be rendered impracticable. A simple statement of the facts involved would seem to be sufficient to convince every American mind not corrupted by British opinions, that the British "anti-slavery" policy is part and parcel of the British system, and therefore must go on as it has gone on until it either overthrows our republican institutions, or England, and indeed all other European governments and European influences are driven from the New World. The *causes* of West Indian "emancipation," therefore, lie deeper and are far wider in their scope, and immeasurably more deadly in their consequences than any temporary schemes of commercial rivalry, as suggested by Mr. Calhoun, to monopolize tropical products.

They strike at the national life—at the heart of republicanism, at the fundamental principle that underlies our system, at the everlasting truth that all who belong to the race are created free and equal; and should it ever be successful, should our people ever become so corrupted in opinion, and so debauched in their instincts as to assent to the British "anti-slavery" policy and "abolish slavery"—distort and transform themselves into equality with negroes, then it could not be long before the forms as well as the spirit of republicanism would disappear from the New World, and whatever might happen in the course of centuries, all that Washington and Jefferson and the glorious spirits of 1776 labored for would be lost to mankind.

While British and monarchical writers, therefore, have labored to corrupt the nation at the heart—to delude the reason and debauch the instincts of our people—to teach them that the negro was a man like themselves, and that the instincts which God gave them for their guidance in these respects were unworthy prejudices—that to retain this inferior and different being in a subordinate social position corresponding with his wants and our own welfare was wrong—an evil, a sin— in short, "enslaving him"—while European writers and their dupes among us were thus at work corrupting the intellect of a great people, the British government have steadily labored to reduce their teachings to practice and to "abolish slavery" in all their American possessions. It has been estimated that something like five hundred millions of money have been expended within the last seventy years to carry out the British "anti-slavery" policy, to abolish the natural supremacy of the white man over the negro, to obliterate the distinctions fixed by the Almighty Creator, and equalize those *He* has created unequal. This vast expenditure is wrung, of course, from the toil, and sweat, and misery of the English laboring classes, and to pay the annual interest on it every laborer in England is compelled to give a certain portion of every day's toil, which is thus taken from the mouths of his children to carry on a policy at war with liberty in America, but which through the monstrous delusions of the day is represented to be the noblest philanthropy! An aristocracy, a class, a mere fraction of the people, have laid this enormous burden on their brethren, their own race—those whom God created their equals—in order to obliterate the distinctions by which the Almighty has separated white men and negroes; or, in other words, to preserve *their* distinctions—those which they have invented, which separate themselves from their brethren, the British aristocracy have mortgaged the bodies and souls of unborn generations of their kind in an impious and fruitless effort to destroy the distinctions that separate races, and equalize white men and negroes in America. The interest for a single year on this enormous sum, this mighty burden laid on the working classes of England, expended on popular education, would doubtless react in a wide-spread revolution and the utter annihilation of those who; under the pretence of philanthropy, or of liberating negroes in America, have imposed these stupendous burdens on the people.

A few years since, an awful dispensation of Providence in a neighboring island swept away in a brief space of time something like three millions of people—but, if the annual interest paid on the debt contracted under pretence of benefiting negroes in America had been applied to the relief of the Irish, probably all or nearly all of these unfortunate white people might have been saved. Indeed, it is reasonable to suppose that, if the money taken from Irish laborers within the last seventy years and expended for the assumed benefit of the negro had been applied to their relief during the famine in Ireland, few if any would have perished, and that awful calamity never would have disfigured the annals of mankind.

It is the practice of some ignorant and superficial people among us to glorify this stupendous misery inflicted on the ignorant and helpless of their own race under the pretence of benefiting the negro. If it had done so—if, instead of an almost equal mischief to the negro, it had done him a boundless good—the crime against their own helpless and miserable people—the poor, ignorant, over-worked, and under-fed laboring millions of their own race—would still scarcely find its parallel in the history of human wrongs. But it inflicted a still greater crime on the white people of the islands—for it has doomed them to extinction—not absorption by the negro blood, as already explained, but entire extinction—that result being simply a question of time. Such, briefly considered, are the causes and the results, so far as the dominant race are concerned, of the British "anti-slavery" policy, which, beginning in the latter part of the last century, has been steadily and vigorously persisted in, and is, probably, in the face of all its failures in respect to its avowed objects, more energetic and active at this moment than ever before. All the islands are now, whether owned by England or other European powers, substantially turned over to the negro. The governments are simply means for working out this ultimate result. England, for example, sends out to Jamaica a governor, secretary, and a few other officials, perhaps to carry on the government of that island. The governor probably selects his council from the white element, for the reason that the intelligence of the negro is incompetent to the functions attached, and in respect to the more important official positions generally, they are, from the same cause, filled by white men, or by those of predominating white blood. But the policy of the government is to place power in the hands of the blacks, and therefore all the subordinate official positions are filled by these people, as, indeed, all the higher and more important places would be if there was sufficient intelligence to perform the functions properly.

A foreign power—an aristocracy of the Old World—employs a machinery, a contrivance, or thing called a government, to exterminate the white population in these islands, and to turn them over to the rule of the negro. Under the English system, political or official position, unlike ours, carries with it social importance, and a negro who is a member of the legislature or a magistrate in Jamaica is elevated, in a social sense, above the white who holds no official position, no matter what his claims may be in other respects. With the same legal and political rights, the same schools, and with largely predominating numbers, and most of the official positions in their hands, which, under the British system always gives social importance, the whole operation of the government is employed to elevate the negro in the social scale, and to depress the white man. Of course, intermarriage or affiliation—that hideous admixture of the blood of different races which God has eternally forbidden, and so fearfully punishes with extinction—is a direct and necessary consequence of this governmental policy.

A short time since the Queen of England knighted a negro, and as this factitious elevation placed him in a social position, quite above the untitled white man of Jamaica, the white woman of fashion would, doubtless, smother the instincts God gave for her guidance, and desecrate her womanhood by an alliance with this creature whom God made inferior, but whom a woman, four thousand miles distant, was pleased to make her equal. The government, therefore—all the governments of the British Islands, and, indeed of all other European powers, are simply instruments that are employed to elevate the negro and to depress the white man to a common level, to equalize races, to obliterate distinctions fixed forever by the hand of the Almighty, and make the negro the equal of the white man. It is no negative or *laissez faire* policy—no neutral or indifferent desire to apply a theory and leave it to work itself out—no mere abstract declaration that all are equal, and therefore should be left free to ascend or descend in the social scale according to their merits; but, on the contrary, the government is an active and all-potent machinery, in constant operation to *force* the negro up, and the white man down, to a common level. And it is probable that people in England look upon this policy as just and proper. The negroes largely predominate in number—why should they not have most of the offices? They have been wronged and oppressed, and are without education, and therefore the higher places must be filled by white men; but why should not they enjoy all the places they are fit for? Such, doubtless, is the notion of those in Europe, who, utterly ignorant of the negro, suppose him a man like themselves, except in his color. But human ignorance and impiety can not change His eternal decrees or alter the works of the Almighty. A middle-aged, respectable woman in England may "Knight" a negro, and declare that *she* thus makes him superior to the common throng of white men, but the black skin, and woolly hair, and flat nose, and gross organism, and semi-animal instinct, fixed by the hand of the Eternal, remains just the same, unaltered and unalterable forever. All that is possible with the middle-aged woman in question, and those who surround her, is to corrupt, to debauch, to destroy, to exterminate, to murder their own blood, to doom the white people of those islands to a fate more horrible than the universal slaughter that swept away the whites of San Domingo. The process of extinction now rapidly destroying the white population of these islands has been already considered, but it may be stated again in this place, for it involves such tremendous consequences that it should be shouted in the ears of the world with the voice of an earthquake. The legal and political equality of the negro necessarily carries after it social equality wherever they predominate in numbers, and when there are no social distinctions of race or blood recognized, when that instinct which God has given us to protect the integrity of the organism, is debauched and trampled under foot—when, in short, the "prejudice against color" is lost, then such depraved creatures do not hesitate to form those hideous alliances that generate mulatto offspring. And when the whole force of government is brought to bear against the "prejudice" that revolts at social equality—the hideous affiliation, the monstrous admixture of blood, the vile obscenity that they may term marriage, follows with equal certainty. But the result of this admixture—the wretched progeny—the diseased and sterile offspring—has a determinate limit, and it is solely a question of time when it becomes wholly extinct. Any one reflecting a moment on this subject—that is, any American whose instincts are healthy and true—would surely prefer that his offspring should perish from the earth rather than to mix their blood with that of the negro; and as the white blood in Jamaica, etc., is rapidly mixing with the negro, and without foreign addition to the white element it must soon be universally tainted with the base alloy; and as all mongrels must of necessity ultimately perish, it is certain that the fate of the white people of these islands is vastly more deplorable than was that of those suddenly swept from existence in the Island of Hayti.

The policy of England in this respect is universally adopted in the other islands. The first step was a war upon the " slave trade"—then " emancipation," then the active employment of the government to enforce the theory of a single race by forcing the negro up and the white man down to an abhorrent, but, of course, impossible level; for those they have transformed into a hideous kind of equality must finally perish, and in the whole tropical centre of the continent, ultimately become extinct. Meanwhile labor, production, and civilization are tending to the same common extinction with the white blood. In Jamaica, Barbadoes, and some other islands where there is yet a considerable white population, the negro, despite the influence of the government, is kept in a certain restraint. He labors little, it is true, but with little patches of land he grows bananas and other products that in that genial clime enable him to live in a certain comfort (to him), and thus— while the same being would rapidly perish in Massachusetts— to multiply himself. The horrible traffic in Mongols or coolies, since the negro was released from labor in the islands, has enabled the owners of some of the former flourishing planta- tions to continue their cultivation, and to furnish in some places almost their former products, and thus to deceive the world and to delude those who desire to be deluded in respect to the non-productiveness of the free negro.

But, as has been shown, the negro neither does nor can labor, in our sense of the word. His dominating sensualism forbids such a thing, while his limited intellect, like that of the child, renders him unable to labor for a remote result, or deny himself immediate indulgence, in order to acquire an ultimate good. In his natural state, and isolated from the white man, he calls into exercise his powerful senses for his immediate wants, and with no winter or barren seasons to con- tend against, and favored with a soil with its many and nutri- tious fruits growing spontaneously all about him, he has little more to do than to pluck and eat. In this way he lives, multi- plies himself, and enjoys an animal existence, which to us seems miserable enough certainly, and, in comparison with his condition at the South, is indeed miserable enough; but to this he is rapidly tending in the West Indian Islands, and the whole power of the British and other European governments are rapidly forcing him into this condition.

In Hayti he is now nearing this final condition—this inher- ent and original Africanism to which he is tending in the whole of tropical America. Seventy years ago the mulattoes rebel- led against the whites; they excited and impelled the negroes to join them; the whites—only twenty-five thousand—were immolated or driven from the island. Then came the conflict among themselves; the mulattoes and mongrels in turn were massacred, or sought shelter in San Domingo, the Spanish part of the island, and the negroes, masters of the field, with their natural tendencies unchecked, without guides or masters, have finally culminated in *Solouque*—a typical negro—a serpent worshipper and *Obi-man*, as chief or emperor.

When the French expedition, under the command of General Le Clerc, failed to recover the island in 1803, and the Haytians, though their independence was not recognized by the French republic, were able, through the aid of the British, to assume the position of an independent power, they commenced a national existence peculiarly favored in many respects. The mulattoes—generally the children of French masters—were many of them highly educated, having been sent to Paris for this purpose in childhood. They had the sympathy of the French people, and indeed of the whole world on their side, for the worst tyrants and oppressors of Europe, while laboring with all their might to crush out the liberty of white men, were then as now deeply interested in the freedom of the black. Moreover, they had the physical as well as the moral support of England, and without a single enemy in the world to embarrass their progress. But though without foreign enemies or wars of any kind to check their advance, with the finest climate and most fertile soil in the world, they have rapidly collapsed into their natural Africanism.

Internal commotions, as now in Mexico, began at once among the mongrels, and bloodshed and misery of every kind prevailed until this element was necessarily destroyed, and the stolid, idle, and useless savagism of Africa became the essential characteristic of these people. Two causes alone have held in check the tendencies to Africanism—the white blood and the surrounding civilization. The mongrel element, though constantly diminishing in numbers, naturally governed, until it became so feeble that *Solouque*, a typical negro and an embodiment of Africanism, of fetichism, and a worshiper of Obi, seized the supreme power and inaugurated savagism. Accident of some kind or other has recently pushed this worthy aside and placed one *Jeffrard*, a *griffe*, or " colored man," or mulatto, in power, who calls himself president, but he will doubtless soon give place to some negro chief. Nevertheless, there is a considerable infusion of white blood still in Hayti, and therefore, the true negro condition—the natural condition when isolated, the condition it has always been in and that it always must remain in when isolated from the Caucasian man—is not yet entirely restored. Again, the surrounding civilization— the contact with Europeans and Americans that commerce or trade in fruits growing almost spontaneously together, with the few adventurous spirits always attracted to such a fertile soil as Hayti would, perhaps, always give to its people a somewhat different external character from the African type.

But if we can be permitted to suppose the absence of these things—the utter extinction of the Caucasian innervation and absolute isolation of the negro as in Africa—then, in the tropics, the same climate with similar soils, in short, similar circumstances to those surrounding him in Africa, of course, the negro type, the negro nature, the negro being, would be the same as it always has been and is now in Africa. On the coast, where he is brought in contact with the white man, where there are a good many with white blood in their veins, who therefore retain to some extent the habitudes of the superior race, the traditions and historic recollections of their former masters are preserved. But in the interior, where the negro is permitted to live out his African tendencies, he has lost all knowledge of the events of seventy years ago. History, religion, even the French language has disappeared, and in their place there is Obiism and African dialects, while probably not one in a thousand has any perception, knowledge, or recollection whatever of *Christophe, Dessalines,* or others of those notorious chiefs who a little over half a century since filled the island with the terror of their names. As observed, the utter

extinction of the Caucasian innervation and absolute isolation of the negro in Hayti, would of necessity end in complete Africanism, and to this end, this final culmination of
savagism the whole British and European policy is now necessarily tending. It is true, the existence of a white government by mere juxtaposition as well as the prestige of power,
holds in check the strong tendencies to Africanism, but the
policy—the official employment of negroes always carrying
with it under the monarchical *regime* social importance—tends
powerfully to degrade the white blood and induce amalgamation, to drag after it, of course, that inevitable extinction of the
mongrel progeny which the Almighty has decreed forever and
everywhere.

Thus, the British " anti-slavery'" policy tends rapidly and
constantly to the restoration of Africanism, to savagery—to the
building up of a mighty barbarism in the very heart of the
American continent—to the establishment of a huge heathenism that shall spread itself over fifty degrees of the most fertile
and beautiful portion of the New World. This, then, is the
legitimate termination of that wide-spread delusion of modern
times, which has drawn into its fatal and monstrous embrace
multitudes of honest and well-meaning men, and while it
already has worked out evils so stupendous as to be almost beyond our powers of computation to measure them, and never
in an instance, direct or indirect, done the slightest good whatever, at this moment it threatens to inflict even greater evils on
the world than those it has hitherto cursed it with. The process through which all this mischief is worked out can not or
need not be mistaken—a man may run and read it, and though
a fool understand it. It is this: 1st. The dogma of a single
race—that the negro is a *black*-white man. 2d. The " anti-
slavery" policy of Pitt, nominally to put down the " slave
trade." 3d. " Emancipation"—and whites and negroes de-

clared equal. 4th. The policy of European governments to elevate negroes and depress whites, inducing social equality and consequent amalgamation. 5th. Absorption of the white blood by mongrelism. 6th. Sterility and extinction of the mixed element. 7th. Restoration of the African type and consequent savagism—a huge heathenism—indeed, Africa itself literally lifted up and planted down in the center of the New World—thus erecting a mighty barbarism directly in the path of American civilization; and which, in all coming time, as the ally or instrument of European monarchists, shall beat back the waves of democracy, and dwarf the growth and limit the power of the American Republic.

The "free negro" in our midst perishes; but in the tropics, in his own climate, he poisons and destroys the white blood, and then relapses into his inherent and organic Africanism, toward which he is rapidly impelled by the British "anti-slavery policy." If that policy could ever be successful—if fifty degrees of latitude in the heart of this continent should ever be permanently turned over to free negroism, or ever occupied by a huge barbarism—which should not alone render the fairest portion of the New World a barren waste, but interrupt that great law of progress which impels us onward, to carry our system, our republican idea of government, and our civilization, over the whole "boundless continent," then, indeed, might the friends of freedom despair of the future. But it is not possible that the rising civilization of America is to be thus broken down by the monarchists of the Old World. The law of progress—of national growth, of very necessity—that has carried us to the Gulf of Mexico and to the Pacific Ocean, will continue to impel us onward, and to restore the rapidly perishing civilization of the great tropical center of the continent. All humane and good men desire that this grand result shall be worked out by moral causes, by the exposure of the monstrous delusion in regard to negroes that has been productive of so much evil; but either through an appeal to reason or to the sword—through the operation of natural causes or through bloodshed and national suffering —the final end *must be* the restoration of the negro to his normal condition, and consequent restoration of civilization in the finest portion of our great continent.

CHAPTER XXIV.

It has been shown in the foregoing pages of this work how that providential arrangement of human affairs, in which the negro is placed in natural juxtaposition with the white man, has resulted in the freedom of the latter and the general well-being of both. It has been seen how a subordinate and widely different social element in Virginia and other States, naturally gave origin to new ideas and new modes of thought, which, thrusting aside the mental habits and political notions brought from the Old World, naturally culminated in the grand idea of 1776, and the establishment of a new political existence, based on the natural, organic, and everlasting equality of the race. It has been seen, moreover, how the great civil revolution of 1800, which, under the lead of Mr. Jefferson, restored the purity and simplicity of republican principles, saved the Northern laboring and producing classes from the rule of an oligarchy, otherwise unavoidable, however it might have been disguised by republican formulas.

It is scarcely necessary to appeal to the political history of the country since 1800 to demonstrate the vital importance—indeed, the measureless benefit—of what, by an absurd perversion of terms, has been called negro slavery, to the freedom, progress, and prosperity of the laboring and producing classes of the North, and, indeed, to all mankind. It is seen that the existence of an inferior race—the presence of a natural substratum in the political society of the New World—has resulted in the creation of a new political and social order, and relieved the producing classes from that abject dependence on capital which in Europe, and especially in England, renders them mere beasts of burthen to a fraction of their brethren. The simple but transcendent fact, that capital and labor are united at the South—that the planter, or so-called slaveholder, is, *per se* and of necessity, the defender of the rights of the producing classes—this simple fact is the key to our political history, and the hinging-point of our party politics for half a century past.

The Southern planter and Northern farmer—the producing classes—a Southern majority and a Northern minority—have governed the country, fought all its battles, acquired all its territories, and conducted the nation step by step to its present position of strength, power, and grandeur. Just as steadily a Northern majority and a Southern minority have opposed this progress, and labored blindly, doubtless, to return to the system of the federalists, indeed to the European idea of class distinctions, and to render the government an instrument for the benefit of the few at the expense of the many.

They have sought to create national banks; demanded favors for those engaged in manufactures; for others engaged in Northern fisheries; for the benefit of bands of jobbers and speculators, under pretence of internal improvements; in short, the Northern majority have labored continually to render the government, as in England, an instrument for benefiting classes at the expense of the great body of the people.

All these efforts, however, have been defeated by the union of Northern and Southern producers, and mainly by the latter. A large majority of the votes in Congress against special legislation and schemes of corruption have been those of so-called slaveholders; and in those extraordinary instances when Northern representatives of agricultural constituencies have proved

15

faithless, and these schemes "worked" through Congress, "slaveholders" in the Presidential chair have interposed the veto, and saved the laboring and producing classes from this dangerous legislation, and the government from being perverted into an instrument of mischief.

Such has been our political and current party history, and from the nature and necessities of things, every "extension of slavery," or every expansion of territory, must in the future, as it has in the past, strengthen the cause of the producing classes, and give greater scope and power to the American idea of government.

The acquisition of Louisiana, of Florida, of Texas, etc., of those great producing States on the Gulf Coast, has nearly overwhelmed the anti-republican tendencies of the North, and rendered almost powerless those combinations of capital and speculation which have always endangered the purity and simplicity of our republican system, and thus the rights and safety of the laboring and producing millions everywhere.

Indeed, it is a truth, a simple fact, that can not be too often repeated, that in precise proportion to the amount or extent of so-called "slaveholding"—of the number of negroes in their normal condition—is freedom rendered secure to the white millions of the North. And when in the progress of time Cuba and Central America, and the whole tropical center of the continent is added to the Union and placed in the same relation to New York and Ohio that Mississippi, Alabama, etc., are now, then it is evident that the democratic or American idea of government will be securely established forever, and the rights and interests of the producing millions who ask nothing from government but its protection, will be no longer endangered by those anti-republican tendencies which in the North have so long conflicted with the natural development of our system, and struggled so long and fiercely against its existence.

of our system, and struggled so long and fiercely against its existence.

If this freedom and prosperity of the white man rested on wrong or oppression of the negro, then it would be valueless, for the Almighty has evidently designed that all His creatures should be permitted to live out the life to which He has adapted them. But when all the facts are considered, and the negro population of the South contrasted with any similar number of their race now or at any other time in human experience, then it is seen that, relatively considered, they are, perhaps, benefited to even a greater extent than the white population themselves.

The efforts, as has been shown, to reverse the natural order of things—to force the negro into the position of the white man—are not merely failures, but frightful cruelties—cruelties that among ourselves end in the extinction of these poor creatures, while in the tropics it destroys the white man and impels the negro into barbarism.

In conclusion, therefore, it is clear, or will be clear to every mind that grasps the facts of this great question, with the inductive facts, or the unavoidable inferences that belong to them, that any American citizen, party, sect, or class among us, so blinded, bewildered, and besotted by foreign theories and false mental habits as to labor for negro "freedom"—to drag down their own race, or to thrust the negro from his normal condition, is alike the enemy of both, a traitor to his blood and at war with the decrees of the Eternal.

THE END.

www.ingramcontent.com/pod-product-compliance
Lightning Source LLC
Chambersburg PA
CBHW040144270326
41929CB00024B/3365